DISABILITY AND THE MEDIA

Disability and the Media

Prescriptions for Change

CHARLES A. RILEY II

university press of new england

Hanover and London

Published by University Press of New England,
One Court Street, Lebanon, NH 03766
www.upne.com
© 2005 by University Press of New England
Printed in the United States of America

5 4 3 2 1

Library of Congress Cataloging-in-Publication Data
Riley, Charles A.
    Disability and the media : prescriptions for change / Charles A. Riley II.
      p.   cm.
    Includes bibliographical references and index.
    ISBN 1–58465–473–2 (cloth : alk. paper)
      1. People with disabilities in mass media. 2. People with disabilities—United States.
    I. Title.
    HV1553.R49   2005
    302.23′087—dc22   2004028282

For Diane C. Riley, M.D.

*A surgeon of immaculate skill and infinite compassion, you guided
me to an understanding of the disability community that informed
my thinking and writing. If only more doctors were like you.*

Nature never did betray
The heart that loved her.

— WILLIAM WORDSWORTH

Contents

Preface

Every time Aimee Mullins sees her name in the papers she braces herself for some predictable version of the same headline followed by the same old story. Paralympian, actress, and fashion model, Mullins is a bilateral, below-the-knee amputee, who sprints a hundred meters in less than sixteen seconds on a set of running prostheses called Cheetahs because they were fashioned after the leg form of the world's fastest animal. First, there are the headlines: "Overcoming All Hurdles" (she is not a hurdler, although she is a long jumper) or "Running Her Own Race," "Nothing Stops Her" or the dreaded and overused "Profile in Courage." Then come the clichés and stock scenes, from the prosthetist's office to the winner's podium. Many of the articles dwell on her success as the triumph of biomechanics, a "miracle of modern medicine," turning her fairy tale into a Coppelia narrative (or a *Six Million Dollar Woman* movie sequel). From the local paper where she grew up (Allentown, Pennsylvania), to national exposure in *Esquire* and *People* and guest spots on *Oprah*, Mullins's "inspiring" saga is recycled almost verbatim by well-meaning journalists for audiences who never seem to get enough of its feel-good message even if they never actually find out who Mullins is.

This is the patronizing, trivializing, and marginalizing ur-narrative of disability in the media today. The mainstream press finds it irresistible, but this steady diet of sugar has its dangers. The cliché has excluded the mature, fully realized coverage that people with disabilities have long deserved. For Mullins, it has translated into well over her Warholian fifteen minutes of fame, bringing her the financial rewards of sponsorships, motivational speaking gigs, and modeling contracts at the expense of being turned into a latter-day poster child. Stories about her rarely get around to mentioning that she was a Pentagon intern while making the dean's list as an academic star in history and diplomacy at Georgetown, or that she is one of the actresses in Matthew Barney's avant-garde *Cremaster* film series.

Mullins is not the only celebrity with a disability to be steamrolled out of three-dimensional humanity into allegorical flatness. All the branches of the media considered here, from print to television, radio and the movies (including advertisements) to multimedia and the Internet, are guilty of the same distillation of stories to meet their own, usually fiscal, ends. For example, even though her autobiography is remarkably ahead of its time in its anticipation of disability culture, by the time Helen Keller had been sweetened for movie audiences in Patti Duke's version of her life, little was left of the fiery trailblazer. In much the same way, Christopher Reeve and Michael J. Fox have been pigeonholed by print and television hagiographers as lab experiments and tragic heroes. Packaged to raise philanthropic or advertising dollars, they perform roles no less constrained than the pretty-boy parts they played on screen earlier in their lives.

What is wrong with this picture? By jamming Mullins and the others into prefabricated stories—the supercrip, the medical miracle, the object of pity—writers and producers have outfitted them with the narrative equivalent of an ill-fitting set of prostheses. Each of these archetypal narratives has its way of reaching mass audiences, selling products (including magazines and movie tickets), and financially rewarding both the media outlet and the featured subject. In some ways, as optimists point out, this represents an improvement. We have had millennia of fiction and nonfiction depicting angry people with disabilities as villains, from Oedipus to Ahab to Dr. Strangelove. The vestigial traces of that syndrome still occasionally recur, although with far less frequency, in current movies or television series and in journalists' fixation on the mental instability of violent criminals. However, today's storytellers, including those in the disability media, are more likely to make people with disabilities into "heroes of assimilation," to borrow a phrase from Erving Goffman's seminal work on disability, *Stigma: Notes on the Management of Spoiled Identity.*

As Goffman knew too well, just as the stigmatization of the villain had its dilatory effects on societal attitudes, so too does relentless hagiography, particularly by transforming individuals into symbols and by playing on an audience's sympathy and sense of superiority. Those who labor in the field of disability studies point out that disability culture and its unique strengths are absent from this story of normalization. Others would simply note that the individual is lost in the fable, an all-American morality tale that strikes one of the most resonant chords in the repertoire: redemption. Like the deathless Horatio Alger tale, the story of the hero of assimilation emphasizes many of the deepest values and beliefs of the Puritan tradition, especially the notion that suffering makes us stronger and better. An able-bodied person falls from grace (often literally falling or crashing, as in the case of many spinal cord injuries), progresses through the shadows of rehabilitation and depression, and by force of willpower along with religious belief pulls through to attain a quality of life that is less disabled, more normal, basking in the glow of recognition for beating the odds.

This pervasive narrative can be found in print, on television, in movies, in advertisements, and on the Web. Its corrosive effect on understanding and attitudes is as yet unnoticed. It is impossible to know the full degree of damage wreaked by the demeaning and wildly inaccurate portrayal of people with disabilities, nor is it altogether clear whether much current progress is being made. Painful as it is for me as an advocate to report the bad news, I cannot help but point out that the "movement" has slowed to a crawl in terms of political and economic advancement for 54 million Americans. The stasis that threatens is at least partly to be blamed on a reassuring, recurring image projected by the media that numbs nondisabled readers and viewers into thinking that all is well.

This study aims to expose the extent of the problem while pinpointing how writers, editors, photographers, filmmakers, advertisers, and the executives who give them their marching orders go wrong, or occasionally get it right. Through a close analysis of the technical means of representation, in conjunction with the commentary of leading voices in the disability community, I hope to guide future coverage to a more fair and accurate way of putting the disability story on screen or paper. Far from another stab at the political correctness target, the aim of this content analysis of journalism, film, advertising, and Web publishing is to cut through the accumulated clichés and condescension to find an adequate vocabulary that will finally represent the disability community in all its vibrant and fascinating diversity. Nothing like that will ever happen if the press and advertisers continue to think, write, and design as they have in the past.

Today's vulgar media productions are an easy target, particularly for one who has worked on the inside for decades. In addition to the precipitous decline in the intelligence level of its content over the past few years, the press is beset with credibility problems that break into its own headlines. Once the *New York Times,* the sober "Gray Lady" that billed itself as the "paper of record" for so long, was exposed as the error-prone hunk of factually erratic Swiss cheese it is, and the venerable BBC confessed to blowing the weapons of mass destruction story and contributing to the suicide of a midlevel bureaucrat, the public trust was finally shaken into a reasonable state of skepticism regarding the machine that delivers its news. The manipulative distortions wrought by "tie-ins" among outlets, the abysmal lack of standards on television, the tasteless fodder of major movie studios, the ad-driven consumer hype of magazines, and the mendacious excesses of ad agencies are out in the sunshine for disgusted audiences to recognize. Even corporate regulators are alert to the toll taken by mergers: many have expressed concern about the way conflict of interest shapes messages and degrades the general quality of both news and entertainment. Clearly the media in general do not present a pretty picture in their current incarnation.

This is not the place for a wholesale reaming of the media's obstruction of the truth, because its maladies go way beyond its pathetic treatment of disability stories, but one or two basic observations on the etiology of the most recent catastrophes may be useful in the context of this focused critique. From an editor's perspective, the revelations that reporters were delivering fiction dressed as fact to the BBC, the *Times, USA Today,* CBS and the *Washington Post* expose more than just the mendacious habits of a few rogue journalists infected with overweening ambition. When a batch of bogus stories make it into the paper or on air, the decision makers in the news organization bear as much of the blame as the reporter who filed the fraudulent stories. Whether in print or on screen, the news product involves far more than the idealistic movie scenario we see in *All the President's Men*—dirt passed from hard-digging reporter to editor to reader—because the levels of managing editors, publishers, and executives who direct the show have to be factored in. Basic judgments regarding newsworthiness, accuracy, bias, logic, privacy, ethics, the quality of sources, even libel are not solo calls. The hierarchy is in plainer view now thanks to the transparency called for in the wake of the recent scandals, as with corporate governance and even accounting; and as our view of the inner workings of the media clarifies, so does our understanding of how the major outlets manufacture stories rather than simply report them. The cynical movie *Wag the Dog,* about the falsification of a war in Albania to divert public attention from White House indiscretions, was even closer to the mark than was thought when it was released. The good old days of journalism may have been reflected in *All the President's Men,* but the restructured media conglomerates begat today's mirror image in *Wag the Dog.* Remember, editors at many publications are paid in equity, and stock prices go up only if earnings are up.

A priority in this study is the evaluation of fellow journalists, always a tricky business but one that is even more problematic in the arena of advocacy media, where the standard of objectivity is conventionally laid aside in favor of stridency. For years I have taught undergraduates in my business journalism classes to regard the impartiality of the reporter—extended through the calibration of the writer's language and the discipline of the editor—as one of the tests of the validity of an article. When I suddenly found myself at the helm of an unabashedly pro-disability magazine I had helped to found, called *WE,* I had to manage the degree of bias that the copy could accommodate without entirely invalidating the reportage. In the pages of that magazine, we attempted to redefine the disability narrative by radically changing the way images and stories were delivered. The story of the magazine's rise and fall is related in the seventh chapter of this book. Doubtless we could have been charged with bias, as any community publication can be. If the needle swings too far to the end of the dial, the reader has every reason to be skeptical about how thorough (or filtered) the factual core of a story might be. One way to punch a hole in any journalist's work is to turn up a missed or suppressed detail that would alter the balance of the piece. To complicate matters further, I will admit here at the start a polemical agenda that invests these pages with personal passion but may also undermine their reception as a "study." To commit oneself to the disability world, even for a period of time in the role of observer, is to be exposed to a furnace of anger at injustices both of a civil rights nature and at the hands of Nature itself. Beneath all the warm and fuzzy stories I ran in my magazine that made a positive difference in the lives of people with disabilities (I counted more than two hundred different writers who made their debut in our pages over the four years), there was a rock-hard substratum of icy anger I now feel regarding the glacial pace of change for this community. I mean to drive my critique deep into this calcified mass of misrepresentations because I share that impatience and resentment. I walked out of the magazine just before it suspended publication, knowing that somehow we had failed in our mission because our impact was ultimately fleeting and shallow. Specific problems that I felt sure we could remedy at least in part through reaching the right audience with a deft mix of language and graphics remain to this day unbudged. Even though we became a story in ourselves, gaining invaluable exposure in the *New York Times, Wall Street Journal,* and scores of local papers as well as on CNN, CNNfn, ABC, CBS, NBC, Fox, NPR, and even Pax (which put together a full hour about one of our fashion shoots), our message finally fell on deaf ears in the newsrooms.

Why do print and electronic media outlets remain transfixed by the medical miracle rather than the human-rights story? How does the old paternalism, the poster-child mentality, manage to hang on? When will they balance mental and physical disability? Why can't press exposure lead to higher employment levels for people with disabilities? How does the cycle of pity renew itself in the nonprofit world (when will the annual black-tie balls give way to yearlong enabling programs)? I pound the keyboard harder when I think of how little the media actually do for the rights of people with disabilities, and how far short our magazine fell. These pages represent an attack—hopefully not a parting shot—that could not be launched in the magazine's pages (and certainly not in the commercially diluted drivel that was our Web site). There will inevitably be civilian casualties as I blast away—those innocent victims who were on our side and especially those who bought into the crafty business opportunity dangled by the magazine's publishers—and I have no doubt many of the journalists and celebrities I name in these pages will not feel they deserve such ire (sorry Oprah).

Friendly fire aside, I do aim to make others in the communications field flinch to recognize some of the inanities they have spread. When you are inside a community that has been subjected to the hit-and-run tactics of the mainstream media, you feel particularly bruised. The infantile attention span of the modern media is pandemic, and the old excuse that the general stupidity of the American public is dragging down journalistic standards is nothing but a smoke screen for lack of skill, anemic critical faculties, and downright laziness in the newsroom. This is particularly true of the mainstream coverage of disability. This study eavesdrops inside the corridors of news organizations and blames both "church and state"—that old division of the editorial and business sides of a media enterprise. When it comes to disability, the church is gutless, clueless, and indifferent. Equally callous, the state is befogged with greed. Once the polling figures for the community reached the 54 million level and economists came up with the $1 trillion in aggregate income, $220 billion in disposable income, the temptation to harvest was too great for advertisers to resist, and this study also takes a good hard look at the sudden discovery of the person with a disability as consumer, raising the question whether Madison Avenue advanced the community's cause or exploited sentimental goodwill among nondisabled consumers while hoping to attract the disabled market by putting actors in wheelchairs. The purpose is to use exposé as an agent of change.

The press perpetuates stereotypes in the same way that it codifies other errors, by repeating the same inaccuracies over and over and not taking the trouble or having the courage and integrity to acknowledge them. This book points fingers. Similar wake-up calls have nudged the press into more judicious coverage of women and minorities. Disability is the all-inclusive minority—it is completely race- and culture-blind—and it will be worth it to land a few punches on the media and rouse them from their torpor to take a more active look at the way in which they address disability issues. My motive is the same today as when I put together the first issue of *WE*—to improve the situation of people with disabilities by bringing the most sophisticated, credible journalistic techniques to their service in the belief that the skillfulness and accuracy of the portrait empowers the sitter. The publishing industry has, by default, turned to confessional literature by people with disabilities as a more valid way to mitigate the problem, but even that avenue has proven to be flawed as the genre is shaped by market expectations. I believe that an Archimedean point is necessary from which this problem can be effectively examined.

A few caveats, however, are necessary. I do not have a disability, and in the eyes of some, as well as within the framework of my story, this poses a problem. I also acknowledge that I came into this story late— I was not around for such landmark events in disability history as the "Berkeley quads" (a group of quadriplegic students who demanded independent living accommodations) and other great breakthroughs of the sixties. I was not even cognizant of the issues in 1990 when President Bush the First signed the Americans with Disabilities Act. The slice of disability history that occured when I was on the scene, starting in 1996, had its own inherent points of interest, but an awful lot of water had already passed under the bridge by the time I was on the beat, and there is no way within the compass of this book, which does not purport to be a history of disability in the media, to account for it all. Nor is there any way to safely project where the movement and its image in the press is headed, except to say that unless some enlightened and competent journalists, editors, filmmakers, and advertising decision-makers come along who demonstrate a higher awareness of this issue, we are destined to be subjected to the same old drivel for generations to come.

This is not a work of theory, and technically not a direct entrant into the disability studies discourse, although I draw heavily on the distinctions made by scholars between the medical and political model of disability, just as I agree that the onus placed on people with disabilities is an exterior, "constructed" environment of physical and attitudinal barriers. I did not want to steer this study into the swift current of disability discourse as it mainly exists in the academy since I hope to stay close to my subject—the media's depiction of disability—in the hope that many of my readers will be members of the press themselves. They in turn have their own analytic literature, from the popular (*Slate, Salon,* the Monday business section of the *New York Times,* the overly long *Vanity Fair* front-of-the-book features) to the intellectual (*Columbia Journalism Review*). Only after running a magazine, writing hundreds of stories, and editing hundreds more, digging through the clips in my research or sitting through the interminable pitch meetings to advertisers, have I reached the stage where I can judge my own work and that of others, discriminate between the specious and the worthwhile, and recognize a few of the telltale signs of advanced thinking on the representation of this wonderful community.

So here is a memo to all producers, editors, and reporters: Wake up! Use your power, make smarter choices, remember that at any moment you could enter that world you are covering, that it does not exist "out there" or in vitro behind some glass membrane that keeps you secure in your editor's chair separate from the subjects of your articles. Now that the economic justification for more sophisticated disability coverage is at hand (the recognition that the community is a major consumer niche), adjust your picture accordingly and stop falling back on the old story structures.

I learned constantly from my collaborators and the community I covered. *WE* magazine was a tight little team that, over the course of four years, embraced an ever wider group of writers and leaders whose support I cherished and often relied on to excess. For this, the following have not only my gratitude but profound apologies. They include, Fran Ahders, Dexter Benjamin, Robert Bennett, Nicole Bianco, Sarah Brewster, Bruce Burton, John Callahan, Andrew Cantor, Belle Gale Chevigny, James Conrad, Fred Asong Eno, Lori Frisher, Stephanie Hammerman, Gordon C. Harper, Tari Susan Hartman, Olga Hill, Henry Holden, Jeff Hoover, Wilson H. Hulley, Nancy Isenberger, Kay Redfield Jamison, Mikki Lam, Ken Levinson, Kitty Lunn, Casey Martin, David McMullen, Terry Moakley, Robert Muller, Claudine Napoli, Maggie Nieves, Les Park, Dianne Pilgrim, Anthony Razza, Anne Rendall, Alberto Rizzo, Francesca Rosenberg, Jill Gray Rosser, Marc Server, John Siciliano, Dick Shephard, Aaron Silberman, Ellen Stohl, John Stovall, Ginny Thornburgh, Jane S. Van Ingen, James J. Weisman, Dr. Ruth Westheimer, Tom Whittaker, John M. Williams, Marilyn Murray Willison, and Alexander Wood. We also included in our family such hotshot celebrities as Andrea Bocelli, Kathy Buckley, Walter Cronkite, Michael J. Fox, Stephen Hawking, John Hockenberry, Marlee Matlin, Christopher and Dana Reeve, Robin Williams, James Wolfensohn, Stevie Wonder. Mayor Rudolf Giuliani was at my side when we launched the magazine and, when I quit, presented an award to me for my service to New York's disabled community, which I glance at on my mantelpiece with pride and gratitude. I reserve particularly fond thanks for George Covington, whose daily phone calls broke the tension of the newsroom, for Dr. Oliver Sacks, who was unsparing in his support of our endeavor and to whom I still owe a very good luncheon (which I should have provided while I still had an expense account), and for the renowned writer Walter Abish, who over one unforgettable luncheon offered generous editorial guidance based on his own experience.

Certain friends viewed my career diversion into publishing a magazine for people with disabilities with enthusiasm, foremost among them my mentor Patrick Cullen, whose long conversations and rigorous questions helped me solve many of the most difficult problems I encountered in writing my articles as well as this book. An overworked editor in chief needs a circle of support, and I have leaned hard on friends including Richard Armstrong, Brian Bernstein, Esq., Asher B. Edelman, Jay Furst, Dr. Susan E. Goodman, Lisa Hahn, Byron Holinshead, Ann and Leonard Kent, Peter and Barb Peck, Kenneth Perko, Anthony Pfeiffer, Ben Primer,

Richard Sellery, S. Prakash Sethi, Edward Strauss, Dr. Marc Wilk, Raoul and Bettina Witteveen, and more.

Committing these ideas to paper has been as exhilarating as it has been painful at times. Throughout the process, I have had the benefit of an extraordinary editorial conversation with Phyllis Deutsch, executive editor of the University Press of New England, whose grasp of the significance of the overall message as well as of the details on which it relies has the firmness of convictions every bit as strong as my own. Having visited our offices during the waning months of the magazine, she even shared firsthand the promise and frustrations of our pioneering experiment in disability journalism. Every sentence of this book has felt the benefit of her wisdom and commitment, for which she has my undying thanks.

Involvement in the issues facing the disability community, for one who is not disabled, usually comes down to having a personal connection. After years in the field, I have the honor of many such connections, but I started with a few. My mother, Isabel C. Riley, modestly and selflessly shared her mother's experience of blindness, and to this day through her volunteer work at the Dartmouth-Hitchcock Medical Center finds time in every week to get to know people with disabilities. My sister Diane, to whom this book is dedicated, is the very model of the compassionate and respectful physician, and my other sister, Robin, as a mother and devoted friend to many people with disabilities, fully understood the depth of my feelings for my colleagues and the people I was covering. Ever compassionate and ready to root for the underdog, having suffered so greatly herself in her earlier life, my dear wife, Liu Ke Ming, perfectly grasped the deep need I felt to serve the community with all my heart during the time I started the magazine, when the schedule was often seven days a week well past the midnight hour, and while revisiting that arduous period for this book. Each of them, along with many of my dear friends, fed me a constant banquet of tips on stories and ideas for the magazine, leads that often led to our finest stories. My cousin and role model Stephen Horne labored on the frontlines in this battle as an attendant in public mental hospitals during the late sixties and early seventies, emerging with a deeper and more tender sense of humanity than any man I know.

Often a deep distress does humanize the soul. I would never have become editor in chief of a magazine for people with disabilities at all if it had not been for my own severe bout of, thankfully, temporary but paralyzing inner pain, the cause of which I decline to disclose but the effects of which were a deeper understanding of what it is to fall and recover, to embark on life's second act. I learned, for the first time, how viciously personal are the torments of discrimination and how wickedly destructive misrepresentation can be. I left my classroom and returned to the news-room in charge of a classic media start-up surrounded by others who had also known what it meant to pick themselves up and start all over again. My rebound coincided with an unforgettable meeting with Travis Roy, whose spinal cord injury during the opening minutes of a hockey game when he was playing varsity for Boston University grabbed headlines a decade ago. Because I am a hockey player myself, and one inclined to the same hustling, go-for-broke pace that cost Travis dearly, the encounter decisively motivated me to take up the cause.

Remedying the shortcomings of the media is a tall order, and much of the analysis to follow is relentlessly negative. That does not imply there are not bright spots, moments of optimism or high achievement that we can celebrate as examples of what is possible in today's media. Without doubt, one of the great voices in this chorus is that of John Hockenberry. In his memoir, *Moving Violations,* he uses "the chronically stared at" as a variant on "the disabled." He identifies "them" with the ones who stare. It is a lesson in point of view, one of journalism's touchstones, that commands our attention. In his virtuosic and authentic prose Hockenberry assures us that there is more than one way to see disability:

> From the beginning, disability taught that life could be reinvented. In fact, such an outlook was required. The physical dimensions of life could be cre-ated, like poetry; they were not imposed by some celestial landlord. Life was more than renting some protoplasm to walk around in. It was more than being a winner or a loser. To have invented a way to move about with-out legs was to invent walking. This was a task reserved for gods, and to perform it was deeply satisfying. None of that was apparent to the people who stared. To them, I was just wheelchair. To me, I was inventing a new life. To them, I was getting by in dealing with my predicament. To them, I was standing on a ledge and not jumping off. To me, I was climbing up to get a better view. There was no place to jump off. Whenever I look down, I can see my feet. They're along for the ride. There's no reason to be afraid.[1]

Charles A. Riley II, Ph.D.
Cutchogue, New York
July 2004

DISABILITY AND THE MEDIA

CHAPTER ONE

Heroes of Assimilation

How the Media Transform Disability

> *Nothing of him that doth fade*
> *But doth suffer a sea-change*
> *Into something rich and strange.*
> —*Ariel, in* The Tempest

O ne in every five people on the planet has a disability and, because of that, is shamefully misrepresented in the fun-house mirror of the mass media. Consigned by the arbiters of what is published or produced to a narrow spectrum of roles, from freaks to inspirational saints, lab rats or objects of pity, people with disabilities have not seen the evolution in their public image that their private circumstances have undergone in the aftermath of political and medical progress over the past four decades. Even the specialized publications, programs, and films dedicated to people with disabilities (and sometimes run by them) present such twisted images that one wonders what bizarre trick is being played on the "last minority," which lags by decades behind other groups—gays, blacks, Jews, women, seniors—who long ago used their economic and political clout to demand changes that at least ameliorated the offensive portrayals of them on screen and in print. Such changes would ultimately be empowering. While image may not be everything, it does perceptibly affect such brass-tack issues for 54 million Americans with disabilities (by far the nation's largest minority group) as unemployment, health care policy, educational and social benefits, and the unquantifiable factor of self-esteem.

As we examine the misrepresentation of people with disabilities in magazines and newspapers, on television and in movies, in ads and on the Web, even in their own memoirs and advocacy press, we cannot neglect the dollars-and-cents dynamic that governs, to far too great a degree, what makes it to the screen or page. There is no way to subtract economics from either side of the equation between representation and power. Whether the scenario reveals a struggling start-up magazine trying to squeeze out a profit on advertising revenues or a colossal national non-profit trying to reach a multimillion-dollar fundraising goal, the strategies behind image and word choices answer to the same fiscal imperative. Moreover, the association of dollars and disability is not uniformly damaging. Among the few bright spots in this survey, one of the most surprising is the relatively advanced state of disability awareness in the advertising industry, where the recognition that the disability niche is an untapped market has led to significant efforts to reach out and touch the disabled spender with remarkably respectful, sensitive image-making and copywriting. These ads are often miles ahead of the magazine or television content surrounding them. In the end, perhaps, they are just as manipulative in the service of a commercial agenda, but that motive is, fortuitously, aligned with the calls for respecting a cultural identity. The portrayal of disability culture is the crucial barometer of much-needed social pressure to recognize that people with disabilities are no longer children in need of handouts. Equality in this case arises from a little less "special" treatment or heroic awe—which further estranges the person with a disability from others—and a little more straightforward marketing.

Whether for better or worse, the metamorphoses of a person's image are controlled by the image maker, not by the one in the picture. Even on a technical plane, tweaking is easy in this era of digital editing and cosmetic surgery, when the human form can be so thoroughly altered that the ethical codes of publishing and broadcasting have been rewritten. People with disabilities have always been sensitive to being stared at rather than embraced. It is just as tiresome to be looked up to as to be looked down on, and in both cases one's appearance is altered. The media have many ways of refracting an image, bending it according to the desire not only to make a profit (or raise philanthropic dollars, essentially the same thing) but to generate fame, shock, revenge, entertainment, or a smoke screen. With all these filters and forces intervening between fact and reception, it is no wonder the story is misshapen at the end.

If you are looking for somebody to blame, begin by scrutinizing the decision makers (not the audience, whose stupidity is too often used as an excuse by media executives to lower standards). The media's systemic failures on the disability beat are just one example of a wider malaise plaguing a declining industry in dire trouble. As a test for measuring how wayward the press can be, the disability community presents a fascinating example of a sustained pattern of missed opportunities and looping, lazy returns to the familiar stereotypes of the angry misshapen villain, the innocent victim, the awesome "supercrip," or the exotic Coney Island freak. The image makers who present these spectacles should know better, but their industries are so insular (and becoming more so, with corporate consolidation) that they are blind to the compelling reasons for improving the situation and deaf to the faint criticism offered so far, which could have alerted them to the insults and problems they create. One surefire way to get their attention is to point out that profits are to be made by recognizing a new way to consider disability, an incentive that cannot be ignored in an industry whose revenue growth stalled years ago.

Pinpointing the Target

The media business runs on demographics. Quantitative measures of who's watching, listening, reading, clicking, and, most important, buying are sliced and diced by marketing experts according to every conceivable category. This systematic analysis of data has advanced way beyond the old herding by race, gender, age, education, and income. That makes the current state of affairs regarding readers and viewers with disabilities all the more astonishing (and frustrating for insiders). The media are alienating an audience conservatively estimated to number in the hundreds of millions worldwide. Estimated by whom? The numbers depend on how you define disability. This alone is one of the politically and economically loaded questions that has dogged the community and its advocates since the earliest civil rights battles enjoined in the sixties, hampering efforts to build support as well as creating what can loosely be called a public relations problem. The media, the politicians, the medical community, and the people with disabilities themselves differ on who deserves to be classed as "disabled." While many involved in the political struggle hope that the heft of the most vast and inclusive number possible (54 million Americans, one in every five) will help the cause, some on the front lines of particular research or legal fights (the deaf offer the paradigm) prefer a narrower set of guidelines. The definitions of disability that weigh most heavily in corporate and political circles involve money and the courts, including not only the text of the Americans with Disabilities Act (ADA) but the historically prior Social Security guidelines and workers' compensation rules, or insurance plans, Equal Employment Opportunity Commission codes and, an up-and-coming trend, corporate diversity policy programs.

This kaleidoscopic array of classes and categories is a legacy of the brief and still relatively obscure history of modern public policy. Its three epochs are echoed in three models of how the media have portrayed people with disabilities, beginning with the patient who is an object of pity or awe (the medical model), succeeded by the protester (the political model, highlighted by the passage of the Americans with Disabilities Act in 1990), and culminating in the latest and by no means fully fledged reincarnation, the consumer who lives with a disability rather than fighting it and the world. The traditional emphasis on the *physical* aspect renders the "sadcrip-supercrip" as two sides of the same coin—one is dependent on caregivers while the other is a miraculous triumph of medical progress teamed with willpower. The transition to a civil rights view allows the physical element to become unremarkable, so attention shifts to the identity issues of a minority culture or, better, the multifaceted life of an individual whose portrayal relegates disability from the foreground to the shadows. This shift also involves a change in point of view, from regarding the person as disabled to recognizing the society and environment as disabling. Understanding how these paradigms succeed one another in both public policy and media contexts is crucial before an assessment can be made of how well or poorly the media serve the community.

Most of us are familiar with the image of the person with a disability as a medical case, as this is the most embedded portrait even in current media. Less attention has been paid to the politically active person with a disability, demanding rights rather than a handout, to the extent that the most reliable historian of the push to pass the ADA called the disability rights campaign a "stealth" movement. When the civil rights agenda accomplishes its economic goals, leading to stronger employment figures especially in terms of white-collar jobs, the consumer model supersedes the political model and solidifies the rationale behind creating a disability media. As a business strategy, the consumer model seems foolproof. Counting on the extant spending power of 54 million Americans, my own magazine as well as other companies in the media and retail sectors jumped the gun on the transition from the civil rights to the consumer phase. Like the major multinationals that bullishly invaded the Russian and Chinese markets slightly ahead of the establishment of a middle class in those transitional economies, we failed mainly because we were too early. This account of disability in the media is not a success story. The optimistic view of a neat linear trajectory from pity to progress defers to a more accurate picture of the hesitant oscillation between entrenched attitudes and short-lived forays into a mature, even comfortable, integrated coverage. The lack of connection between political empowerment and media representation is one of the reasons this anomaly is so intriguing.

The Politics of Representation

The emergence from the medical model can be tracked to the early legislative history of disability policy. If you want to examine a current law that follows the "medical" path, turn to the Social Security rules, which rely on limitations of function as determined by an examination in a doctor's office. These rules are not far removed from the welfare qualifications that governed pensions for injured veterans of the Civil War and World War I. They also take up where the federal rehabilitation efforts to assist victims of industrial accidents, today known as workers' compensation, left off. By 1921, forty-five states had enacted laws requiring medical and financial assistance for those injured on the job (work-related diseases were added much later). In the same decade, effective lobbying on behalf of blind and deaf people resulted in relief laws that offered financial assistance specifically for those disabilities. At that point, only a handful of activists, mainly in the blind community, were uncomfortable with the underlying assumption that people with disabilities could only be beneficiaries of state assistance. There was still a long way to go before a widespread movement to promote independent living would be inaugurated.

In 1935, Franklin Delano Roosevelt signed the Social Security Act, which created assistance programs for adults with specific physical disabilities as catalogued in the text of the law. Under the New Deal, public policy remained focused on the physical impairment of the person with a disability, and the rules drifted toward becoming an incentive not to work since one could lose the federal payment if one's earnings reached a certain level. Flush with tax revenues during the prosperous fifties, the Eisenhower administration amended the Social Security Act in 1956 to create Social Security Disability Insurance (SSDI), a cash-benefit entitlement for workers with long-term disabilities that was federally mandated but left the eligibility determinations to the states. Originally confined to workers between the ages of fifty and sixty-four, by 1960 the lower age limit was removed, and the entitlement applied to anyone with at least ten years' paid work experience whose impairment was "of such severity that he is not only unable to do his previous work but cannot, considering his age, education, and work experience engage in any kind of substantial gainful work which exists in the national economy, regardless of whether such work exists in the immediate area in which he lives or whether a specific job vacancy exists for him or whether he would be hired if he applied for work." While the medical determination of impairment was still integral to the legislation, one can detect the subtle way in which the worm was turning toward civil rights questions in the way in which the question of employment was edging into the policy picture.

In the sixties, architectural and labor issues rose to prominence in disability policymaking. Attention was shifting further away from the medical condition of the "patient" and toward the inability of the built environment or workplace to accommodate a person with a disability. In 1968, Congress passed the federal Architectural Barriers Act which made public buildings and transportation accessible. The opening of the workplace, at least as federally funded, followed five years later with Section 504 of the

Rehabilitation Act of 1973, which outlawed discrimination against people with disabilities who were "otherwise qualified." Although Beltway insiders viewed Section 504 as a minor provision in a $1.55-billion federal aid package for people with disabilities, it made Richard Nixon the first president to sign a civil rights law that prevented discrimination against them. It stipulated that no federal agency, public university, defense contractor, or other organization that was selling to the federal government could discriminate against a person "solely by reason of . . . handicap," an echo of the Civil Rights Act of 1964. Then, as now, there was no "affirmative action" aspect to the bill, which means that there are no provisions for favoring a candidate with a disability over a nondisabled one in roughly equal comparison. In the backlash articles that have recently dominated media coverage of disability laws including the ADA, this is one of the most frequently recurring errors. Another magnet for negative press attention is the high cost of mainstreaming students with disabilities. In 1975, the public schools were the target of the first Education for All Handicapped Children Act (subsequent Individuals with Disabilities Education Acts have essentially been expansions and reauthorizations).

By the late eighties, there were fifty such acts of Congress regarding disabilities, many of which tinkered with the definition of disability, usually in a way that broadened and clarified it in response to a movement that was gaining power and notoriety. A number of sit-ins and demonstrations, most famously the student protests for a deaf president at Gallaudet University in 1988, alerted lawmakers to a constituency that was growing more politically active. That year, a group of thirteen Reagan appointees sitting on the National Council of the Handicapped drafted the first version of the ADA. They were prodded by the charismatic Justin Dart, Jr., whose father was head of the "kitchen cabinet" of California plutocrats who had backed Reagan for the presidency. The council differed from the administration in turning its back on benefits and entitlements to directly address discrimination. Republican senator Lowell Weicker sponsored the first version in its unsuccessful first attempt at passage in 1988 (it was virtually ignored while the Iran-Contra controversy raged). The text of the bill was rewritten to appease business interests (unlike other civil rights laws, it would require expenditures for accessibility) by Democratic senators Tom Harkin of Iowa and Edward Kennedy of Massachusetts. The Senate debate was particularly emotional. In his speech on the floor, Harkin used sign language so that his deaf brother could understand, while Kennedy drew on his own family experiences (his sister is developmentally disabled, his son a below-the-knee amputee because of cancer). Orrin Hatch broke down in tears relating how he had carried his brother-in-law, who slept in an iron lung after polio, up the steps of a

Mormon temple in California. The bill was signed into law by President George H. W. Bush on July 26, 1990, and took effect in 1992. President Bush also had family ties to the "silent army" behind the bill—he and his wife, Barbara, had lost a three-year-old daughter to leukemia, and their sons Neil (learning disability), Marvin (colon removed), and George W. (recovering alcoholic) are all people with disabilities.

That was how the mother of all disability designations, the text of the Americans with Disabilities Act, was created. It is supposed to be the rule of thumb for detecting discrimination in the workplace. Curiously, the ADA does not specify particular medical conditions, as most of the earlier laws did. This alone reflects the shift from a medical to a civil rights view of disability. The ADA reads: "The term 'disability' means with respect to an individual (a) a physical or mental impairment that substantially limits one or more of the major life activities of such individual; (b) a record of such an impairment; (c) being regarded as having such an impairment." In the disability trade, this is viewed as a "social," "sociopolitical," or "civil rights" model as opposed to the old-fashioned, stigmatizing "medical" or "impairment" model. For a journalist, this definition is the abracadabra unlocking a vastly broader range of story possibilities, all of which lend greater interest and dignity to the people with disabilities profiled because they are suddenly business leaders, artists, teachers, farmers, and real people engaged in the same enjoyable or infuriating activities we all share instead of remaining in the passive position of being patients "for" whom something needs to be done. From the perspective of building a magazine or broadcast company, this also means that people with disabilities are a viable paying audience, too. "Disability is not an outcome, it's an input," says Don Lollar of the Centers for Disease Control. "Disability is a demographic variable—just like age, sex, racial ethnicity, socioeconomic status—and it needs to be seen that way, as opposed to a negative health outcome."

The leading thinkers on disability policy recognized the significance of abandoning the old view of people with disabilities as "abnormal." Activists rightly shunned the "medical" model as discriminatory, because it immediately places disability in the category of a deviance or illness that needs to be cured. In an important policy briefing titled "Negative Media Portrayals of the ADA," the National Council on Disability, a Washington-based advocacy group, clearly distinguishes between the old and new models:

> Social Security disability laws are based on the medical model approach, which considers disability to be a person's deviation from the "norm"— a defect, infirmity or ailment—and are designed to be limited to a restricted

group of eligible recipients. The ADA is based on a social or civil rights model and its protections should be available to all who experience discrimination on the basis of disability . . . The medical model attempts to cure or rehabilitate disability; if treatment or rehabilitation is successful, the individual no longer is disabled. If that proves impossible, the medical model envisions that "patients" should be taken care of through long-term health care and income support benefits. At a fundamental level, Social Security disability benefits programs are premised on a medical model approach to disability; they seek to provide income support for people who are found to be totally unable to work due to disability.[1]

Along with the legal redefinition embodied in the ADA, the most prominent writers on disability have set their own parameters, some of them radical and some tending more to the idea of mainstreaming. One of the gentlest and most tolerant theories is the notion of a continuous spectrum including a wide range of disability and ability (think of the relative degrees of hearing or visual impairment, paralysis, epilepsy, diabetes, learning disabilities, or even the range of conditions associated with HIV infection). This view is expressed in a report by Beth Haller, an expert on disability and the media, on the press's predatory attitude toward the ADA:

Sometimes the view that the population splits neatly into two groups on the basis of the presence or absence of disability is not expressed directly, but is displayed in a "we/they" attitude toward persons with disabilities in media coverage. According to this simplistic conception, the task involved in determining who should be covered by the ADA is simply to draw a bright line between those who have a disability and the rest of the population who do not. Anyone who is on the non-disability side of the line but claims to be protected by the ADA is automatically deemed to be a deceitful, malingering, greedy imposter. Such views represent a terrible oversimplification of a much more complicated reality.[2]

Another, more militant point of view from within the disability community casts the blame on the "temporarily able-bodied" (as the nondisabled are jokingly called) for creating a world in which people are thrust into the role of "the disabled." As James Charlton, a Chicago-based activist, has written, deftly invoking the language of the ADA as an example:

Disability is socially constructed. For example, if a particular culture treats a person as having a disability, the person has one. Second, the category "disability" includes people with socially defined functional limitations. For instance, deaf people are considered disabled although many deaf individuals insist they do not have a disability. People do not get to choose whether they have disabilities. Most political activists would define disability as a condition imposed on individuals by society. This definition is mirrored in the Americans with Disabilities Act of 1990: "The term 'disability' means with respect to an individual (a) a physical or mental impairment that substantially limits one or more of the major life activities of such individual; (b) a record of such an impairment; (c) being regarded as having such an impairment."[3]

I would add that the media are complicit in this construction of disability because it defines the ways in which people with disabilities are "regarded," enforcing stereotypes that prolong the "domination" (Charlton's term) that has kept the community down. Although the ADA model is fairer than the medical one, it still splits the world into disabled and nondisabled. This isolation may suit the agendas of those who would opt for a separate disability culture (the radical Deaf with a capital D example comes to mind); it strikes me as inclined to bracket people with disabilities as "other." This estrangement is too obvious in the media. By consigning most stories about people with disabilities to the "back-of-the-book" sections of newspapers or magazines (the soft news on broadcasts), and by using inappropriate language that has long been proscribed by activist groups ("wheelchair-bound," the "handicapped," the lingo of victimhood), editors and producers insidiously serve to bolster the economic and attitudinal status quo of past decades. The mainstream media become a significant component in a structure Charlton aptly characterizes as circular: "In the case of disability, domination is organized and reproduced principally by a circuitry of power and ideology that constantly amplifies the normality of domination and compresses difference into classification norms (through symbols and categories) of superiority and normality against inferiority and abnormality."[4]

More charitably, to elude the paranoia of promulgating a conspiracy theory, the "oppression" is often unwitting or unintentional, caused by well-meaning but ignorant editors and writers, filmmakers and producers who think that by casting a spotlight on how "obstacles are overcome" they serve to improve the lot of the subjects they have chosen. Charlton, along with many other activists and scholars, is quick to pounce on the toll this "benign" misrepresentation takes:

> What images of disability are most prevalent in the mass media? Television shows depicting the helpless and angry cripple as a counterpoint to a poignant story about love or redemption. Tragic news stories about how drugs or violence have "ruined" someone's life by causing him or her to become

disabled, or even worse, stories of the heroic person with a disability who has "miraculously," against all odds, become a successful person (whatever that means) and actually inched very close to being "normal" or at least to living a "normal" life. Most despicable are the telethons "for" crippled people, especially, poor, pathetic, crippled children. These telethons parade young children in front of the cameras while celebrities like Jerry Lewis pander to people's goodwill and pity to get their money. In the United States surveys have shown that more people form attitudes about disabilities from telethons than from any other source.[5]

This paternalistic syndrome translates into economic and political deprivation for people with disabilities, whose status is irreparably harmed by the images projected to the nondisabled world through print and electronic media. Two of the most material among the many signs of its destructive effects are the horrific unemployment figures for people with disabilities (hovering at a steady 80 percent even before the last recession) together with the dwindling ranks of disability-specific publications and programs, a downturn we will examine in the fourth chapter. In other words, even as the situation of other minorities continues to improve, the material signs of acceptance of people with disabilities in the workplace and the mainstream are declining.

One development that concerns advocates who have worked in the disability field for decades is particularly worrisome: the umbrella of the ADA is perceived to be shrinking. This reverses a trend. Legislation defining disability rights began with deafness, blindness, and various mobility impairments such as spinal cord injury and amputation, the so-called physical disabilities, and rapidly expanded to include AIDS and "mental" disabilities from the most serious, such as bipolar disorder, to such controversial conditions as recovery from drug and alcohol addiction, attention deficit disorder (ADD), and Asperger's syndrome, an autism-like condition that makes children react strongly to any change in their routine.

Fifteen years after President Bush signed the ADA into law at a ceremony on the White House south lawn one July afternoon, most in the community are concerned that the broad-brush coverage of the law is being severely curtailed by court decisions, including those of the Supreme Court, which has lately swatted down a number of complaints by questioning the qualifications of the plaintiffs to claim disability. Only one in ten ADA suits is won by the plaintiff, a statistic that now gives lawyers pause. As a policy brief from the National Council on Disability states, "Although Congress intended the ADA to provide broad coverage so that discrimination on the basis of disability could be addressed comprehensively, the courts have construed the ADA's definition of disability very narrowly to make it quite onerous to satisfy. The current legal standard established by the Supreme Court is a strict and demanding one that makes it difficult, and, at times, nearly impossible to prove that one has a disability under the ADA."[6]

The present state of legal affairs makes the ADA look like a sloppily written, unenforceable piece of legislation, but historians of disability beg to differ. It was the product of more than two decades of legal and political discussion regarding how disability should be construed. By eliminating many of the prevailing distinctions (including physical versus mental as well as the older "deserving" versus "undeserving" based on the heroism of returning veterans), the ADA affirmed a pandisability unity the community had only recently shown. Although most people place physical disabilities well ahead of so-called mental disabilities with regard to almost any criterion, in fact there were provisions in the sixties set by the Department of Health, Education, and Welfare for the inclusion of mental disabilities and even alcoholism and drug dependency in the rules.

The political fight for the ADA brought together activists from various groups in cross-disability alliances, notably between the Deaf and blind camps, that do not otherwise harmonize. Why would these rivalries exist in the first place? In part, the fragmentation persists because competition for philanthropic dollars can turn one group against another. There is, moreover, a hierarchy of disabilities that sets up its own discriminatory perversities. It is reflected in the way the press and entertainment industries assign coverage or allot roles, casting according to the visibility and sentimental associations of particular disabilities. Television in particular loves to spotlight the blind person or wheelchair user rather than the amputee or someone with cerebral palsy. The "cuteness" of Chris Burke in the hit comedy *Life Goes On* made it seem as though Down syndrome were telegenic, whereas fear of death haunted the visible signs of AIDS too much to make it palatable for television viewers. This condition-by-condition hierarchy also partitions the disability press into various disability-specific segments, each with its own issues and stances, making assimilation of people with disabilities—if that is indeed the goal—a more and more remote possibility. Even a cursory glance at the accumulated directory of 1,400 disability publications and broadcast outlets published every two years by the National Telability Media Center in Columbia, Missouri, in conjunction with the First Amendment Center at Vanderbilt University, confirms this fragmentation. The hundreds of newsletters devoted to specific conditions represent the overwhelming majority of disability publications. These overshadow by far, in terms of circulation alone, the publications or programs that attempt to cross disability lines. One law may be enough to embrace all these subgroups, but so far no single publication, Web site, or other organization has come along that makes everybody happy.

Where Were the Media?

The distinction between the medical and social models is of paramount importance to an understanding of the media and disability. Nearly all the problems in the representation of people with disabilities can be traced to imposition of the medical model on what would otherwise be compelling and newsworthy narratives. One of the most candid assessments of the problem is offered by Joseph P. Shapiro, a reporter for *U.S. News and World Report* and author of *No Pity,* by far the best history of the disability rights movement and the meeting-by-meeting, demonstration-by-demonstration story of the ADA's passage. Shapiro's own experience as a reporter offers insight into the stubborn way that the representation of people with disabilities would not quite conform to the political and social models that were evolving. The precursor to his definitive history was an article on the mounting excitement of the disability movement he wrote in February 1988, which his editors at *U.S. News* would not publish under the "slug" (category) of politics, where it belonged, because they had the same knee-jerk response to the story idea that most editors had in those days especially, immediately chucking it into the medical bin.

A month after he completed it, with the news peg and numbers threatening to go stale, Shapiro managed to convince the *Washington Post* to run the article. But it appeared as an op-ed rather than a political piece, in the health section of the newspaper. As Shapiro and others have pointed out, the medical "ghetto" into which disability stories are shunted robs them of their impact and impugns their news value. This robbed the movement of public relations leverage during the fight to pass the ADA. As Shapiro relates, the press completely missed the importance of the story:

> The media were of little use to the disability rights movement as it sought passage of the ADA. The reason is that journalists have been too slow to understand the new civil rights consciousness of disabled Americans. As a number of writers have shown, press coverage of people with disabilities has tended to fall into one of two stereotypes: the sad, unlucky disabled person, in need of pity and charity, or the plucky, courageous disabled person, celebrated for overcoming a disability and performing seemingly superhuman feats, whether it is holding a job or scaling a mountain. One is the image of Tiny Tim; the other that of the "supercrip."[7]

This state of affairs continues to haunt the role of disability stories in the press. Ideally we would be able to track the advance in status from the medical to the political to the consumer stages along a chronological continuum that runs parallel with shifts in media coverage from one beat to the next, health to policy to business and lifestyle, but the grim reality is otherwise. While the legal status of people with disabilities in the United States has evolved steadily at least through the second of these three stages, the media has not kept pace. Just as Shapiro described more than a decade ago, examples of the medical model persistently dominate the mainstream press, portraying people with disabilities either as tragic figures or triumphant "supercrips" (usually athletes and entertainers who "overcome" their obstacles). Playing on raw emotions and the public's passion for the victorious underdog, these personal sagas make for gripping reading in the human interest section of your local newspaper. When a celebrity is "stricken"—Christopher Reeve, Michael J. Fox, Montel Williams, or Lance Armstrong—the editors and producers of national news organizations fall all over each other to run a mass-market variation on the theme, but in terms of narrative structure the celebrity story is simply the same notes scored for a symphony orchestra rather than a string quartet. This plangent melody is also important to the house or gans of the major disability organizations, which play their versions as fundraising anthems.

Some magazines and television shows have moved on to the political and even consumer stages, particularly when there is breaking news to "peg" a story on, such as the Gallaudet protests in 1988, the passage of the ADA in 1990 or the subsequent Supreme Court decisions on ADA-based cases, or, in a widely covered product launch, the introduction of a Barbie doll in a wheelchair by Mattel in 1997. These breakout stories are more the exception than the rule, especially in the mainstream press, owing in part to the quiet state into which the political movement has passed as well as the recalcitrance of the media in the face of pressure to change.

Just having a positive media presence may strike some as a sign of progress. After centuries of either demonization or invisibility, conditions that still prevail in many parts of the world (notably Asia), disability emerged blinking into the light of public consciousness in the late nineteenth century. The medical model is the descendant of the Dickensian legacy of the poster child, which dominated coverage of disability well into the 1950s. Shocking as it sounds, it survives in the ad campaigns for nonprofits as well as the annual rite of the Jerry Lewis telethon, still the primary source of media exposure to disability for most nondisabled Americans. Right behind the telethons in terms of mass appeal are the "miracles" trumpeted by Oprah Winfrey or other television producers bent on delivering the nightly wow factor. Such narratives only perpetuate the tendency to consign disability to an issue of the body. Because many of the largest specialized publications and productions devoted to disability are actually vehicles of charity, designed to raise funds to cure an illness or mend severed spines, they have an inherent medical bent. The good they do in the lab or operating theater (there is no denying that the telethons alone have raised well over a billion dollars for treatment and research, including the monumental assignment of tracking the genes that cause some conditions) is meant to offset the sociopolitical harm of keeping people with disabilities in the passive position of being recipients. The conundrum for these groups is finding a way to keep the funds flowing without resorting to the time-tested pity and fear tactics that the medical model provides.

That means refocusing attention on the rights of people with disabilities. The political model was a late bloomer in the media, especially by comparison with the treatment of other minority groups. On screen it emerged in such highly charged films as *Children of a Lesser God* (1986) and *Born on the Fourth of July* (1989), which drove home the point that people with disabilities were long overdue for recognition and a drastic revision of their place in society. As the battle for the ADA in the late 1980s heated up, editors and reporters realized that a disability article could be hard news rather than soft, a breaking political story for the front page instead of a sweet human interest piece tucked into the back of the issue. An important catalyst for change in this regard was the entry into the newsroom of writers and editors with disabilities, whose personal experience could challenge the stereotypes and pull such stories out of the medical ghetto onto the front page or into the op-ed section. One of the genuine heroes of this integration of the newsroom is John Hockenberry, a star correspondent on NBC's *Dateline* who has covered war stories from Bucharest to Baghdad.

Hockenberry's prominence and his ability to make sure his assignments are frontline, lead material are the exception, not the rule. More often, reporters with disabilities are confined to "their" beat, and that means medicine. The prevailing ignorance regarding the importance of retrieving disability stories from the health or human interest sections and offering them their rightful place in the news section distinctly limits the community's impact as a political constituency. The medical model is more than just a theoretical category or a "slug" in a magazine. Consider the numbers alone. You do not need to be a statistician to perceive that the population of people with disabilities in the United States would shrink appreciably if SSDI instead of ADA numbers were used. The former links Social Security payouts to doctors' evaluations and state approval, strictures that keep the statistics low. The ADA, by contrast, initially flung its arms out wide to signal to attorneys and activists the willingness of the federal government to recognize a vastly more diverse array of disabilities.

The Consumer Model by the Numbers

For the consumer model to prevail, the figures have to add up. The current estimates of the size of the total disability population come from a wide range of sources, the most frequently cited of which are the United Nations, for worldwide numbers, and the U.S. Census Bureau, both of which agree that one in five people worldwide have some kind of disability. According to the 2000 U.S. Census, the most recent available, 49.7 million Americans aged five and over had a disability, accounting for 19 percent of the population. Of these, 5.2 million were between ages five and twenty; the core magazine and television audience of 30.6 million were between twenty-one and sixty-four; and 14 million were sixty-five or over, which in the eyes of some in the community is stretching the purest definition of disability because of the link between age and such problems as deafness and vision or mobility impairment. The census numbers are considered by advocates and promoters of disability commerce to be low, particularly with regard to so called mentally disabled as well as deaf and hard of hearing Americans, and charges abound that sloppy census takers skipped many respondents who were deaf or developmentally disabled. Another reason the numbers are vexed is that the Census Bureau conducts other surveys measuring disability, including the Survey of Income and Program Participation (SIPP), surveys that use different questions and that in 1997 estimated the number of people with disabilities at 53 million, or 19.7 percent, using a more extensive set of criteria regarding the measurement of functional difficulties ("Do you have difficulty lifting 25 pounds?"). The trouble is that many people who may have difficulty lifting a twenty-five-pound weight would also contend that this does not have an impact on their daily activities, so they would not necessarily tell a census taker that they have a disability. The figure most often kicked around by activists as well as by media executives trying to pull advertisers is 54 million Americans, an upward revision of the census figures used by such advocacy organizations as the National Council on Disability.

The evolution of the census questionnaire is a crucial factor in these shifting numbers. Back in 1970 the question was whether or not the person had a "transportation handicap." But that mistakenly measured problems with the environment rather than the person. By 2000, the questions were focused on blindness, deafness, or severe impairment of or limitations on physical activities as well as difficulty in learning, remembering, or working at a job. In the eyes of advocates, this perpetuates the "medical" view of disability by dwelling too much on function. It clearly skews the count toward physical disabilities (affecting mobility, sight, or hearing) at the expense of the so-called mental disabilities (bipolar disorder, ADD, recovery from drugs or alcohol).

Among the key statistics of interest to advertisers, who write the checks, are education and income levels, as well as a breakdown of the overall numbers by categories of disability. According to a March 2001 supplement to the census's Current Population Survey, the mean earnings of full-time workers age sixteen to sixty-four with disabilities were a dismal $33,109 (compared with $43,269 for the nondisabled), and only 11 percent had college degrees (72 percent had high school diplomas or higher). A cheerier statistical picture, used by most disability publications to keep their page rates up, was presented by the Harris Poll number 59 of October 2000, which zeroed in on employment issues and the effects of advances in medical care on the unemployment rate (more people with severe disabilities live longer, but are unable to work). Sponsored by the National Organization on Disability, which speaks on behalf of both mental and physical disabilities, the poll pointed out that people with disabilities are an increasingly large percentage of the American population, partly because of longer life expectancy rates due to better care, and that the proportion of adults with disabilities who graduated from high school increased from 61 percent to 78 percent between 1986 and 2000 (when the survey of 997 noninstitutionalized people aged eighteen and over was conducted by phone and online).

Coverage, advertising, casting, budgets, technology (such as closed-captioning), and other business variables pondered by media executives depend in large part on the raw numbers assigned to various types of disability. While 25 million have mobility impairments of some kind (difficulty walking a quarter mile or climbing a flight of ten stairs), the hardcore, visibly disabled group is generally perceived to be the 2.2 million who are wheelchair users and 6.4 million who use canes, crutches or walkers. This accounts for why most ads, TV programs, movies, or magazine photos include wheelchair users as the token person with a disability. Another defined constituency is the 8 million deaf or hard of hearing Americans (the National Association of the Deaf says it is more like 13.4 million hearing impaired and 1.8 million deaf). Reaching the deaf and hard of hearing circle has always proven to be one of the most difficult media challenges, in part because of the debate over the linguistic autonomy of American Sign Language, which purists would say excludes English-language publications. They prove to be the toughest demographic to win over, even for disability publications. Another challenge is reaching the 7.7 million readers who have difficulty seeing the words and letters in ordinary newspaper print even with glasses. The forgotten group is the 14.3 million with so-called mental disabilities, which includes 1.9 million with Alzheimer's, senility, or dementia, and 3.5 million with learning disabilities, a number that is already probably way out of date after a veritable epidemic of autism since these figures were gathered in 1997. Unpleasant as it is to ponder, there is a pecking order in the disability community that reflects public opinion, and at the bottom are two other groups that qualify for nondiscriminatory protection under the ADA, people with AIDS (just under 1 million), and those in recovery from drugs and alcohol (Alcoholics Anonymous has over 2 million members).

Common Cause

With all those juicy demographics ripe for the picking, and the rise of the person with a disability as a consumer, it still surprises me that as late as 1996 there was no cross-disability magazine on the newsstands to lure advertisers with promises of an untapped minority niche market far bigger than any other in publishing history. So I helped start one, and called it *WE*. When we assembled our staff and first story list, we actively sought a pan-disability platform and the most flexible possible definition of disability. Our position was in part motivated by profit (bigger circulation, so can't we all just get along?). We also genuinely felt that the success of the magazine would depend on building bridges among the many disability groups that were then, well after the unifying fervor of political struggle had abated and during the malaise of an economic downturn that was leaving many behind in the job market, a jigsaw puzzle of antagonistic forces. Advertisers soon pricked up their ears to hear that there were millions of Americans out there with a disability, with $1 trillion in aggregate income. And, even from the start, we had no trouble getting mayors, senators, and presidential candidates on the phone, along with high-level executives from major U.S. corporations eager to trumpet their corporate diversity programs and hawk their disability-friendly products.

Yet from a purely practical standpoint, the cross-disability coverage posed some tricky questions that needed fast answers regarding the editorial mix of every issue. My job was to make sure somehow that each constituency had its representation in the magazine at some point in the yearlong cycle. Finding articles about amputees, wheelchair users, blind or deaf people was never tough, but we needed to be more inventive to make sure epilepsy, cerebral palsy, multiple sclerosis, and muscular dystrophy were spaced out across issues rather than clumped together in one. Our third issue drew roars of disapproval from the publisher—"too many wheelchairs"—and the counterpoint between physical and so-called mental disabilities was always a delicate issue, as was AIDS, after the Supreme Court decision in 1999 to include it in its legal definition of disability as impairing a major life function. There was an obvious economic incentive for us to cast the net as widely as possible and include every conceivable category of disability in our own projections of the audience we had in mind: we wanted to suck in advertisers with the most amazing possible numbers. The more the merrier was our motto. The novelty of the concept was itself a challenge, and many veterans in the disability field wondered if we could pull it off. Tari Susan Hartman is one of the premier experts on civil rights, a longtime advocate who in 1979 started the Screen Actors Committee of Performers with Disabilities, co-chaired an important arm of the President's Committee on Disability, authored the first book of guidelines on disability etiquette for journalists, and founded a dynamic communications consulting firm in California that recently teamed with the Nielsen National Research Group in a breakthrough data project to measure the disability market. As one of the original prophets of the consumer model, and a rare example of an advocate who functions as well in the corporate boardroom as in the political caucus room, her perspective is invaluable. She observes:

> The specialized media was born out of the disability rights movement of the 1970s and rolls on the shoulders of the civil rights and women's movements. There is, however, an important distinction—disability is a bicultural experience. Unlike people of color, those from specific nationalities, religions, tribes, cultural groupings, etc., most people with disabilities do not come from or are aware of a rich lineage—that is the glue connecting one generation to another with group identity, pride, and shared history. Therefore, it is harder to understand and therefore cover, market to and understand, this "disability community" accurately. We have had our news media victories, and still the backlash continues from some sectors of the business community, from some fear-driven companies and industries who really don't want "us" as customers. I guess they don't realize our money is as green as the next guy's.[8]

Although we were on the lookout for ways to build this consciousness of common ground and expand the disability family, not all people with disabilities shared our views. In addition to the predictable outcry from homophobes against the ruling on AIDS, there were many who refused to be lumped together with people who have so-called mental disabilities or, far more virulently, with the subset (also covered under the ADA) of people in recovery from drugs and alcohol. One significant consideration in all this was the possibility that the line separating disabled from nondisabled could become so blurred as to lose all significance, robbing people in need of "special" treatment or the benefits of their status or simply obliterating the need to consider disability as a basis for identity at all. As counterintuitive as this may sound in the context of a book on how disability is presented in the media, the desire that one's disability be singled out and represented as such represents the polar opposition to the invisibility that also haunts the community. When disability status is conferred so widely as to become ubiquitous, it becomes meaningless, in the eyes of those who resent the inclusion, for instance, of an ever wider spectrum of behavioral conditions such as autism, ADD, Asperger's, and bipolar disorders. This presents a dilemma because, while politically or economically it is handy to have large numbers to cite, on an individual basis the dilution of disability as a category can be anathema. In a recent essay on "neurodiversity" that appeared in the *New York Times,* Amy Harmon observed the reluctance with which new additions to the disability movement have been received: "As the number of Americans with brain disorders grows, so has skepticism toward the grab bag of syndromes they are being tagged with, from A.D.D. to Asperger's to bipolar I, II or III. But in a new kind of disabilities movement, many of those who deviate from the shrinking subset of neurologically 'normal' want tolerance, not just of their diagnoses, but of their behavioral quirks. They say brain differences, like body differences, should be embraced, and argue for an acceptance of 'neurodiversity.'"[9] Everybody's a winner, as they say at the Special Olympics.

The Passing Lane

On the opposite end of the spectrum, there are those who refuse to be identified as disabled. While proponents of disability culture would accuse them of being in denial, they would invoke their right to privacy and their justifiable fear of discrimination, even violence (the rape statistics for women with disabilities are horrendous). On an ideological plane, their assertion is that their achievements and lives in general ought not be measured by disability yardsticks. As Stephen Hawking warned me near the beginning of my run as editor in chief, he was not about to be characterized as the world's greatest disabled astrophysicist, nor did he think much of the Paralympics and other "special" events: "Judge us in absolute terms." This is a stern test for a journalist, particularly when the overarching message is that life is great with a disability. Although the gay media can proudly go around "outing" celebrities, ethical and legal codes regarding privacy render this approach to disability journalism impossible. One of the reasons the representation of people with disabilities in the press is such a fascinating problem is due to the complexities posed by this question of identity.

Prominent voices in the disability studies field wrestle with the question of "passing" (pretending to be nondisabled) posed so forcibly by the Canadian sociologist Erving Goffman. In the late fifties, examining how mental patients could constructively reintegrate into society, Goffman prepared his brilliant delineation of how people with disabilities are stigmatized, eventually offered in his book *Stigma: Notes on the Management of Spoiled Identity.* This remarkably prescient foray into the identity politics of disability remains the bible of many thinkers in the field. Sadly, it is still on target in our body-conscious world, whereas most of the references to African-Americans, Jews, and homosexuals seem dated. Goffman's treatise hinges on the duality of inside and outside. Managing stigmas is largely a question of what happens in public. Mass media vehicles such as magazines and television are a paradigmatic example of how this plays out. The popularity of disability comes at a price. Goffman has an answer for an important question: Why would people with disabilities remain bracketed as marginal no matter how they are presented? He conjures the superb metaphor of the stigmatized person as a "resident alien" in the mainstream:

> The special situation of the stigmatized is that society tells him he is a member of the wider group, which means he is a normal human being, but that he is also "different" in some degree, and that it would be foolish to deny this difference. This differentness itself of course derives from society, for ordinarily before a difference can matter much it must be conceptualized collectively by the society as a whole. . . . Thus, even while the stigmatized individual is told that he is a human being like everyone else, he is being told that it would be unwise to pass or to let down "his" group. In brief, he is told he is like anyone else and that he isn't—although there is little agreement among spokesmen as to how much of each he should claim to be. This contradiction and joke is his fate and his destiny. It constantly challenges those who represent the stigmatized, urging these professionals to present a coherent politics of identity, allowing them to be quick to see the "inauthentic" aspects of other recommended programs but slow indeed to see that there may be no "authentic" solution at all.[10]

In one paragraph, Goffman hits many nerves. From the left-handed compliment implicit in the word "special" to the responsibility of being a credit to one's disability and the secret shame of passing, he reminds us of so many of the emotional subtexts that most magazine or television profiles never even approach. This is one of the reasons that memoirs have turned out to be such an important genre. The platform of the writer is his or her disability, and the scope of the genre allows for an in-depth exploration, beyond the usual limitations of a magazine story, of an issue as touchy as this. The problem in journalism often boils down to the confinements of "writing to space" (adhering to the word count), but too many articles wind up skimming the surface, adhering to the public persona. A more introspective examination of disability's personal ramifications is left to a fast-growing subdiscipline in the humanities rocketing along the path earlier taken by African-American, postcolonial, and women's studies, and queer theory. The concept of a dual identity is a common denominator linking disability studies with these other areas. Most academic experts in the field focus on the rift between society and the individual with disabilities, which necessitates a disguise or an attitude. In this regard, disability studies has taken up the marginalized stance of many other similar subdisciplines. For any journalist hoping to understand the subtler aspects of the community's complexity, this is essential reading.

The literature of the movement is divided among advocacy journalism, memoirs, and academic studies. A key theme in many works is the prosthesis, which goes far beyond the material replacement parts to which that term usually refers. For some, the narrative of their lives or a medium itself (a favorite example is the Internet) is likened to a prosthesis, because the narrative or the medium performs a useful function. For others, such as the blind French scholar Henri-Jacques Stiker, the prosthesis connotes replacement: "The image of the maimed person and of the society around him becomes prosthetic. Replacement, re-establishment of the prior situation, substitutions, compensation—all this now becomes possible language."[11] The scary endgame in this scenario is a homogeneous culture in which that loathed dividing line between disabled and "normal" has been eliminated, but only because (it seems almost like eugenics) the disabled end of the spectrum has been lopped off:

> The trick consists in this: in a liberal, prosperous, and technologically advanced society, means can be found so that the disabled no longer appear different. They will be admitted on the condition that they are perfectly assimilated to the able-bodied. This assimilation may initially take the form of a sustained exclusion: limited resources, specialized institutions, separate work places, etc. But the moment will come when exclusion is no longer a problem: it is itself working on behalf of effacement. The time will come when the disabled will no longer be able to raise their voices and many will no longer have the desire or the taste to do so. What are you complaining about? What would we complain about? Complaint becomes impossible, this is the direction in which we are going. "If you are like everybody else, even though you got here by a detour, why should you have anything to say?"[12]

Taking off on Stiker's point, there is a school of thought that says writers with disabilities ought to foster their otherness, to wield the narrative prosthesis more like a weapon than a crutch. This rejects the "heroes of assimilation" approach that Goffman identified. The later "reactionary" defiance of assimilation is not always practical within the economic constraints of commercial publishing—my lifestyle magazine would not have survived if we had taken that tone—but it does reflect the frustration felt by writers and readers with disabilities at the long history of misrepresentation. One of the leading advocates of this position is David T. Mitchell, who writes in the volume *Narrative Prosthesis:*

> The power of transgression always originates at the moment when the derided object embraces its deviance as value. Perversely championing the terms of their own stigmatization, marginal peoples alarm the dominant culture with a canniness about their own subjugation. The embrace of denigrating terminology forces the dominant culture to face its own violence head-on because the authority of devaluation has been claimed openly and ironically. Thus, the minority culture deflects the stigmatizing definition back on to the offenders by openly advertising them in public discourse. The effect shames the dominant culture into a recognition of its own dehumanizing precepts. What was most devalued is now righted by a self-naming that detracts from the original power of the condescending terms.[13]

One of the most valuable ethical lessons of my foray into the field came early in my tenure as editor in chief: not everybody likes you to speak for him or her. It was embarrassing to have people with disabilities hand back a free copy of the magazine I had offered to them when they realized its premise, but the message sunk in. I was not visibly a person with a disability, and they were not pleased to be identified as such. One of the reasons that the texts considered to have the greatest validity in the field are written in the first person is summarized in the slogan "Nothing about us without us." Yet anyone who knows the media business will admit that it is collaborative in nature, an amalgam of agendas and ideas answering to an array of motives, often ulterior. For a hermeneutic tool that may help us understand how the media and the subject with a disability (including an author) complement one another, we can turn to a controversial topic that comes from the disability field. "Facilitated communication" is a much-derided method of assisting people with severe developmental and physical disabilities, including autism, to communicate using physical support for them as they spell out messages on a keyboard or letter board. At Syracuse University there is a Facilitated Communication Institute (six-part video series for only $250) claiming that it allows, after a lifetime of silence, those who cannot speak to suddenly and unexpectedly find a linguistic code and disclose their latent intellectual skills. In a long study published in 1995 by the American Psychological Association's peer-reviewed journal *American Psychologist,* the skeptical authors (John W. Jacobson, James A. Mulick, and Allen A. Schwartz), skewered the theory and its supporters, as well as the media, for popularizing facilitated communication particularly as it is used to make allegations of sexual abuse against people with disabilities (like repressed memory therapy, another hot-button issue in psychology). They reported that controlled research has shown facilitated communication to be a fad—worse, a fake—controlled by the assistants and pushed by overzealous educators, social theorists, human services advocates, "postmodernists," and profiteers. The article raises a couple of interesting philosophical points, including the eradication of the disability distinction in yet another way:

> It is perhaps a short leap from a position that people with disabilities should have a full range of opportunities to the position that people labeled as disabled are, in fact, not disabled at all. Indeed, one could suggest that the professional community has somehow confined such individuals through unflattering descriptions that say more about the limitations of Western society than the limitations of people. Are all organic and functional deficits to be redefined as cultural sequelae, incapacities with meaning only as they relate to the fit with societal demands? Or, is there an objective foundation to disability that can be defined, quantified, and measured, a foundation that has something to do with unusual characteristics and features of the actual development and performance of an individual?[14]

As we examine the uneasy way that media and people with disabilities hit and miss each other's meanings, I wonder if facilitated communication, including its shoddily manipulative undercurrent, is not an apt description of the muddled agendas and codes in the media's representation of disability. Here we have journalists with little experience of disability in charge of writing or producing the story, or writers with disabilities doing their best to impress editors and book buyers who are nondisabled with narratives that are dramatic enough to be worth publishing, and readers who have limited capacity to care or comprehend trying to take it all in. As a writer, editor, and teacher I perceive a great deal of facilitating involved in all this communicating, and consider it an important question to separate the voices of disability from the intermediaries—so that the authentic voices may be clearly heard.

CHAPTER TWO

whose Life is it Anyway?

The Use and Abuse of the Disability Memoir

I will turn diseases into commodities.
—Falstaff, in Henry IV, *part I*

We had the good luck of starting *WE* magazine right in the middle of the golden age of the disability memoir, when earth-shaking revelations were coming fast and furious from the laptops of glamorous celebrities including Christopher Reeve, Lance Armstrong, Kirk Douglas, Montel Williams, and Michael J. Fox. These were joined on the shelves of the book store chains by memoirs of such second-tier media fixtures as Andrea Bocelli, Gabriel Garcia Marquez, and John Hockenberry, and by those of more insightful if less *Access Hollywood* types including Kay Redfield Jamison, a major-league advocate for the rights of mental health patients who at the time was short-listed for surgeon general. Book publishers worldwide were enjoying surprise best sellers such as Hirotade Ototake's *No One's Perfect,* which lasted for months on the top of the Japanese lists, or a slim and poetic volume by the French fashion editor Dominique Bauby that, even after the author's death, held the number one ranking. Week after week the review copies and bound galleys would arrive at our office from publishers large and small, an endless library chronicling life with epilepsy, multiple sclerosis, autism, blindness, deafness, Down syndrome, obsessive-compulsive disorder, and addictions of all kinds. To feed the maw of public curiosity about cyclists fighting testicular cancer and other medical dramas that in previous generations would have remained unspoken (even in my mother's time, the word cancer was seldom uttered in polite conversation, and some people still refer to it in hushed tones as "the big C"), a bizarre sort of competition among writers and wannabes with disabilities began to simmer. This was business, not altruism. Book publishers, beset by industry consolidation and straining under the weight of celebrity and political autobiographies for which they had vastly overpaid and which they were now getting back as returns, having printed well over the numbers of copies that could be digested by the marketplace, suddenly found a rich vein of high-margin material that dovetailed neatly with the self-help and spirituality categories. The books were full enough of aphoristic sound bites to be Oprah-friendly, so that a quick television spot could translate into hundreds of thousands of books moved. Consider this banality from *Morrie: In His Own Words:* "It's very important to be kind and loving to yourself. Befriend yourself in the same way you feel compassionate and gentle with other people. If you practice the principles of grieving, accepting, and forgiving yourself, you will be making a start in that direction."[1] As Hallmark found decades ago, that sort of saccharin sells.

The Morrie books are the all-time leader and prime example of this "who would have thought" best-seller craze. The originator was a slim volume called *Tuesdays with Morrie,* which describes encounters between Morrie Schwartz, a retired Brandeis University professor of sociology who has late-stage ALS, and his former student Mitch Albom, a successful sports journalist with ESPN. It offers what the callow subtitle calls "an old man, a young man, and life's greatest lesson." The book took off when Ted Koppel devoted three half-hour segments in prime time to his interviews with Schwartz. Soon the wisdom of the old professor was all around us, in stereo, with books on tape and disk as well as an ABC television movie starring Jack Lemmon (produced by the inescapable Oprah) and an off-Broadway play. More than 80 million "units" have been sold so far, and the book has been parked for four years on the hardcover best seller list. It spawned a paperback instant best seller, and then Doubleday, which published the original hardcover, through its Delta subsidiary issued a paperback of Schwartz's own ruminations, despite the fact that he had died in 1995, four years earlier. In all, the Morrie franchise produced world-record quantities of both sap and royalties.

On the strength of the Morrie books and knockoffs, publishers and booksellers rejiggered their marketing plans. Right near the self-help and psychology sections, Borders stores in New York and California began sporting a disability section. It was no secret in the community that five-figure advances were being offered to the hastily pulled-together stories of nobodies and their mothers, often with film rights. Agents went on the prowl for writers with a trace of palsy or chronic anything. Given the incentives, fame and fortune, the temptation to play up the drama intensified with every successful made-for-television movie or best seller. The insipid *Tuesdays with Morrie* has taken on legendary quality not only in the publishing field but in the "disability industrial complex." The horrifyingly simplistic "Chicken Soup" series, which uses an elaborate coding system to identify various illnesses and conditions in the thousands of sob stories it receives daily, is loaded with disability narratives that follow the basic "overcoming" recipe of normalcy, injury, recovery. The boom has also brought revisionist histories and biographies, such as the re-editing of Helen Keller's life and biographies of John F. Kennedy, Glenn Gould, Lord Byron, Francis Bacon, and Franklin Delano Roosevelt emphasizing the disability angle. Even disability studies, in lockstep with many other academic disciplines, took a screeching turn toward first-person revelations. At national conferences, one of the most popular sessions became memoir readings, and seminar papers were delivered on selling the book and movie rights to one's story.

All this was great for the publishing industry (the "Chicken Soup" machine alone buoyed the quarterly reports of Amazon, Borders, and Barnes & Noble). Did it bring any benefits to the disability community beyond the royalty checks? The rush to publish such intimacies has been a mixed blessing. On the one hand, as case studies commanding broad audiences, these autobiographies have spread the word and introduced millions of temporarily able-bodied readers to the innermost details of life with a disability from the point of view of the person with a disability. There is a substantial difference between the impact on public awareness of a book such as Lance Armstrong's *It's Not about the Bike* (700,000 copies and massive press coverage) and an article on testicular cancer even in the *New England Journal of Medicine* (circulation 200,000). The more that such books accomplish in breaking the silence surrounding disability, the better off the community ought to be, much as the literature of AIDS, led by Larry Kramer and Tony Kushner, forced recognition and acceptance where there had been much resistance.

Within the community, the writing, interpreting, and teaching of autobiographical texts took on ever greater importance. As the eminent scholar David Mitchell observes in the preface to the collection *Narrative Prosthesis:* "In order to be disabled, one must narrate one's disability for others in sweeping strokes or hushed private tones. And this narration must inevitably show how we conquer our disabilities or how they conquer us. The lack of other options refuses us the pursuit of anonymity in ordinary involvements."[2] On the positive side, there is instant credibility in the first-person voice, which cuts straight through the "facilitated communication" knot and lands straight on "nothing about us without us." Yet at a certain point, inevitably the writing takes a turn. To capture the attention of an agent or editor, thousands of readers, and a movie studio, writers naturally pander to expectations of pathos and "courage in the face of adversity." The narrative that sells preempts the narrative that empowers in a trade-off that perpetuates the stereotypes that satisfy the nondisabled readers who economically support the books. This phenomenon in U.S. publishing history can be traced back to the instant success of Helen Keller's *Story of My Life,* which from its inception as a magazine series was a moneymaker for its young author and an affirmative, "inspirational" story for her millions of fans. As a model for disability memoirs to come, it offered a dramatic structure of loss and recovery, hopelessness giving way to a dramatic breakthrough, that readers have come to expect from all subsequent variations on the theme. F. Scott Fitzgerald, no stranger to disability (his own memoir, *The Crack Up,* is an early version of the so-called mental disability narrative followed by William Styron and others) once declared, "There are no second acts in American lives." The disability memoir is all second act—its very premise is the triumph of recovery and forward motion.

On the other hand, there is an academic tendency toward folding back on a literary text, reflecting on the canon, the genre, the ambiguities of a particular text—this is what we scholars do in seminars or on paper. The theoretical process of second-guessing, analyzing, and questioning exerts its own pressure to structure the critical narrative in a certain way, generally with added complexity and symbolism. As banal as it sounds, since academic careers depend on publication and peer (as well as student) evaluations, there is a built-in reward system for arcane, overwrought theory and critique both in the publish-or-perish track and in the teaching track, and disability studies is putting the grist of the memoir through the mill much as other departments ground up queer confessionals, rap murder accounts, and rape testimony. Much like the maw of commercial publishing, the maw of theory masticates nearly any fare, although certain food groups on the menu are not as well received as others. The memoirists who ascend to places of privilege in the classroom, such as Harriet Johnson, Mary Johnson, Nancy Mairs, Kenny Fries, Temple Grandin, and Stephen Kuusisto, are usually active in advocacy, while others are chewed up and spit out (Keller, Oliver Sacks, and poor Christopher Reeve). In an essay on the teaching of disability memoirs, G. Thomas Couser of Hofstra University relates the genre to ethnography, emphasizing the clash of cultures between the community and the "outside world." This leads to a paradox:

> The problem of disability autobiography lies in the fact that what Western autobiography has valued (that which distinguishes the individual from others) the medical model of disability has devalued (some deviation from normality in the individual's body). Autoethnography may offer a way out of this bind for life writers, critics, and teachers, because it speaks of disability as a condition that is affirmative rather than destructive, defining rather than confining. It is this subgenre that is most likely to realize the counterdiscursive potential of disability narrative. Disabled bodies have long been cultural signifiers whose meaning has been largely determined by

nondisabled people; today disabled people are signifying on their bodies in their own ways with their own voices. Their testimony should be an integral part of the exploration of disability in the humanities.[3]

Helen Keller, the Matrix

Many scholars in disability studies call for "a literature of our own," written in such a way that the interpretation as well as the facts are coded according to disability culture instead of the point of view of people who do not have disabilities and who therefore construe a narrative according to either the medical model of the case study or, just as unacceptable, the "inspirational" model of Morrie and his ilk. The mother of all disability memoirists, of course, is Helen Keller. Now over a century old, her best-selling *Story of My Life* continues to stir controversy, as it did from publication (by Doubleday), when its teenage author was accused of plagiarism and deceit by jealous factions in the disability community. The best way to reexperience Keller's pathbreaking book today is in a reissue that presents three texts in one, combining her unexpurgated text, including notebook entries, with the accompanying texts of her teachers Anne Sullivan and John Macy and her letters, mainly to Alexander Graham Bell, to whom the book is dedicated, and others that open the documentary trail to a revisionist reading. Keller's memoir by its success laid the groundwork for the inspirational bestseller but is written with a lack of self-pity, remarkably restrained for the era, that lifts it to a level a cut above the current examples of the genre. It also turns out to be a seminal example of the difficulties posed by the authorship question when "facilitated communication" is involved. Keller finger-spelled the text into the hand of Anne Sullivan, her teacher, and there were charges from the book's earliest appearance that Sullivan and Macy, who married her, had taken a heavy-handed role in leading Helen to express "her" story in their own, loftily literary style.

Keller was a celebrity at age eight, following in the tradition of other deaf-blind children who had demonstrated their skills before crowds. The autobiography began as a six-part series for *Ladies' Home Journal* in 1902, for which Keller was paid the princely sum of three thousand dollars, a fat fee for an undergraduate lit major at Radcliffe. Keller was and is an industry unto herself. There was never any denying her mass-market pull—after the first-serial bonanza with *Ladies' Home Journal* and the magazine's strong newsstand numbers, the book sold through the millions. Then the performance rights kicked in, as the autobiography spawned a play, *The Miracle Worker,* by William Gibson that had its debut on Broadway in 1959. The audience was vastly expanded when a film version was released in 1962. Like Anne Frank, Keller became a standard text in the school canon, locking in course adoption orders that guaranteed millions more in book sales. Of the major nonprofits that have raised millions of dollars with her likeness and texts, the largest beneficiary by far is the New York–based National Foundation for the Blind, for which Keller acted as spokesperson through the sixties and which still works the association relentlessly.

The text of the memoir is sharper, grittier and in many ways more ahead of its time than the play and movies derived from it. Keller in her own voice is far less prone to cliché and sentimentality than her champions, the Broadway producers and movie moguls without disabilities who played the pity card for profit. In one of the excerpts from her notebooks published in the new edition, she expresses impatience at being treated as a walking saint by her fellow Radcliffe freshmen: "Once someone wrote to me that in his mind I was always 'sweet and earnest,' thinking only of what is wise, good and interesting—as if he thought I was one of those wearisome saints of whom there are only too many in the world! I always laugh at these foolish notions, and assure my friends that it is much better to have a few faults and be cheerful and responsive in spite of all deprivations than to retire into one's shell, pet one's affliction, clothe it with sanctity, and then set one's self up as a monument of patience, virtue, goodness and all in all; but even while I laugh I feel a twinge of pain in my heart, because it seems rather hard to me that any one should imagine that I do not feel the tender bonds which draw me to my young sisters— the sympathies springing from what we have in common—youth, hope, a half-eager, half-timid attitude towards the life before us and above all the royalty of maidenhood."[4] There are, granted, plenty of sappy moments as well in *The Story of My Life:* "Is it not true, then, that my life with all its limitations touches at many points the life of the World Beautiful? Everything has its wonders, even darkness and silence, and I learn, whatever state I may be in, therein to be content."[5]

Her celebrity made her, even from age eleven, the target of jealous detractors in the disability community. One of her earliest and most ardent champions was Michael Anagnos, the director of the Perkins Institute for the Blind, where Annie Sullivan had trained. After breaking with Keller over a perceived slight in one of her published stories, he leveled one plagiarism accusation after another, suggesting that she was hardly "fluent" in English and that she used color and other visual metaphors in ways she could not have an epistemological basis for understanding. He eventually dropped this bombshell: "Helen Keller is a living lie."

This charge has not dimmed Keller's star. The bookish young Radcliffe undergraduate, who studied Milton, Tennyson, and Wordsworth and who was avowedly taken by the Little Lord Fauntleroy novels of Frances Hodgson Burnett, was nothing if not a gifted mimic, turning her own story into a version of such poetry and dime novels she loved. Even in an age when American universities are facing massive plagiarism scandals involving both their students and their faculty, Keller's borrowing seems an endearing habit. In his introduction to the re-edited volume of the autobiography and documentary materials, Roger Shattuck, a literary critic and historian whose previous books include a related study, *The Wild Boy of Aveyron,* generously compares Keller's autobiography to the *Odyssey.* He points out that the word "miracle" occurs twice in the book, but not in the famous water pump scene. It is used in relation to the drastic personality change Keller undergoes when she is tamed by Annie Sullivan, who also was, I feel it is important to emphasize, a person with a disability (she was partially sighted after a bout with trachoma, a viral eye disease). In Shattuck's opinion, Keller's rote learning of literature was a way to "fill in the map of life." She led a double life between reading (the mediated world she found through Annie Sullivan and books) and direct touch. Pursuing the logic of the Anagnos claim against her, Shattuck writes about Keller as an example of the literary imagination reclaiming a world stolen by lost hearing and sight. From Plato to Pascal and beyond, the imagination has struck many thinkers as duplicitous and deceitful, but Shattuck and others, including Cynthia Ozick, who devoted a two-part series in the *New Yorker* to her own meditations on Keller as writer, have a different view. As Shattuck explains in the afterword, "Helen Keller had plagiarized her very personality, that she had a prosthetic identity, made out of words, a secondhand soul."[6] The role of the prosthesis in Keller's story is similar to its recurrent instrumentality through so much of my own consideration of the way people with disabilities are represented by themselves and others. One historical footnote regarding the link between Keller and Alexander Graham Bell, a stalwart champion of her work, whose father had invented a system of communication by hand for deaf-blind people and whose wife was deaf: The primary function of the telephone when it was invented was to be a hearing aid. For Keller, the medium of literary language was a multipurpose, inventive, compensatory, and, most important, powerful prosthesis, her barrier breaker. This "wordmindedness" Shattuck compares to the isolation of the verbally mighty but physically confined Emily Dickinson, but he also rightly points out Keller's willingness to appear on stage in major New York vaudeville palaces and her unstinting advocacy efforts. In her willingness to testify before Congress and badger the administration on the issue of jobs for people with disabilities, she was the predecessor to Christopher Reeve and Michael J. Fox. It is Keller as writer, however, that fascinates Shattuck: "That flood of words gradually built up around her an artificial replica, a simulacrum of material reality. . . . She believed in the reality of that book-created world, however, because everyone else around her confirmed its existence. What she learned from books was there for her to verify through her remaining senses of touch, smell, and taste."[7]

Ozick follows Shattuck into the thicket of the plagiarism accusations and considers Keller's authenticity in a long profile of Keller that appeared in the *New Yorker*. As a fiction writer and critic long associated with identity politics, Ozick makes a fascinating match with Keller for a review article of this kind. Most of her long profile is a straightforward hagiography of Keller the disability rights activist, but the primary agenda is a celebration of Keller the writer. Ozick relates Keller's book to a splendid thought of her beloved Henry James: "We work in the dark." This is all by way of welcoming Keller into the club of fiction writers, those who, as Shattuck also suggested, construct reality from literary materials. Ozick writes:

> She was a warrior in a vaster and more vexing conflict. Do we know only what we see, or do we see what we somehow already know? Are we more than the sum of our senses? Does a picture—whatever strikes the retina—engender thought, or does thought create the picture? Can there be subjectivity without an object to glance off? Theorists have their differing notions, to which the ungraspable organism that is Helen Keller is a retort. She is not an advocate for one side or the other in the ancient debate concerning the nature of the real. She is not a philosophical or neurological or therapeutic topic. She stands for enigma; there lurks in her still the angry child who demanded to be understood yet could not be deciphered. She refutes those who cannot perceive, or do not care to value, what is hidden from sensation: collective memory, heritage, literature.

What the Market Will Bear

Keller's text appeals to eighth graders as well as literary theorists, pushing the envelope of imagining disability in ways that even the skeptics would have to admit are valuable. Most disability memoirs, however, operate on a far humbler intellectual level, which is vastly more remunerative. They also tend to be death centered. One of the problems with the Morrie syndrome is that neither Schwartz himself nor Mitch Albom, the sports columnist who was his student at Brandeis and became his Boswell, ever lets us forget that Morrie is dying of rather than living with a disability. Albom needs the reader to know he can kiss his old professor, lift him up, touch him. He gets into the camera angle, as in this sappy scene from *Tuesdays with Morrie:*

> "Sometimes, in the mornings," he said. "That's when I mourn. I feel around my body, I move my fingers and my hands—whatever I can still move—and I mourn what I've lost. I mourn the slow, insidious way in which I'm dying. But then I stop mourning."
>
> Just like that?
>
> "I give myself a good cry if I need it. But then I concentrate on all the good things still in my life. On the people who are coming to see me. On the stories I'm going to hear. On you—if it's Tuesday. Because we're Tuesday people."
>
> I grinned. Tuesday people.
>
> "Mitch, I don't allow myself any more self-pity than that. A little each morning, a few tears, and that's all."[8]

This is followed by Albom's homily on the self-pitiers he knows and how they should put a daily limit on their whining. Morrie interrupts him to say he himself is "lucky" and we're back to that square. The book presses all the obvious buttons, facilely skimming such topics as emotions and death, the book of Job, the "embrace of aging," money and values, facing reality. In the later volume, *Morrie: In His Own Words,* it is non-stop homilies: "If you are ill, you can experience more freedom to be who you really are and want to be because you now have nothing to lose."[9] Early on, something about the language of both books bothered me. Morrie is "ill," "afflicted, "diminished," even "dying." Neither book has the word "disability" in its pages. I queried Albom on the rationale behind this curious omission, but he never answered my e-mail.

When *Lucky Man,* Michael J. Fox's sloppily written memoir, was published in 2002 it made one significant contribution to the conversation by raising the question of what happens when a concealed condition is "outed." The book is anything but a typical disability memoir. To sell product and simultaneously push his admirable agenda for stem-cell research, Fox released an unwieldy hybrid of boring Hollywood tell-all, recycled late-night talk-show anecdotes, and medical case history rendered as stand-up comedy, drunk-alogue, and sappy made-for-Oprah self-help testimony. However, it redeems itself with a coda on his second career as an activist. For more serious students of the disability movement, this is worth the price of the book. A theme throughout, overplayed in the context of his whining account of the paparazzi violating the privacy of his wedding in Vermont, is Fox's battle with the press for a bit of private space. My curiosity was piqued by a rapid flurry of setbacks he had experienced beginning in 1997, when two Boston-area gossip journalists started sniffing around the airport and hospital where Fox was undergoing radical treatment for his Parkinson's. I was in on the act relatively late, when *WE* joined the bandwagon of press coverage launched by an article (prepared with Fox's participation) in *People* timed to coincide with an obnoxious prime-time interview by Barbara Walters. We threw together a cover story on Fox with a sidebar on Parkinson's, dubbing it "Into the Maelstrom" (I quoted the Edgar Alan Poe story for a touch of class) and emphasizing the challenges he faced not from Parkinson's but from publicity. Fox had been driven into the light by the tabloids, especially *National Enquirer*. One day a reporter standing in the middle of the quiet Upper East Side Manhattan neighborhood where he lives screamed "Parkinson's" at the rear bumper of his cab, and he knew the genie would be out of the bottle soon.

Fox miscalculated (or perhaps he is just being disingenuous in the memoir) how much coverage his "outing" would receive. All through the memoir he harps on a self-congratulatory fascination with the press he generates, the little Canadian boy on all those magazine covers—more than once in the narrative he revisits a newsstand in Los Angeles to stare at his image. Yet when the *People* magazine article is in his hands, he is surprised that Todd Gold, the reporter, would move beyond the interview (which incidentally was conducted in the Los Angeles office of Fox's publicist following meetings with Dream Works and ABC executives discussing the decision to go public). As Fox writes: "However sincere my upbeat and philosophical approach to the illness, in the press coverage the subjective reality of my experience with Parkinson's would inevitably be juxtaposed with the objective reality of the disease, in all its destructive cruelty. The rules of good journalism demanded as much. Doctors, scientists, and in all likelihood, other patients would present a grim picture of this crippler of nearly one and a half million Americans—and in the process, force me to take a fresh look at it myself."[10] Here is the celebrity with a disability revealing what the press coverage looks like from his angle, a fascinating moment for those of us who had been in the pack of hounds pursuing him.

The *People* story was on its Web site just before Thanksgiving 1998. Fox recalled having second thoughts: "It quickly became clear that I was *the* big news story over that holiday weekend. My revelation was the lead item on all of the network newscasts, there were hourly updates on the cable channels, and above-the-fold headlines in big city newspapers throughout the United States and Canada. . . . What I dreaded most was being cast as a tragic figure, a helpless victim. TV's erstwhile boy-next-door stricken by an incurable disease, transformed into a frail object of pity. *Poor bastard.* . . . While some in the media (the usual suspects) were stressing the maudlin and sensational angle, in the vast majority of the reports, the overall tone was surprised but respectful—and concerned. In man-on-the-street interviews, members of the public offered expressions not so much of sympathy, as I feared, but of genuine empathy, as well as heartfelt wishes for a positive outcome. Even better, much of the follow-up coverage centered less on me than on Parkinson's disease itself."

That part of the book has merit in that it raises important questions and offers an inside scoop on how intrusive and insensitive the media can be. Sadly, not all of the book remains on this plane. Here's the rhetoric: "I have referred to it in interviews as a *gift*—something for which others with this affliction have taken me to task. . . . Coping with the relentless assault and the accumulating damage is not easy. Nobody would ever choose to have this visited upon them. Still, this unexpected crisis forced a fundamental life decision: adopt a siege mentality—or embark upon a journey. Whatever it was—Courage? Acceptance? Wisdom?—that finally allowed me to go down the second road (after spending a few disastrous years on the first) was unquestionably a gift—and absent this neuro-physiological catastrophe, I would never have opened it, or been so profoundly enriched. That's why I consider myself a lucky man."[11] You will not receive any extra credit for picking which of these quotations made it to the reviews, into the publicity, onto the jacket, and, naturally, *Oprah.*

Another celebrity memoir in the same puffed-up, commencement-address vein is the more recent *Blindsided,* by Richard Cohen, a television executive (former CNN and CBS producer with three Emmy awards on his shelf) who has contributed a slim volume on living with multiple sclerosis (MS) and colon cancer. The book was swept onto the best-seller list on a tide of publicity owing at least in part to the logrolling efforts of his wife, the talk-show host Meredith Viera, and his other connections in the business. Nobody should begrudge Cohen his good luck with the press. However, his self-pity and pitiful prose are ready targets. Most journalists are smart-asses, particularly among other journalists or in private, and Cohen lurches between the sarcasm of the New York media wise-cracker and the standard Hallmark mode. Unfortunately, there is little of an analytic or reflective nuance in between. He whines:

> There is little one can do to find ways out of the darkness. When the kids go to their mother for help with homework, it is all too obvious why they walk around me. I can find simple instructions baffling. Soon the children are helping me. My frustration feeds their own. . . . My feelings of help-

lessness will not go away. Humiliation is sitting with a child who calls out to Mom in the next room for the answer to a question I could have provided easily. My cognitive crimes are punishable with the unintended insult followed by searing self-doubt. This is not my leg or foot or hand, but my mind.[12]

Could you imagine giving this book to a person with MS, a family member or someone who wanted to learn more about living with MS? A later confessional paragraph is similarly weak headed:

I must rise above the culture of perfection and remember that I can be even if I can no longer do. I am learning to acknowledge weakness, accept assistance, and discover new forms of self-definition. My formula has changed. I do not read self-absorbed men's magazines or go to Vin Diesel movies. A new male ideal will have to do and might even save me. I will just have to create it. I cannot allow myself to be held captive by old dreams.[13]

The fanfare that greeted *Blindsided* drowned out the fact that most of it is written in a minor key, a rare choice in the genre of celebrity disability autobiography. Even though the book is a downer, among the blurbs are benedictions from Christopher Reeve ("profoundly moving") and Tom Brokaw ("moving, inspiring, and instructive. May we all be so brave and caring in our own families"). Inside the covers, however, the message is even more riddled with guilt and conflict than Fox's comparatively cheery self-deprecation. "The diminished man must find a way to live, though stripped of his power," Cohen professes, reverting to an attitude toward disability that predates Helen Keller.[14] You would think that Cohen had endured enough casting conferences in the CBS headquarters to know better than to dog a story with such a tenebrous character, but here he is in a double portrait with his famous wife: "I am the beleaguered character feeling small next to the beautiful leading lady who has grown larger than life."[15] At this point his editor ought to have penciled into the margin, "We're wallowing here."

Keeping It Real

By contrast, there is the disciplined humility alternating with virtuoso recklessness of John Hockenberry's *Moving Violations,* published to critical and community acclaim in 2000 and still one of the finest disability memoirs on the shelf. Although I take issue with the long passages devoted to the car accident that made Hockenberry a paraplegic, I mitigate my doubts by admitting they are also beautifully written. There are moments when it seems he is trying to play to the balcony, or conform to the editorial formula of the successful disability memoir, as when he laments: "Every leap year I remember the lost day. I am always chasing it, determined to win it back."[16] Hockenberry is more than just a television talking head. He is a playwright and investigative reporter (having started at NPR in news). He knows how to grandstand:

> As surely as the accident tore my body, altering and ending its function, the experience planted seeds and etched riddles that have been my companions ever since. I can be back in that car in my mind even today. It is a gift to learn the fabric of unpredictability. We are taught to see the world as a big machine. On the fringe, chance intervenes like a lottery ticket. There are fabulous winners and the horrible losers. In the middle is everyone else, the hopeful players. The demoralizing effect of this worldview is everywhere.[17]

More than most celebrities with disabilities, Hockenberry has adroitly navigated the perilous channel between advocacy and mainstream media by turning up at community events such as awards ceremonies and taking the occasional assignment on the ADA or new technology for people with disabilities while primarily covering foreign affairs and national politics. His commentary on disability issues commands the attention of both the community and a general audience that knows his face from television, making him an invaluable pivot player in the media for the cause. Because I share most of the community's deep respect for his achievements and have a jealous writer's grudging admiration for the quality of his prose, I rank him at the top of the current autobiographical crop. Here is why:

> I float through forests of pedestrians on the sidewalks of New York, Chicago. A wheelchair presses its advantage on the pavement, streetsmart, good with cargo, fast and smooth. While walking measures out landmarks in running shoe bounces or high heel castanets, rolling glimpses a city in pans and dolly shots . . . a pedestrian movie with a soundtrack of breathing. The spaces in the pedestrian traffic are liquid passageways that open and close. I weave my way through the people as sunlight passes through a crowd of skydivers on its way to the ground. I live in the blank spaces between the business suits and the gridlock.[18]

Partly because it is similarly so well written, Stephen Kuusisto's *Planet of the Blind* was a breakthrough in the genre. In a disclaimer, the author, an activist who graduated from the Iowa Writers' Workshop and has taught at Hobart and William Smith colleges, indicates that he changed names to protect the privacy of a few individuals in the story. Kuusisto was a part of the *WE* magazine family from early on, contributing a first-person column and stories on guide dogs (he is a prominent staffer at Guiding Eyes for the Blind, one of the country's leading guide-dog schools), and was a frequent guest at panels or events we sponsored. Born three months premature, his retinopathy has affected him all his life, but he is particularly adept at allowing the sighted a glimpse of what he does see, in the form of splendid descriptions of light and imagery punctuated by classical and literary references ("Dear Jackson Pollock, I've entered your *Autumn Rhythm*"), scenes that I relish if only because they are such a refreshing change from the down-home, monosyllabic, cross-stitch "wisdom" of the Morries of the world. One of the best passages is a scene in a supermarket where a mother and child are wondering how a blind man eats, while he is more worried about how he and his dog Corky will get to the checkout counter and have to go through the ritual humiliation of having his food stamps counted out for him by the cashier. Kuusisto, like Hockenberry, is particularly strong at responding to the response of others:

> I want to follow this mother and child through the tall laundry soap displays and tell them that the world doesn't end. I imagine telling them that the blind are not hungry for objects. I want to take strangers by the hand and tell them there is no abyss. Under the tower of Coke cans Corky and I pause, and I wonder about the discrepancy between my blindness as a symbol for others and the reality that I'm not all blind people. I'm only one man, a slightly bent and middle-aged man with a bad back. I've been successfully guided here by an exceptionally beautiful dog. I suspect that we may look accomplished, but behind this tableau—man and dog—I'm as lost as any of you. In fact, I'm more lost. I've entered this supermarket because I need something for lunch, and though I'm here now, I require help to find the tuna fish.[19]

As with Hockenberry's book, there is a redemptive quality to genuinely brilliant writing. Since we are in the realm of books, it makes sense to consider the cross-cultural appeal of well-crafted prose for readers with or without disabilities who simply appreciate the display of skill at the service of sound thinking. I admire this technically grounded, broader base of Kuusisto's "platform," a buzzword among agents and editors for the position and authority of the author. Usually this is just a selling point, but it serves as well to define another species of access, as important to the disability cause in its way as physical access, which permits readers with or without disabilities to draw near enough to the subject to make up their own minds about its importance. Based on the wide-ranging admiration for his style, Kuusisto extends his message of blindness as a universal condition ("I'm as lost as any of you") without either evoking pity (the nondisabled medical model) or provoking defiance (the community's posture). Toward the end of the book, Kuusisto offers a purple passage about walking across the Brooklyn Bridge so exquisitely felt and expressed it would turn any writer green with envy:

> My eyes fill with violet silhouettes, tricks of the air, shapes made by the cables of the bridge, a cluster of grapes hanging in the open air. No, it's a turn of the century gas light, still standing out here. I'm stock-still, filling myself—every microscopic and meandering raindrop inside a man must be replenished with another. I picture myself holding the sieve of Theocritus above my head, the water falling in streams through my hair. It occurs to me that my experience of the Brooklyn Bridge is so completely cerebral it is in fact a kind of metaphor, an imaginary headdress like those body-length hats worn by Tibetan women. In my version, the bridge falls over me in layers of amethyst, gold, purple and silver. These are the threads of being.[20]

One of the only rivals to Hockenberry and Kuusisto came from an unexpected quarter. A slim volume arrived for review in our offices in 1997 from Knopf that was preceded by accolades for its sophistication and for being its nation's *Tuesdays with Morrie*. Part of the hype over *The Diving Bell and the Butterfly* involved the way the book had been written. The writer was Jean-Dominique Bauby, and he died just two days after the book was originally published in France, where he had been the high-flying editor in chief of *Elle* until a rare sort of stroke affecting his brain stem caused him to be "locked in," able to blink his left eyelid and force a smile or grimace to convey his moods or intentions. Living in a grim naval hospital on the English Channel, he had blinked his way through an alphabetic code to compose the entries in the book with a scribe at his side, a process I knew well having spent a day in the company of a similarly "locked in" former orchestral conductor turned artist named Walter Engel. A board with the alphabet rearranged in order of the frequency with which letters are used is held in front of the speaker or recited to him, and by a blink of the eye he chooses, letter by letter, the message he is trying to send. During my interview with Engel, I learned to help, as one sometimes does with a stutterer who is a friend, by completing words or thoughts and allowing the conversation to flow, but the pace is excruciating for everybody, listener, interlocutor, and speaker. "Elegant" is overused as a description of French style in writing, as it is in many areas, but the word seems inescapable as a descriptor for the spare, funny, exquisitely observed and expressed entries in this Mallarmé-esque swan song. It is heavy on the metaphors but not on the self-pity, and bears a grudge nobly against offensive parties. A current of complaint moves through the book and flavors it like a good strong red-wine vinegar in a soup, as when he describes annoyances from the thoughtless orderly who turns off the television in his room halfway through a crucial soccer game to the fly that rests on his nose one visitorless Sunday. But he escapes: "My diving bell becomes less oppressive, and my mind takes flight like a butterfly. There is so much to do. You can wander off in space or in time, set out for Tierra del Fuego or for King Midas's court. You can visit the woman you love, slide down beside her and stroke her still-sleeping face. You can build castles in Spain, steal the Golden Fleece, discover Atlantis, realize your childhood dreams and adult ambitions."[21]

Given the biographical ironies of reading a posthumous translation, it was still astonishing to note the switches in tense Bauby used to invest his text with grammatical indications of the philosophical issues he was addressing. One chapter, "The Ladies of Hong Kong," in which he wonders what became of a chair with his image on it in a Hong Kong hotel bar, begins, "I loved to travel."[22] That would have been cut from *WE* magazine as a "downer" note, but in the context of being a posthumous work, and as a moment of candor however tough on the reader as well as the writer, it works powerfully.

A highlight of his wanderings in the decrepit and depressing labyrinth of the old hospital was the time he spent contemplating the glass-encased bust of the Empress Eugénie in the foyer (the hospital was originally a children's institution under her patronage) and fantasizing about meeting her during a royal visit:

And then one afternoon as I confided my woes to her likeness, an unknown face interposed itself between us. Reflected in the glass I saw the head of a man who seemed to have emerged from a vat of formaldehyde. His mouth was twisted, his nose damaged, his hair tousled, his gaze full of fear. One eye was sewn shut, the other goggled like the doomed eye of Cain. For a moment I stared at that dilated pupil, before I realized it was only mine. Whereupon a strange euphoria came over me. Not only was I exiled, paralyzed, mute, half deaf, deprived of all pleasures, and reduced to the existence of a jellyfish, but I was also horrible to behold. There comes a time when the heaping up of calamities brings on uncontrollable nervous laugher—when, after a final blow from fate, we decide to treat it all as a joke. My jovial cackling at first disconcerted Eugénie, until she herself was infected by my mirth. We laughed until we cried.[23]

The role of the unexpected in the French existentialist tradition, and especially the *écart* (shock) value that means a text has struck home, is quietly astir in this passage. Bauby gently mocks the odd cries and quirks of his fellow inmates before launching another nimble fantasy: "Far from such din, when blessed silence returns, I can listen to the butterflies that flutter inside my head. To hear them, one must be calm and pay close attention, for their wingbeats are barely audible. Loud breathing is enough to drown them out. This is astonishing: my hearing does not improve, yet I hear them better and better. I must have butterfly hearing."[24]

As editor in chief of a lifestyle magazine, I was more than a little fascinated by the oneiric richness of the Bauby story, in part because during the time I ran the magazine I had recurring nightmares of losing my own mobility, sight, or hearing. I was at one point also tormented by what I felt was a hypocritical terror of having a child with Down syndrome or other disability for which "dangerous pregnancies" are named. As a professional courtesy, editor to editor, I scrutinized with admiration the way in which Bauby delivered his story. The "miraculous" patience of his writing method aside, Bauby defied his journalistic principles (no potshots at *Elle* here) in structuring his memoir. Although he has up-front material about why he is in the hospital, and can be unstinting regarding the day-to-day indignities of rehab, he saves the account of his last "normal" day and his stroke for the penultimate chapter, recounting these events with an objectivity and detail that are cinematic (an analogy he often draws in the book). This elicited a loud "aha" from me as I came to the final pages because a staple of journalistic method is the so-called inverted pyramid, a schematic organization of a story that mandates coverage of the most significant information in the first few paragraphs while material of ever dwindling urgency is relegated to the bottom of the story, where inattentive readers who have given up on the piece will miss it but still have the basics. Bauby inverted the canonic inverted pyramid as he constructed his book. He also interlaced it with lyrics from a Beatles song, using as the title of the chapter "A Day in the Life." The effect is chilling and at the same time irresistible, a welcome diversion from the usual manipulative stratagems of the disability memoir.

The Antidisability Memoir

Three memoirs by writers with disabilities whom I know personally intrigued me for the ways in which they eluded the conventions of the disability narrative. When George Steiner's bookish and rewarding *Errata: An Examined Life* appeared in 1997 I copped a review copy for the magazine, eager to add to my shelf full of his works (from the great critical studies *On Difficulty* and *Extraterritorial* to his thematic view of Antigone and linguistic writings, his has been a prolific and critically important career) and sure that I would find a passage or two on the disability issue to single out in a review. The same season, Peter Brook, the immensely influential theater director, released his memoir, *Threads of Time.* Just last year, I received Walter Abish's *Double Vision.* I was curious about how this great novelist, author of *How German Is It* and *Eclipse Fever,* would illuminate the disability experience with a talent so immense that I along with many others expect him to win the Nobel Prize for Literature. Yet none of them directly relates either the cause or the effects of his disability (Steiner does not have use of one arm, Brook spent his childhood in rehabilitation from spinal disfigurement, and Abish lost an eye). They concentrate, for "identity" issues and the sense of being an "outsider," on such topics as Jewish heritage or the solitude of the artist.

Call it the "antidisability" memoir for the sequestration of disability in a story that is not shaped by it. The resistance to placing disability in the foreground among writers for whom other questions predominate need not be construed by advocates of disability culture as "denial." The making of a writer, especially three as ethereal and even frighteningly highminded as Steiner, Brook, and Abish, is not as warm and friendly, even sexy, as the plunge and recovery of the disability trajectory as traced by Hockenberry, Reeve, or Fox. Whether this coolness is a triumph of privacy rights or a matter of striking a small blow for discretion against the battering we all take from heavyweight confessionals, these three books struck me as important exceptions to the trend toward high disability drama. Their very reticence seems to prove the point that life goes on with a disability indistinguishably from what one might call "normal" life, annulling the various impediments by which disability disrupts. Activists would deplore this suppression of disability culture in much the same way that many African-Americans resent Colin Powell or Tiger Woods for being "too white." I confess I respect the approach Steiner, Brook, and Abish have taken for its dignity and self-control, its resistance to market forces and other temptations.

The three books can be categorized as intimate testimonies of the reader (Steiner), the writer (Abish), and the man of the theater (Brook). Because they each skirt disability and yet we know they are written by men with disabilities, whenever the story draws them close to the subject (a discussion of another person or character with a disability) our attention and curiosity are piqued. In Steiner's *Errata,* for example, Stephen Hawking makes a cameo appearance, and there is a riff on DNA and the optimistic possibilities of progress toward a haler and healthier image of man. Other passages more obliquely touch on questions of intense interest to anyone in the disability field. Steiner is an avowed opponent of theory, ruthlessly so in the "lit crit" sphere, so one would hardly dare to overlay the following exquisite passage with an I-told-you-so response from a book on disability studies. And yet, the embrace of difference has multiple meanings in this case. The context is a childhood fascination with the widely varied heraldry of European coats of arms, precursor to Steiner's brilliant work as a decoder in linguistics and literature:

> I grew possessed by an intuition of the particular, of diversities so numerous that no labor of classification and enumeration could exhaust them. Each leaf differed from any other on each differing tree (I rushed out in the deluge to assure myself of this elementary and miraculous truth). Each blade of grass, each pebble on the lake-shore was, eternally, "just so." No repetition of measurement, however closely calibrated, in whatever controlled vacuum it was carried out, could ever be perfectly the same. It would deviate by some trillionth of an inch, by a nanosecond, by the breadth of a hair—itself a teeming immensity—from any preceding measurement. I sat on my bed striving to hold my breath, knowing that the next breath would signal a new beginning, that the past was already unrecapturable in its differential sequence. Did I guess that there could be no perfect facsimile of anything, that the identical word spoken twice, even in lightning-quick re-iteration, was not and could not be the same?[25]

There are similar passages in most conventional disability memoirs, rhapsodies to the singularity of the body or moment, but what a difference the framing makes when the disability is unspoken. Much of the same tension informs Peter Brook's *Threads of Time*. At the pinnacle of the arts, there are certain leaders whose work either directly or indirectly lets the connoisseur know that the creator is acquainted with disability. Among the great theater figures of our time, both Robert Wilson and Brook deploy certain suggestions and allusions that tip off this understanding. Of the many epiphanies and turning points that the highly receptive Brook chronicles in *Threads of Time*, the pivot point in his childhood is captured in one fleeting sentence:

> There were two merciful years of idleness, thanks to illness, first in a long basket on wheels called a spinal chair and later in the Swiss mountains with my anxious mother all to myself, talking to grown-ups, wondering why the shadows in the snow were a luminous blue, devouring Edwardian housemaids' novelettes left on the bookshelves of *pensions de famille*, or else unmentionably wicked books forbidden in England and available at railway bookstalls in what were called Tauschnitz editions.[26]

From that point on, Brook shot to a maturity that his public-school mates and teachers could not even begin to understand, and his precocious grasp of literature and drama led rapidly to his becoming the wunderkind of British theater. Pursuing pattern in these disparate volumes, we note as well that this is the moment when Brook becomes and perceives himself as "different," not because of his disability but as a result of changes incurred during that period of confinement (a staple of many authorial memoirs; from Lord Byron to T. S. Eliot, Marcel Proust, and Thomas Mann, the catalogue of authors who followed this route is long). When a book is released, the author is often available for interviews. I had my chance with Brook, and he was far more interested in chatting about Oliver Sacks, who had been his inspiration, than about himself. Such reticence is far more attractive than the self-flagellating humility of a memoir like *Blindsided,* and it shows in Brook's text as well as in his theater work. Viewing the assembled audience as individually "dis-membered" but in a group "re-membered," Brook pointedly compares what he does to healing. One of his greatest triumphs in the theater was *The Man Who,* a staging of Oliver Sacks's brilliant *Man Who Mistook His Wife for a Hat,* for which Brook split the famous repertory company's days between visits to the neurology wards of the Paris hospital La Salpêtrière, Charcot's historic neurology school, and the rehearsal studio. He recounts the experience in his memoir:

> We saw the mind painfully losing its faculties and then losing the memory of what it had lost or else compensating for the deficit with a sudden and unpredictable burst of excess. We followed the complex systems of adaptation through which an apparently diminished mind reconstructs a world in which it then lives to the full. The patients in many cases became our best allies, helping and correcting with interest and humor our imitations so that what we did became more and more faithful to their state. In this way, the outside form became increasingly real for the actors, and the more they entered it, the more their own imagination came to life and began to play a role. The patients were no longer "cases"; we could now feel the full and often rich human being within the restricted range of movements that we had first witnessed with such distress.[27]

Brook saves his aria on understanding for the finale: "I have witnessed no miracles, but I have seen that remarkable men and women do exist, remarkable because of the degree to which they have worked on themselves in their lives. This is my only certainty, and it has been the quest for this 'something' elusive that has guided me, however often it has been forgotten or ignored. . . . When I first became articulate, I felt that everything could be explained; now I see what a disservice I would commit if

I attempted to explain here in a few neat phrases what has guided me over the years, because I do not even know. Not knowing is not resignation; it is an opening to amazement." [28]

The slight nod made by Brook to an experience of disability in childhood and the meditation on physical perfection in Steiner's book are overt gestures compared to the poker face Abish assumes in his memoir, *Double Vision*. Its counterpoint between "The Writer" and "The Writer-to-be" yokes his fictional and nonfictional styles. Stripped of its jacket, the library version of the book loses its most vivid connection to disability, the author's portrait showing his black eye-patch. As a reviewer for the *New Yorker* whined, nowhere in the book is there a mention of why he wears the patch, an editorial elision that we should focus on in the context of our agenda and of his previous work (the *New Yorker* review makes Abish look evasive in not mentioning his monocular vision in the memoir.) The ascetic aspect of Abish's modus operandi is manifest not only in the themes he chooses but in his habit of repeated questioning. The cool detachment of his authorial voice, and even those of his characters, embodies restraint. Very little of the emotional interior is spelled out in his masterpieces of short fiction, collected in the volume *The English Garden,* or his novels, including *How German Is It* and *Eclipse Fever*. In these books and in *Double Vision* the questions are real rather than rhetorical.

Traces of disability, wisps of oblique observation rather than confession, are all that is left by the winnowing process of Abish's relentless irony. Attuned by personal acquaintance with the author and by my own agenda, I find the quick gestures to be all the more meaningful. Early in the volume he briefly mentions trying hypnosis as a remedy for chronic trigeminal headaches. Five years before its publication, during a long lunchtime conversation in which he counseled me generously and thoughtfully on how the magazine could evolve (Abish in person has all the warmth and spry curiosity that his lead characters seem to lack), he let me know he was at work on a memoir and that a central element in it would be "pain"—certainly a theme that readers with disabilities would identify with readily. By the time *Double Vision* arrived, in 2004, the pain had been sublimated, transferred in perfect Abish fashion to the discomfort of the reader, who winces through long passages on the misfortunes of the cultivated and baffled Abish family as they are driven from Viennese comfort to war-torn Shanghai and Israel. In a chapter devoted to his time in Cologne, he inserts a two-sentence paragraph, set off by line spaces from the rest of the chapter, that is both impersonal in tone and highly personal (whose "overcome emotional privation" are we talking about at its end?): "Now and then I'd spot someone with a cane, limping badly, or a grim-faced individual missing an arm or a leg. In this particularly austere setting, this vestige of the war is like a marker to a barely overcome emotional privation."[29] As with Brook and Steiner, the disability in sight is someone else's business. There is one confrontational moment in Abish's book that does involve his monocular vision. It is delivered without comment in a tight little paragraph from the section on Berlin. The tension between the American writer and the Germans he has portrayed in his most famous fiction is palpable throughout the memoir, so the cultural clash has been imminent all along. This is as close as the book comes to an overt treatment of the author's disability:

> Seeing me cross a deserted street against the light, an offended motorist on a cross street stopped in midtraffic to upbraid me at the top of his lungs. "What business is it of yours? I yelled back, my voice matching his in loudness. Surprised by my furious rebuttal, he sounded aggrieved: "You're wearing an eye patch . . . your eyesight is impaired. You might get hurt!"[30]

Give Abish, Steiner, and Brook credit for taking the high road. It is not as fashionable, or as profitable, to focus on becoming a writer, an intellectual, or an avant-garde theatrical director as it is to play the disability card in contemporary publishing. The deliberately inaccessible, even infuriatingly disengaged posture of the writer as played by Steiner and Abish, or the somewhat more public persona of the film and stage director in Brook, does not lend itself all that readily to hugs and tears. Their books do, however, offer a signpost to a "postdisability" style of memoir writing that might someday be the capstone of assimilation among autobiographers. Having reached the point where it is socially unremarkable, disability recedes into the background.

Faking It

Telling lives and telling lies are often related. A bizarre twist in the representation of disability came toward the end of my tenure at the magazine. The next-to-last of hundreds of pieces I wrote for the magazine was a book review that could not have been more apt. It panned an outrageous, appalling, admittedly fascinating "metaphorical memoir" called *Lying,* written by the snide instigator and author of the controversial, highly touted *Prozac Diary* and *Welcome to My Country* as well as the more recent, equally infuriating *Opening Skinner's Box.* Lauren Slater's genre-bending book (fiction or nonfiction, flip a coin) is an experiment in fakery. It embroiders along the lines of a seminal psychoanalytic idea advanced by Donald Spence in 1981 that narrative truth and historical truth diverge,

calling into question the face value of information surrendered by a patient in a psychoanalytic session when a "well-constructed tale" has its
own rewards (as exemplified by Freud himself). As Spence, addressing analysts, concludes, "If we listen actively and creatively much of the time,
there is no longer any clear line where reconstruction stops and construction begins. We have seen that ours is an archeology of descriptions,
not of images, and that language is always getting in the way between
what the patient saw or felt and the way this experience appears (variously transformed) in the analytic conversation. We never make contact
with the actual memory or dream; language is always the elusive go-
between. As a result of the multiple meanings of much of our data and as
a result of the fact that we have no systematic means of decoding these
meanings, we must always assume that for any given interpretation actually made there are any number of other candidates that could be made
and have equal claim on our attention. We are only just beginning to
understand how unwitting interpretation and background assumption
combine to produce a particular interpretation at a particular time; as we
understand the process in more detail, we will become more sensitive to
the way in which context can influence content."[31] Had Slater been more
honest, a laughable proposition, she would have directly acknowledged
Spence's work in her brief and troubling book.

There are doctors cited, but Slater makes them up and composes their
texts in a parody that is at least skillful. She has a good ear and can write,
dangerous skills in the hands of a successful parodist. She makes up experts and inserts their texts in her own. The philosopher from the University of Southern California who supplied the foreword? A fake. The neu-
rologist whose case-study journal article about Slater is inserted in the
center of the book? Faux. The pretense is that she has epilepsy, and in a
shifty afterword she supports her shocking spiral of deceit, a fake memoir
that is a page-turner I have to admit, behind trendy postmodern theories
of the signifier and signified. The title and subtitle, *Lying: A Metaphorical Memoir,* sport the Borgesian qualities of evasiveness and labyrinthine
self-referentiality. In the introduction, an early mention of "creative nonfiction" has us on alert. "What makes this book disturbing is its incremen-
tally rising refusal to state the facts of the illness about which she writes. By
the end of the book, the reader is, indeed, left to wonder whether, or to what
degree, Ms. Slater has suffered epilepsy, or if she has used the disease as a
meaningful metaphor to convey what are otherwise unutterable experiences in her life."[32] The half dozen commas in that last sentence are a sput-
tering sign of indecision and frustration all on their own. The introduction,
along with the afterword, attempt to elevate the analytic vocabulary, claiming that she touches "a new kind of Heideggerian truth, the truth of the lim-
inal, the not-knowing, the truth of confusion, which, if we can only learn

to tolerate, yields us greater wisdom in the long run than packaged and parceled facts."[33] On the one hand, this sounds like a White House defense counsel trying to make special prosecutors back off. On the other, arriving at an advanced stage of "Heideggerian truth" would be an achievement in a genre—the disability memoir—that has grown stale with cliché and minor prevarications of its own. The two-word first chapter, under the part-title "Onset," is clever: "I exaggerate." The text that follows is standard fare, beginning with the author's childhood recognition of difference, moving on to her struggle with parental ignorance and suspicion, dwelling on the diagnostic and treatment phases, and then celebrating her embrace of differentness—same old, same old, you could say, with a few interesting curves thrown in to keep us on our toes because it is also the story of the growth of a writer from childhood through anguished teen years to finding a literary voice. A recurring confession is the intense hunger for praise for a story well told, whether from mommy dearest, schoolmates daring her to write graffiti in red marker on the wall, impressed doctors, Hallmark contest judges, or the John Gardner stand-in who is the nineteen-year-old's randy mentor at Bread Loaf and calls her a genius the morning before deflowering her. It was the "Pavlovian association between words and love."[34] Desperate to be popular in junior high school, for example, she lies her way into a party:

> But no matter how much makeup I wore, I was still a girl with epilepsy, a girl who pissed herself, a girl convulsed; was there a way to make sickness sexy? That was the year I read nineteenth-century novels, in which tubercular heroines coughed up blood, and died in feather beds. I bought foundation two shades lighter than my actual skin. I wore a dark velvet ribbon like a choker around my neck, and I took my Medic Alert bracelet off my wrist and sported it instead as an anklet, the scarlet serpent dangling down. And still, Sarah Kushner did not invite me to her party Friday night. Danny Harris wouldn't like me. "I am dying," I whispered to Sarah in English class one day. "You're dying?" she said to me. "What's wrong?"
> "Cancer," I said.
> "I thought you had epilepsy," she said.
> "Epilepsy causes cancer," I said. "Can you believe it?"
> She believed it. She invited me to her party lickety-split, and Haskell Crocker danced with me, and Danny Harris held my hand, and every girl brought me pink punch, such beautiful punch, with foamy globs floating on top, and slices of orange and lemon in it. Sweet. Sweet.[35]

The guilty pleasure of enjoying the book is in part fed by our complicity with Slater, being in on the prank, having the key to the dramatic irony, until the suspicion that the joke is on us begins to creep in. She admits she exaggerates, invents, even plagiarizes. One wonders when the lying is going to catch up with her, and there are bouts of loneliness and moralizing that renew our faith in her eventual integrity. From the point of view of a disability advocate, it is unthinkable to write off a cri de coeur from one of our own, but it is also unacceptable to let an outsider get away with concocting a best-seller, stealing her pink punch in the publishing game, by making up a disability. In a chapter titled "Amazing Grace" she shows up at Alcoholics Anonymous and dupes them as well with her tearful tale that draws applause and admiration. Listeners gush, "Oh my god, that was so honest." Recovery insiders recognize this as the "drunk-alogue" that showcases newcomers at meetings, where the autobiography always begins "My name is so and so" and then heads toward "and I am an alcoholic." It is, in addition to being the first step in a twelve-step program that has helped millions, also a dramatic performance, the edgier the better, that leads to hugs and clapping, acceptance and even fame. Slater's trick tempted me into worrying that my magazine, too, had become one long drunk-alogue served up for advertisers, awestruck readers without disabilities, the media, and the amusement of others who relish that whole smug sense of "there but for the grace of God go I."

In the afterword to Slater's *Lying,* the mirror of analysis flashes again: "All I know for sure is this. I have been ill much of my life. Illness has claimed my imagination, my brain, my body, and everything I do I see through its feverish scrim. All I can tell you is this. Illness, medicine itself, is the ultimate narrative; there is no truth there, as diagnoses come in and out of vogue as fast as yearly fashions. Line up all the DSMs, the book from which mental health professionals draw their diagnoses, and you will see how they have changed, how they have radically altered from decade to decade, depending upon the Zeitgeist. . . . Therefore, despite the huge proliferation of authoritative illness memoirs in recent years, memoirs that talk about people's personal experiences with Tourette's and postpartum depression and manic depression, memoirs that are often rooted in the latest scientific 'evidence,' something is amiss. For me, the authority is illusory, the etiologies constructed. When all is said and done, there is only one kind of illness memoir I can see to write, and that's a slippery, playful, impish, exasperating text, shaped, if it could be, like a question mark."[36]

While it is wickedly difficult to poke a hole in Slater's postmodern argument if you abide by the theoretical parameters of the debate (privileging metaphor, scorning accuracy), there is a realization as well that she has led us into a cul-de-sac within this labyrinth. The word "ultimate" is tossed around a great deal in the disability press, and it makes people with disabilities into cliff dwellers, always on the edge of "mind-blowing"

revelations and achievements that demand but one verbal mode, the su-
perlative, a grammatical marginality as limiting as any political or social
marginality.

Meanwhile, any reader well versed in the disability memoir as genre is
waiting for the lab results to come back and tell us whether the pathol-
ogy of the author's disability is physical or mental. Along the way she slyly
hints at Munchausen's disease (a psychological syndrome that would have
compelled her to fake epilepsy and other ailments to get the attention of,
principally, her distant and eccentric mother) as well as borderline personality and bipolar disorders. She even gives autism a try. At its best
Slater's accent on stylish writing produces moments of sensual sprezza-
tura, particularly in the lavish accounts of the synesthetic experience of
the epileptic aura (the jasmine smell, the kaleidoscopic colors), but the
downside, frankly, is that Slater's odd trick is mainly a nasty bit of bull-
shit that, were it to attain popular coolness, would offend many and send
others sliding into cynicism. Including this writer.

After Slater, what? Accuracy, sincerity, the "honest" pursuit of the
truth, wanting the gist of life with a disability—all are called into question in a moment such as this, when for the dollars or the notoriety a
writer is prepared to play so casually with deceit, expectations, and, of
course, those powerful stereotypes that the disability memoir has worked
so hard to codify.

CHAPTER THREE

Getting It on Paper

Revising the Disability Story for the Print Media

Optimists write badly.
—Paul Valery

One of the first things a journalist does upon starting with a new magazine or paper is to get hold of the in-house style sheet and a stack of back issues to become familiar with the editorial voice of the publication. My compact blue three-ring binder of Reporter's Guidelines never left my desk at Time Inc. The first copy a reporter turns in, often written as a respectful parody of recent clips, inevitably needs "styling" by editors and copy editors more familiar with the organization's standards, but a sharp writer who wants to gain points for submitting "clean" copy does everything possible to follow the template. Major news organizations, including the *New York Times,* BBC, and Associated Press (AP), even publish their stylebooks, which have become reference guides for journalism classes and aspiring writers. Dedicated to mundane matters of punctuation and reporting methodology, they are hardly controversial or noteworthy, except insofar as they offer a root-level view of the progress and problems in how the newsroom handles such "special situations" as disability stories. In 1987, for example, the *AP Stylebook and Libel Manual* was modified to read: "Do not describe an individual as disabled or handicapped unless it is clearly pertinent to the story."

The idea to develop guidelines related to disability discourse originated in the 1980s at the University of Kansas's Research and Training Center on Independent Living (RTC/IL), directed by Dr. Jim Budde. In 1984, the center launched a "Media Watch" campaign asking media and consumer organizations to update their terminology. One of the priorities from a political point of view was helping uninitiated reporters on the politics and policy beat get up to speed on terminology they would need to cover the congressional debate over the ADA. Nearly a decade later most editors would spot a blooper like "handicapped" and delete it right away, but not all. The *New York Times* allows a number of "handicap" mentions to slip through the cracks every year, and there have been 256 instances of "wheelchair-bound" or "confined to a wheelchair" in the past seven years alone according to the *Times*'s own Web site search engine, which also lists 271 instances of "homebound" in relation to people with disabilities who work at home (as many writers do, for heaven's sake). Even the interior design section, where one would expect a slightly more sophisticated editorial team to be at work, is still riddled with instances of "handicapped" in conjunction with accessible architecture (as of 2004).

Most of the most egregious errors seem to pop up in the metro and national news sections, or sneak into stories by freelancers in the arts and entertainment weekend sections, where the editing standards, we now know thanks to the Jason Blair scandal and all the public breast-beating the *Times* has done, are particularly lax. In 1990, the year of the ADA, the American Society of Newspaper Editors (ASNE) issued its own set of guidelines, focusing on, for example, whether deaf or Deaf was appropriate. It is appropriate as a cultural distinction: the uppercase D is used for signers and those who consider themselves members of the Deaf community. The ASNE also, at the prompting of AIDS activists, urged members to lay off using "victim" in conjunction with AIDS because it connotes affliction, a correction, by the way, as important for polio, MS, or any number of other disabilities, just as people living with or surviving cancer are not victims (thanks to Susan Sontag for that one). A helpful checklist from Easter Seals (reproduced in full as appendix A to this book) is even more direct: "Omit mention of an individual's disability unless it is pertinent to the story." Just that step would alone eradicate half of the most insulting gaffes in print today. Ask any African-American reader of newspapers and magazines what a difference it has made in their experience of the news to note the progress made by news agencies in the past decade in *not* mentioning an individual's race when it is not crucial to the story.

Watching Our Language

The Easter Seals guidelines also warn against drifting toward the two polarities of "supercrip" or "patient" in overdramatized stories, urging writers to emphasize instead a more fully integrated version of ordinary people living ordinary lives, working and playing side by side with others, "experiencing the same pain/pleasures that others derive." It offers a list of trip words that should similarly be posted on the editorial bulletin board: "COURAGEOUS, BRAVE, INSPIRATIONAL and similar words routinely used to describe persons with disabilities. Adapting to a disability does not necessarily mean someone acquires these traits." Curmudgeons will sound the alarm over political correctness, but the avoidance of stock phrases and clichés is a point of professional pride among the better class of journalists, as any reader of William Safire's column will aver. Periodically at Time Inc. we would receive memos about phrases or words that had been overused lately, and occasionally these raised eyebrows, as when we were advised not to use "articulate" as a modifier for African-Americans.

Focusing on the linguistic baseline already reveals the shortcomings of most print outlets in disability reporting. The basic people-first logic of giving up "the disabled" and "disabled people" for "people with disabilities" (including "people with epilepsy" rather than "epileptics") is still a struggle, after more than a decade of use, for many writers and editors who prefer an easier fit for the tight word count of a column design. An even longer delay seems to keep "mental retard" in print, apparently still a baffler for many local newspaper editors who long ago should have become acquainted with the terms "developmental disability" or, better, "so-called mental disability."

The disability community has its own version of the n-word, which is "cripple," and it is "only for use among us." The trendy moniker, sometimes abbreviated to "crip," confers "disability cool" in its facetious, not to say militant, tone, raising the same discomfort as the n-word among outsiders. Cheryl Wade, a performance artist with multiple sclerosis, says, "It's visual, strong—feels like a good, gnarled fist." As does "gimp," which reached its peak popularity in the nineties thanks in part to an Oscar-winning documentary on the artist Dan Keplinger, who calls himself "King Gimp." This term also has a militant side, but it too is for use by people with disabilities only, precisely for the discomfort it causes in others. Believe it or not, Ann Landers's column—both the questions and her responses—still uses "crippled child" or "cripple" despite the fact that her editors would quickly nix Negro. As a temporarily able-bodied writer, I could never bring myself to use "crip" on its own. Fortunately, a few other once-fashionable terms such as "physically challenged," "differently abled," and the cutesy "handi-capable" have gone by the boards as awkward examples of terms used by nondisabled writers trying too hard to find forced euphemisms. If you go this route, why not use "inconvenienced"? (a real suggestion submitted to a $50,000 contest once sponsored by the National Cristina Foundation to find a new term). Two of the words we stringently banned at WE magazine were "special" and its opposite number, "normal." For advocates, "special" infers segregation. As John R. Woodward fumed in a 1991 issue of the Disability Rag, "It's the label we put on segregated programs, a euphemism, a word introduced by do-gooders to sugar-coat their control of our lives. 'Special' infantilizes and trivializes the identity of a disabled person. If you are disabled, you are not 'special'; you are disadvantaged and oppressed."[1]

The Power of Placement

While style sheets are one way to forcibly uncouple outdated if ingrained terminology from current referents, a broader conceptual change in print journalism is still necessary. As recent studies confirm—the most up-to-date evidence is the newspaper you're about to toss out—for too long disability stories have been consigned to three ghettos in the news mix: medical, local coverage of charity events, and "soft" human-interest usually devoted to "supercrip, sadcrip" cases. The first two share the same problem, in that they turn people with disabilities into passive recipients of government, a nonprofit's or a hospital's support, even as they continue to emphasize the physical aspects of illness, cure, and rehabilitation. The antidote to this type of condescending coverage is just an extension of "people-first" diction, in that it views people with disabilities as individuals with civil rights and a culture of their own.

And stories of their own, I would add, as a former editor in chief. Without making the spurious claim that *WE* magazine solved once and for all the many problems of disability coverage in media, we did pioneer a new approach to basic genres including the profile, "think" piece, design or travel feature, dining review, and column. The most important innovations we made occurred on the structural level of the organization of the pieces. There are discernible formulas for almost all the print pieces you read—outlines that can be taught and copied according to which information, sources, commentary and "color" are deployed. One of the basic lessons all journalism students endure is the "inverted pyramid," an image of the typical story that places the most up-to-date and important information at the very top of a narrow-based form, the bottom of which (where the reader is most likely to give up on a story) holds the least vital facts or quotes. As a visual guide to the order in which the elements of a story ought to appear, the inverted pyramid has yet to be displaced. One of its blessings is the chronological lassitude it allows the writer, who is urged to break strict past-present-future order to privilege a fact or quote that has overbearing significance (the classic example is the account of a town meeting at the end of which a councilman is assassinated, an event that should rise to the top of the pyramid in place of a rehash of the soon-to-be-whacked councilman's opening statement and last words). In terms of that metaphor, one of the first stipulations in my marching orders to first-time contributors was a rejiggering of the typical order of paragraphs so as to drop the medical and "hard-core" disability information to the bottom of the inverted pyramid, especially for profiles.

As we will see, most publications foreground the cause of a disability and the rehabilitation narrative when profiling a quadriplegic (like Reeve), obeying a long tradition in print coverage of replaying the accident and capitalizing on the ooh-ah factor of the medical miracle by which the subject of the story is still around to tell the tale. This steadfast habit even holds for most biographies and memoirs, which, perhaps as a selling point, usually lead with the car accident, bear mauling, shooting, or other fell disaster that appeals to the bloodlust of the contemporary reader (and editor). I specifically instructed my writers to confine the cause of disability to the last third of the article (if it was noted at all) while foregrounding the current career or achievements of the subject and following with the color and quotes that would affirm the *life* part of living with a disability. With Reeve, for example, we waited until we had him "on the job" and trailed him around the set of his remake of *Rear Window*. There were two reasons the magazine could get away with this unconventional reordering of the standard tale: our readers already knew the grim particulars of cervical injuries and rehabilitation, and pictures of people in wheelchairs, using canes, or wearing hearing aids made much of the recital of diagnosis and treatment superfluous. Don't tell a reader what he or she knows, and in all likelihood would prefer not to recall.

In terms of disability advocacy, this fits neatly with the importance of avoiding the representation of people with disabilities as case studies, but my motivation also entailed the basic economy of a two-thousand-word feature, more of which could now be devoted to the positive, the pity-free, the painless, and the profitable (remember your advertisers). It would have taken a full two- to three-hundred-word mininarrative to adequately explain Chuck Close's unusual spinal cord injury and its misdiagnosis, space that I was much happier to give to an account of his wondrous painting process on a movable easel he had designed after seeing a similar setup in Willem de Kooning's studio. I chose the latter route because I was confident that my readers, tired of seeing rehashes of what they already knew about the spinal cord and its vulnerability, would prefer to learn about how Chuck Close paints his pictures, and I hoped that some would appreciate the novelty of our shift in focus. To give this a philosophical rationale, the more pages we devoted to the "lifestyle" pleasures of the post-injury phase, the more we affirmed the importance of everything but the limitations of the disability.

Our magazine underwent an evolution with regard to the balance of information. In our first issues, we followed the example of other media in the disability field and carried a number of research stories under the slug of "medical frontlines." The articles we ran included a paean to the Miami Project to Cure Paralysis and to the Shriners' hospitals, both major forces in the fundraising circles we were hoping to crack to help our circulation by obtaining their mailing lists. Eventually, we pulled back significantly on our medical coverage, not because we were heeding the proscriptions against the "medical model" in disability studies, but because there were so many strong, colorful, important stories to tell that did not involve the incessant promises of cures. Finding stories to replace the "frontlines" pieces was never my worry—stories about real people were pouring over the transom every day. Although I sometimes wish we had more vigorously pursued the political and ethical debates over stem cell research, I am proud of the fact that most of our later research stories pursued design breakthroughs in prostheses, cochlear implants for people who are hard of hearing, even a similar camera device that is being tested to help blind individuals see again. These pieces were consonant with our pressure on architects and product designers to remove the external barriers surrounding people with disabilities, which is in line with the all-important point most disability studies make about shifting the focus from what is wrong with the person with a disability to what is wrong with the environment around him or her. With the right story, the right apportionment of information, and the right language, it all fits together— disability culture informs journalistic style without neglecting the market demands of advertiser and reader for entertainment and news.

Get Me Rewrite

This meshing of advanced thinking and economics is more the exception than the rule in print journalism, unfortunately. Turning to some of the major publications, in addition to spotting the persistent linguistic errors, it is too easy as well to find the continuation of old habits of thinking. Mainstream magazines such as *People* or *Vanity Fair* are so addicted to selling physically attractive celebrities that disability poses a challenge to the visual and narrative momentum of an issue. Fortunately for editors, a tried-and-true formula for the disability story exists that has the feel-good component necessary to offset the discomfort of an image or detail that disturbs. The hero gamely smiles while the article extols his or her "courage in the face of adversity" and other celebrities chip in a platitude on what an inspiration, etc. This story surfaces every few issues in *People,* for example, to add a "serious" moment to the mix of bubbly profiles and star news.

One expects greater sophistication regarding disability etiquette from the *New York Times,* and to a certain degree the Gray Lady is more proper, but in the end she disappoints. One of the supposed strong points of the *Times* is its coverage of health care policy and abuses, including medical ethics and patient rights, in the context of which one would anticipate more attention to be devoted to the situation of the disability community. The Washington bureau has made half-hearted attempts to cover stem cell research whenever Reeve or Fox was in town but has fallen well short of its potential in entering the debate on this important issue. The exposure of the internal self-policing of the editorial desks after the Blair scandal revealed a corporate culture obsessed with identity politics, particularly ethnicity and gender, but as yet not a word in the "Public Editor's" column has mentioned the inclusion of disability in the often frantic, and costly, diversity efforts. On the positive side, running a couple of first-person stories (including a cover story and a major feature in one year) in the Sunday magazine section by Harriet McBryde Johnson, a noted advocate, was a step forward in terms of the sheer amount of space devoted to the voice of the community on topics of huge importance politically, such as independent living and the controversy over the eugenics of Peter Singer. Johnson is an outside voice, however, and we should judge the *Times* more on its day-to-day practice.

In that regard, I find that the *Times* will get off a good shot now and then but narrowly miss the target of up-to-date disability awareness. For example, in the Week in Review of October 19, 2003, under the dateline Rome, correspondent Frank Bruni filed a long trends piece about the pope's deliberate effort to make public the effects of his advancing Parkinson's. Bruni was onto a fascinating and timely topic, if shading somewhat toward what advocates would call the "medical model" and certainly using a celebrity to pitch a disability story. Yet in the piece, presented with an opportunity to address a complicated set of questions regarding privacy and disability awareness, Bruni remains either coy or unaware of the existing debate regarding the responsibilities of figures as well known as Mohammad Ali, Janet Reno, and the pope to the community of people with Parkinson's. One problem with the story is that it is permeated by an air of surprise that the pope would showcase his disability, even that the *Times* would dedicate much space to the issue. This seems innocuous. For one thing, it does not take much background in Christian theology to understand the religious justification for the strategy ("the meek shall inherit the earth" and so on). Bruni's angle seems more appropriate to an FDR-era respectful distance from world leaders than to the relentless scrutiny our own time:

> To a degree that arguably no other public figure of his stature has done, John Paul, 83, has decided not to hide his physical deterioration from public view, not to shrink from a spotlight that allows all the world to watch him wither by painful fit. It is a gripping sight, inspiring to some people and uncomfortable for others, and it is the result of an unusual combination of personal

motivations, pastoral responsibilities and the special circumstances of his office. It also defies convention and expectation in societies where old age is often venerated but infirmity is usually concealed. Many famous people elect to be remembered as younger and more physically vibrant, and they leave the stage when they can no longer stride briskly across it.[2]

Praising the pope for his message of perseverance (although, unlike an elected politician or corporate chief executive officer, the pope scarcely has much of a choice in that resignation is not an option), Bruni wonders that the pope has not been "curtained off" by family and the Vatican, as Ronald Reagan was, or Woodrow Wilson after his stroke in 1919 (he left office two years later), not to mention the later examples of Strom Thurmond and Attorney General Reno. Had the *Times* editors read their Sontag they might have found better verbs than "battling" and "struggling" for the pope's life with Parkinson's, and one wonders whether Bruni's fingers hesitated above the keyboard before describing the way the way the pope's head "lolls" or he is seen "drooling." This is not to question the veracity of the observation, but the choice of including it in the piece is a matter of taste, and I think the Easter Seals journalism review board would have opted to elide. In the end, Bruni elects to punt, falling back on the old cliché of courage in the face of adversity: "Other Catholic leaders and people who know the pope say he also believes that any suffering he endures has value, providing people with an inspirational image of courage." In a section of the *Times* where ideas and trends supposedly hold sway, we're justified in expecting a more advanced stage of thinking on disability.

Yes, the New Yorker

It is not difficult to find worse examples of disability coverage. As this book was heading into the homestretch in late 2003 and my thoughts turned to its chances for reviews or media attention, I happily noticed a spate of major articles related to disability appearing in mainstream publications, including a massive, eleven-page feature about Christopher Reeve in the *New Yorker* of November 10. At first it was exciting to pick up this distinguished magazine and see that editor in chief David Remnick had budgeted so much space for one of those good, old-fashioned, full-blown *New Yorker* profiles—Remnick and I had been student writers at Princeton when the venerable John McPhee, who perfected the genre in that magazine, was our campus god. On the basis of column inches alone the Reeve piece encouraged me to believe disability was finally getting its due in the *New Yorker*. The opening spread even had the obligatory Richard Avedon portrait of Reeve, framed in the artsy (even morbid) black border. The portrait was a stunner, even for one who knew Reeve personally and had followed his career with professional interest. The Hollywood good looks are history. Bundled in three layers of cardigans, his breathing tube snaking down the front like a big white zipper, Reeve peered out in apparent bemusement. His brow was furrowed, his head waxed and held in the embrace of a black wheelchair rest that sticks out on either side like an appendage. He looked as if he had been made up for a science fiction movie. The shock effect was bound to hit the million *New Yorker* readers: "Oh God, look at poor Christopher Reeve. Now he has no hair." Even if the picture was a bit macabre, at least there would be the long story, I thought.

Then I read the piece. One may as well be up front about the tenor of the following critique, at the avowed risk of offending everyone from the article's author, Jerome Groopman, a professor of medicine at Harvard, to the *New Yorker*'s editor in chief Remnick, who signed off on it, and all the editors and fact-checkers in between. From the lede (shoptalk for opening sentences) to the kicker, this debacle is not-knowing-where-to-look bad, so inept as to be offensive not just in terms of disability etiquette but in terms of acceptable codes of student reportage. It seems almost impossible that it could have found its way into print in 2003 in the soi-disant "best magazine in the world" (although most professionals would save that fanfare for the *Economist*), and it is precisely because it appeared in the *New Yorker* in 2003 that it so miserably falls short of the expectations one would have for what might have been—this old story once more—a breakthrough for the press coverage of disability. I was not even through the first page of this hopeless recycling of the Reeve saga as it had already been done to death by *People* and Barbara Walters when I had to put the issue down and ask myself where in Cambridge Dr. Groopman had been hiding all these years as the vocabulary of disability evolved, and why his editors had left their blue pencils in the drawers. There, at the bottom of the first page, was the signal that tipped my growing impatience into angry dismay, a reference to columnist Charles Krauthammer, "who is wheelchair-bound." At that violation of the stylebook, I picked up my pen to mark the article's further problems. Barely a paragraph went by without extensive underlining, exclamation points, and warning flags. The last major article on Reeve when he was alive, and it was a mess.

Scrutinizing the piece with the eye of an editor or journalism teacher, we begin with the "slug" or section heading under which the story appears both on the contents page and on its opening page: "Annals of Medicine." Right away, we are in the realm of "medicalization," the pigeonhole to which the representation of disability has been confined for centuries. While Groopman eschews honorifics (perhaps the magazine style sheet, as with the *New York Times* in most instances, prohibits either Dr. or M.D.), a quick turn to the contributors' page at the front of the book yields the backstory—he is Recanati Professor of Medicine at Harvard and one of those "literary docs" (the current favorites are Sherwin Nuland and Peter Selwyn, but the ur-phenomenon was the late lamented Lewis Thomas). The title of an upcoming book plugged in the bio, *The Anatomy of Hope: How People Prevail in the Face of Illness,* tips us as to what to expect in the article. On either side of that colon are two of the great white clichés to which Reeve in particular had fallen prey, "hope" and "prevail." Whenever you heard the off-putting, and oft-expressed, animosity of wheelchair users particularly targeted toward Reeve, it had little to do with the person, who was utterly charming and a potent force in advocacy. It was incited by the use of the celebrity as a "symbol of hope" with all the attendant promises. Even when he died at age fifty-two in October 2004, as this book was heading to press, the sentimental hagiographies continued to overshadow the serious legacy of political work. If anything, there was a crescendo of bathos. The media tributes to Reeve never strayed from the "Superhero To the End" script (the headline, from *USA Today,* was the basic theme on which hundreds of papers played their variations). His own son Matthew's documentary, *Courageous Steps* and Barbara Walter's 20/20 elegy "Portrait in Courage" were just two examples of a raft of nearly identical, hopelessly sentimental broadcast programs. This is, for those who have lived with spinal cord injury for decades, tantamount to denial. It becomes an affront when it is so public. The headline for the *New Yorker* story, in this context, has a double edge. Within the community "the Reeve effect" is one thing—rage at callow submission to exploitation—while in the context of the *New Yorker*'s optimism before a mainstream audience it is the opposite—admiration for heroic willingness to be a pioneer in research. The deck, or subhead, steers right into the "prevail" lane: "Can an actor's determination to walk again change the way medical research is conducted?"

Even before reading the piece, considerations of genre arise. To briefly defend the editor's choice, one of the redeeming factors in running the piece in the science slot should have been its broad-brush gesture, as what is called a "think piece," toward placing Reeve in a pivotal role as a catalyst for change in the nation's research practices and policies. The question in the deck was a strong and important one. The *New Yorker* had recently pulled off a number of strong articles on medical and ethical issues involving vision research and autism, and has had a strong track record of AIDS coverage. But this coverage was intended to satisfy much more than the readership's fascination with science writing (or hypochondria). From the cynical point of view that I had to adopt as editor in chief and shareholder of a media company, it is no coincidence that as travel and luxury advertisers pulled their pages following 9/11, one of the only growth areas in ad revenues has been the pharmaceutical sector, courtesy of the major drug companies pumping up brand recognition of new drugs to stomp out generics, led of course by Pfizer and Viagra. Any savvy publisher was going to lobby for "supporting" those sponsors editorially with beefed-up health coverage. The sacred separation of church and state is all very well in flush times, but the lean issues of 2001 and 2002 called for strategic measures. In medical terms alone, the article should have pushed its point about Reeve heralding progress in research methodology harder. Thirteen paragraphs in, it mentions "causing a revolution" in the clinic, the laboratory, and the government but then lets the assertion hang for fifteen thousand words before feebly returning. A stronger focus on that "revolution" would have been more interesting, especially coming from the laptop of a Harvard Medical School professor, surrounded as one expects he is by old-school practices and attitudes. However, the substance of the article does not support the claims of its billing, which is nothing new in journalism. Headlines and decks are slapped on by editors deep into the process. Their function is to tease and, when used as cover lines, to sell. The *New Yorker*'s newsstand edition uses a Seymour Hersh or John Updike to lure nonsubscribers, like me, with bylines or topical and catchy headlines. Many a head in magazine publishing has as little to do with what follows as car names with what is under the hood.

Even so, there were alternatives to the way this piece could have been assigned and framed within the context of the magazine's mix of articles. This may sound like Monday-morning quarterbacking, but the editorial decision-making process begins with the assignment, the matching of writer and topic, the budgeting of pages in the book, their placement and layout. Much as I relished the long format, dead center in what is called the feature well (prime location in layout real estate because it is far from ads, minimally invaded by cartoons), I questioned the category or slug and the writer. The advocates are right for deploring the knee-jerk medicalization of Reeve, especially when in this case an alternative would have made a statement in and of itself. Along those lines, the *New Yorker* has its own battery of big-gun regulars who could have assessed the Reeve "effect" in their arenas, including not only movies and drama or celebrity culture but also sociology, philanthropy, and, the choice I would have made, politics. Turn loose a Capitol Hill insider and assess whether anybody in Congress really considered Reeve a match for the forces behind

Bush who are holding up stem cell research. The article's proportions would be instantly rejiggered, from maximal medicine and minimal advocacy to an inside-the-Beltway strategy investigation that, given the *New Yorker* audience, would have required minimal explication of the medical and legal parameters of the stem cell debate. A year before it became a crucial campaign issue, this would have been crystal-ball journalism.

At the time, the three figures in the disability world who provided multifaceted possibilities to editors faced with choosing which department of a general-interest magazine they belong in were Reeve, Magic Johnson, and Michael J. Fox. They were regulars on both lightweight and heavyweight programming (*Access Hollywood* and MSNBC), presences on the red carpet, princes of the black-tie fundraising circuit, and laudable pains in the congressional asses during public committee hearings on research budgets and policies. The nonprofit organizations they founded have it both ways—celebrity wattage for maximal donations and serious clout through testimony. So do the editors, who can run the celebrity's profile for Hollywood ratings and make a redemptive medical or political story much sexier. That is the real meaning of the "Reeve effect," and had the article been true to its headline it would have shifted focus from the medical to the political angle. When I started my magazine, former colleagues from Time Inc. I might bump into at White House press conferences or editorial panel discussions inevitably asked, "What are you going to do after the Reeve story?" as though he were the only name in town and my inevitable cover boy. This made me nervous in those crucial early months as we bumbled through the problems of establishing our marketability on Madison Avenue and our credibility on the disability "street," where Reeve was boringly overexposed at best, and provoking at worst. Two years into our run, when we made our deal with the devil and ran the Jerry Lewis cover, we were obviously over that initial trepidation about community approval, but for the first year the cover problem was torn between courting people with disabilities who would make readers want to look inside for a reflection of their views (Heather Whitestone, Stephen Hawking, George Soros, John Hockenberry) and attracting advertisers with the usual blend of name recognition and upscale assocations (Elizabeth Taylor, Muhammad Ali, Princess Diana, Itzhak Perlman, Paul Newman, Michael J. Fox, Andrea Bocelli). Once in a while we could score points with both readers and advertisers, as with a sexy Marlee Matlin cover.

Every first Monday editorial meeting in our bimonthly cycle inevitably raised the question of when the Reeve cover would run. Early on we had decided that a celebrity cover was an effective leading edge of the wedge we wanted to drive into the market. Attractive and recognizable, "affirmative" and positive, it cleared a path for the "real people" inside the issue—the further back in the book you paged, the less glamorous the photos and stories were, from the celebrity profile and fashion up front, professionally shot and styled, to the 35-millimeter slides of people in their living rooms that accompanied our short autobiographical pieces in the final pages of the book. I wasn't proud of that visual and verbal diminishment but viewed it as the price we needed to pay to break into the market. It worked. After our first issue had gone out to thirty-five thousand names on our bought mailing lists, we were pleased with the 3 percent return as measured in the reply cards torn from issues and sent back to us. In the second mail bin we ever received from the Upper West Side Manhattan post office branch around the corner from the office, where one of my interns and I would go and haul home the responses to our mailing-list efforts, a subscription card had come in from Dana Reeve, Christopher's wife, which we saved for posterity. He was family, but that did not automatically make him cover material. In fact, despite many encounters with both Dana and Christopher Reeve over that inaugural year of the magazine's existence, and my own admiration for the advocacy work they were doing, I held off putting him on the cover until well into our track record, when I had a news peg that was not just a charity appearance or medical "breakthrough"—of which there were too many, frankly, to be creditable. "Rehashing Reeve" simply was not an appealing headline. When he completed the shooting for his remake of Hitchcock's *Rear Window*, which he both starred in and directed, I had my premise, and it dovetailed beautifully with the proemployment, promainstreaming agenda we were pushing. With Reeve on the job, a built-in teaser for film buffs (Reeve vs. Hitchcock), and the cover timed to the release of the movie in 1998 on HBO, we had news, we had substance, and we cast him as an active star instead of a passive guinea pig. A point-by-point comparison between the *WE* cover story, written by freelancer Todd Shapera from notes he took on the set as well as interviews, and the *New Yorker* piece would be unfair to "the world's greatest magazine," in part because (my God it sounds presumptuous to say) our sophisticated audience was so much better equipped to handle a postdisability take on Reeve and we were not blinded by the beam of "hope." I would also contend that we put together a better feature, paragraph by paragraph, on technical merits.

Returning to Dr. Groopman's efforts, let us pose some hardball questions regarding journalistic standards at America's leading news organizations. Word count is not the cardinal measure of quality, or gravitas to use a buzzword that is on the verge of overstaying its welcome in the media business. Conciseness has its merits. Intimacy between writer and subject, similarly, is no guarantee that the reader's best interests are served.

As to serving the agenda of the subject himself, in this case advancing the cause of aggressive spinal cord research, let us remember that flipping along to the end of eleven pages when bored at the beginning can lead to the whole article being abandoned before the quote arrives that delivers the point the subject probably had in mind when consenting to the interview (in this case, one has to wait thousands of words for the pearl of Reeve's final thinking on research, which is far too long). The article gets a C for basics, including the proportion of background to news value (the only discernible news peg seems to be Christopher Reeve loses hair), diversity and quality of sources, factual content, and writer's bias, particularly as evident in Dr. Groopman's clumsy cameo appearances in what I might jokingly call a journalistic house call.

After a scenic opener at Reeve's gorgeous and accessible Bedford mansion (done before, five years ago, in *People* when he first invited journalists in, and dozens of times since including by television crews and local newspapers), the article segues into three breathlessly overwritten paragraphs on the drama of Reeve's equestrian accident eight years earlier. Not only is this a blatant regurgitation of earlier accounts including Reeve's own in the autobiography *Still Me* (which Groopman mines for quotes, a no-no among prouder professional journalists), but it stoops to shameless ghoulishness: "Reeve flipped forward and suffered what doctors call a hangman's injury . . . death by hanging often results from suffocation, and Reeve was heard to say, I can't breathe . . . if he had landed with his head one-sixteenth of an inch to the left he would have died instantly." One way to make old news interesting is to play up the drama, but in terms of the medicalization syndrome this just plunges the reader further into a view of Reeve as a body on a gurney. Then Groopman abruptly shifts gears into comedy in a gratuitous, snide remark that any alert editor would have blue-penciled with the marginal comment "tasteless." Observing that Reeve's daughter Alexandra is a current member of the Yale polo team, the writer adds, behind the back of his hand, "The Reeves are clearly not a superstitious family."

By now we know Dr. Groopman is inside the house (he has described himself being ushered from the front door to the office by an assistant) and bent on showing us his bedside manner. He reports on Reeve's breathing and gasping (an ongoing issue in his rehab, including his work on the set of *Rear Window,* was his ability to go without a respirator for hours), we have his weight and height duly recorded (214 and six-foot four), and we see the effect of alopecia areata, as observed in the Avedon photo. Reeve is talking about the need for change in the research community while Groopman undermines the exchange by observing that "his words were as carefully chosen as those of a Presidential candidate."

The doctor sticks to his examination as Dana, who has a nonspeaking role in this scene, delivers lunch. Explaining to us that Reeve could eat anything he likes, with assistance, Groopman observes that the patient's lower body was not as "shrunken" as that of the typical quadriplegic, that he was immobile except for the pointing of the index finger. The average joe is always fascinated by the hidden details of disability life, as John Hockenberry mercilessly points out in a fantastically funny passage about Oprah and sex in his memoir. Groopman obliges: "I asked him if he could move his legs. 'A bit,' he said, adding that he now exercised regularly in a swimming pool." The doctor-as-writer is doing his job, administering a checkup and reporting back to us on the patient's condition, whether or not Reeve was a miracle (Groopman feels his recovery was "a mystery"), and, eventually, recommending the treatment strategy culled from a battery of research options he evaluates in the body of the story. In addition to pushing us further into "medicalization" than most journalists would even have the capacity to go, the doctor-patient scenario ends up, I feel, way out of bounds in the final paragraph of the story. This is skipping ahead, and I sympathize with any writer who has to come up with a kicker to such a long piece for a literary magazine such as the *New Yorker,* but the schmaltz of the final paragraph is beyond the pale even of Barbara Walters and her similar lovefests with Reeve. Groopman, like Walters, violates the distance a journalist should maintain: "When I was first introduced to Reeve, I had placed my hand gently on top of his. At the end of the afternoon, I asked him if he had truly felt it. 'Of course!' he said, surprised. Then he paused, and for the first time his voice was infused with emotion. The warmth of human skin, he said, was the sensation he valued most. 'Feeling my children's touch again—that's been the most amazing thing.'" Cue the violins.

It sounds curmudgeonly, but this is unadulterated pity mongering. It does wonders for the doctor's image as a tender, sympathetic humanist but completely undermines the authority that is most needed, as does the admission a paragraph before that Reeve's "rhetorical vigor and robust appearance made it impossible not to be caught up in his vision." If a doctor submits to sentimentality, and cannot assemble a story according to basic investigative principles, then what is he there for? Like Walters and others who have romanticized Reeve, he is just another fan, a voice from the chorus, and in Goffman's terms an "other." What would have been immeasurably better would have been Groopman using his professional criteria to evaluate his own observations as well as articles and charts to report on the progress of the spinal cord research Reeve advocated, but that would not have made gripping copy, the ooh and ah stuff that sells.

As for the meat of the story, Groopman needs to take Reporting 101.

The first test for an article of this length on a scientific topic with a political spin is mustering the sources. Quantity counts, but so does quality as judged by expertise and impartiality. To stir controversy, passionate partisanship adds color, but to inform, the writer needs to find spokespeople with the ability to lay aside axes that beg for grinding. As a benchmark, let me revert to standard journalistic practices. For pieces a third of this length in the science and technology slot for *Fortune,* a magazine for which I used to work, the writer and reporter who split the data gathering would regularly interview twenty or more experts on both sides of the coin (if the picture remained unclear at the end of that month-long process, double the number of sources). In the published article, we would quote about half of them, with full attribution. The geometry of arranging quotes, diagonally balancing pros and cons and subtly tipping the story in the direction the editor or writer has chosen to support, is a skill in itself. By the time editors were done with cuts, many quotes were left out, but on-the-record sources both pro and con had to be part of the final mix. I enumerated Groopman's live sources (those he had evidently spoken with directly, after the inevitable Reeves) and came up with a grand total of seven, six researchers plus one of their patients.

Their qualifications as neuroscientists aside, there is a prevailing problem with the quality of this roster: they are all "contrarian" researchers in the spinal cord field, supporters of the "he'll walk again" position, who obviously tumbled from Reeve's Rolodex. First up is V. R. Edgerton, a neuroscientist at UCLA, who starts the ball rolling: "When scientists think they know something works, it becomes difficult to get new ideas accepted." This is a suitable premise and a juicy quote. There is nothing wrong with starting off with a strong thesis. The problem lies in failing to produce an antithesis. After Edgerton, one of his ardent supporters, Dr. Anton Wernig from the University of Bonn, is invoked, and his radical therapy regimen laid the foundation for the work of John McDonald of Washington University in St. Louis, who plays a prominent role in the *New Yorker* article for helping Reeve attain movement in his feet in the pool (as seen on TV). As the article points out, McDonald's high-profile patient, and the research dollars involved, have helped build a big institute in St. Louis where forty patients are undergoing treatment (including a little girl cited in the piece). Another beef of mine about the article: the only dollar amounts given are the half million Reeve spends on medical expenses per annum, two-thirds of this covered by insurance, and the $13 million in grants conferred by the Christopher Reeve Paralysis Foundation each year. But by the time we are finished with the "ebullient" McDonald ("As far as I know, no human being has ever been reported to have substantial recovery after two years when he had no recovery in the beginning. Chris

shattered that myth"), we are conscious of a serious point-of-view problem with the article's sources. They are basically all on the payroll. Late
in the piece, four other cutting-edge researchers, two Europeans, an Is-
raeli, and one from Rutgers, are quoted, and a fifth, Dr. Honyun Huang
in Beijing, is also discussed via enthusiastic reports from one of the three
(it was too difficult to place a call or send an e-mail to Beijing?), all of
them contributing to the optimistic picture that the regeneration of spinal
cord tissue is on the horizon as long as the research can carry on, and all
of them recipients of or prime candidates for Reeve research dollars.

Please do not mistake my own point of view. I cheered every wiggle of
his toes, too, and want like hell for those stem cell projects in Israel, Spain,
and Beijing to work out, for the innovators to win Nobel prizes, and for
their treatments to give hope to every friend of mine with a spinal cord
injury. Everything in the article supports my own beliefs, in other words,
so it seems odd to nitpick, but the cause is better served by balanced journalism than by a rigged puff piece. Even though I am "pro-Reeve" myself, I could scarcely overlook the problem that the article was an inside
job, right down to the testimony of the mother of a six-year-old quadriplegic, like Reeve a patient of McDonald the miracle worker, who dutifully echoes the consensus: "Every step that he makes, that he moved a
finger or moved a toe, for us, we know how incredible that is. That would
be like me running a marathon. Seeing the progress he is making, it keeps
us going."

Owing to either laziness or cowardice, the dissenting voices are drowned
out. In the paragraph from the first page that so annoyed me at the start,
Charles Krauthammer is cited not "live" but in a very old quote after Reeve
was shown in the "disgracefully misleading" (Krauthammer's words, my
sentiment) mutual fund ad that was the low point of the 2001 year Super
Bowl for most people with disabilities (to be considered in chapter 5, on
advertising). It used a simulation of Reeve's head superimposed on a man
walking down a runway. Krauthammer is cited as one of many "advocates for the disabled" (another Groopman blooper—Krauthammer has
been criticized by advocates for being so aloof) who would not buy Reeve's
promise to walk again. Why not call Krauthammer for an updated take
on Reeve? As a fellow Harvard Med School grad, a wheelchair user because of a spinal cord injury (diving accident), and a fantastically well-
connected Washington insider (he studied politics at McGill and Oxford,
shaped psychiatric research policy under the Carter administration,
wrote speeches for Mondale in 1980, and files stories and columns from
Washington for *Time* and the *Washington Post* when not appearing as
a wonk on all the major networks), he would have been the ideal source
for this article. It is difficult to reach him for comment but not impossible

(I did it, and I wasn't calling from the *New Yorker*), and one would assume he and Groopman, both Harvard men, could have had quite a conversation. It never happened.

After critics among "the disabled," there are only two other references to anti-Reeve sources. Midway through reporting on McDonald's successful attempts to electrically stimulate the regeneration of neurons, Groopman admits: "Claims about Reeve's recovery were initially met with skepticism by scientists." Some pages later, there is a cautionary note: "Some scientists think it is absurd that a layman can help determine funding decisions." The alert reader will have already picked up on the weakness here: not one name is provided. The insertion point for a dissenting point of view is available in a paragraph devoted to that old journalistic stratagem, the confrontation of the interviewee with clips from his critics:

> When I spoke to scientists, many complained that Reeve's impatience could lead to premature conclusions or faulty data. Nobody, however, would speak on the record. "He has gotten impatient when he's heard the answer 'We don't know enough,'" one researcher said of Reeve. "You can almost hear him say, 'well you're not the one on the respirators.' And yet doing something just because someone's situation is desperate—that's not acceptable." *Nature*, the scientific journal, published a news article last May about how researchers felt pressured by Reeve and other advocates. When I showed him the piece, his tone was icy. "If we push, that's our prerogative," he said. "And scientists, of course, have the right to push back."

The final quote of the paragraph is a keeper—concise and vivid in its summary of the tension between Reeve and his critics. What precedes it, however, is embarrassing. In fact there *are* critics on the record vis-à-vis Reeve—specifically bioethicist Arthur Caplan—but the article fails to produce them in their own voices, a glaring fault. The line about not going on the record ironically made Reeve look like a spoiled, intolerant despot who used his money to intimidate professional researchers, which is far from the case. Certainly with four pages to go it would be ridiculous to invoke the "not enough space" excuse. Finally, I had to wonder why Groopman could not invoke his own qualifications and voice doubts in propria persona about the important issue, so crucial as well to FDA decisions and familiar from the AIDS battleground of the eighties, of public pressure and research protocols.

My nitpicking of the article could go on, from both the disability and the journalism perspectives, but it is time to let the estimable *New Yorker* off the hook. You never know how bad or good a magazine is until it covers something in your backyard. The news cycle being what it is, this magazine will never in the near future revisit the scene of this crime. But Reeve deserved better treatment. People with disabilities, especially those sitting in wheelchairs after spinal cord injuries, deserved better. So did the frontline rehab workers and researchers, and the readers.

As for Groopman, his star turn continues in the context of a movement in his profession called "narrative medicine," a novel approach to the doctor-patient relationship now taught at Columbia University's medical school and championed since 1999 by Rita Charon, an internist with a doctorate in literature. Reinforcing the notion of medicine as an art, and making welcome use of literary texts and even critical theory as part of a wholistic treatment strategy, its aim is to create a "narrative competence" to go with other skills a doctor brings to the diagnostic situation. Groopman and Abraham Verghese are often cited as perfect examples of the empathetic application of narrative medicine, and Groopman is an adviser to a pilot program at Harvard Medical School requiring first-year students to write a book about a patient's yearlong progress. One of the most fascinating aspects of this theory is the creation of a "parallel chart" that records in detail the doctor's emotional responses to a patient. Setting aside for a moment the clinical value of this invention, I think there is a great deal to be learned for writers and editors here. As Charon teaches her third-year medical students, the analysis of the parallel chart is more than a writing exercise designed to awaken the emotional lives of doctors. It is a reflective process that offers a specialized vocabulary for decoding elements of contingency and chance, intersubjectivity (the writer's relationship to the reader), genre, and diction, all with particular attention to the ways in which the narrative shapes the perception of the patient. Combined with the patient's narrative, or pathography, the value of these documents lies in the awareness they stir that can lead naturally to some of the reforms disability advocates have been unsuccessfully pushing for years. One can imagine a "parallel notebook" for journalists, for example, that records the reporter's reflections on a disability profile in time for the adjustments in language and structure to be made—that is, before publication. Like the ethnographic, sociological, and anthropological examinations of the clashes between disability and mainstream cultures, this bifurcated approach could make it possible for journalists and editors to ask these questions of themselves: Have I fairly and accurately represented this person with a disability? Does my diction pass the tests for acceptable language? Have I tried too hard to shape a narrative that dramatizes at the expense of reflecting the real-life experience? If it were me, is this the way I would want to be portrayed? Dr. Groopman, try this remedy at home.

CHAPTER FOUR

I'd Like to Thank the Academy

Losing Focus on Disability in Movies and Television

So may the outward shows be least themselves.
—*Bassanio, in* The Merchant of Venice

To pan television and movies in toto for their perpetually offensive treatment of disability would require a book in itself, but I hope in this chapter to skewer enough of the worst offenders—Hollywood directors and stars, television sitcom writers, and, surprise, Barbara Walters—to raise hackles or at least suspicion about most of the others. From Lon Chaney's *Hunchback of Notre Dame* (1923) to Cuba Gooding's *Radio* (2003), Jamie Foxx's *Ray* (2004), and beyond, so much money has been made off the backs of various real-life and fictional people with disabilities that, like the memoir, a media-stock analyst could identify a lucrative niche of the film industry spun from this theme. The fiscal and critical success of such films and shows is precisely why the electronic media owe far more to the disibility community—respect, fairness, good taste—than to any other minority, and yet their brainless and patronizing take on the subject adds injury to insult especially by contrast with the way the industry has been instrumental in advancing the human rights of other minorities. One might have supposed that with the advent of so-called reality TV this situation might be primed to change, because the day-to-day coping mechanisms of people with disabilities are both real as can be and fascinating to outsiders, but there is evidently far more box office appeal for American viewers in gay interior designers than in wheelchair users. In Europe, by contrast, the third year of reality television brought casting calls for people with disabilities, often announced through community Web sites such as the BBC's Ouch. Like the hokey sets, with their inane circles of tiki torches or Dr. Strangelove lucite lecterns, the reality shows are just as fake as their movie and sitcom counterparts, preferring perfect bodies or at least fashionable geeks to people with visible or invisible disabilities. Movies, television, even reality shows all have their limits when it comes to the tolerance of on-screen disability, unless of course taste is thrown to the wind and a series on the mating of "little people" (*The Littlest Groom,* a low point even for the abysmal Fox) is offered up to the Nielsen gods. The fall 2004 season of *Survivor* included an amputee. By the same token, Hollywood since the advent of the talkie has never hesitated to mine the disability vein for schmaltz and laughs, and revenues.

The safest nomination bets for Oscar gold, year after year, are disability flicks. The Academy adores feel-good stories starring major names willing, briefly, to forgo their customary leaps from burning buildings or steamy bedroom exploits to jerk tears from devoted fans with a sanitized impression of some poor sod with a disability. The big star spends a few days, maybe a whole week, chatting up patients and doctors in addition to reviewing medical footage of tics and spasms, drooling, and wobbling to be practiced before the mirror while the writers fill in the blanks of screenplays so hopelessly derivative of "classics" in the genre that one wonders if there is a workbook generally available in the California public library system with templates for the blind, deaf, returning veteran, and degenerative muscular or neurological disease movies. As predictable as the script itself are the critics' responses (the inescapable "brave" and "inspiring" end up in bold face in the full-page ads) as well as the acceptance speeches on Oscar night, thanking a "victim" and/or researcher who is momentarily blinded by flashbulbs at the afterparties before returning to the obscurity of his ward or lab. Weeks later, victims and doctors are forgotten as *Entertainment Tonight* moves on to the next story about an actor checking into rehab.

While *WE* magazine was at its peak, we were blessed with a few of those magical Oscar-night moments that used people with disabilities to "unforgettable" effect, as when Muhammad Ali brought down the house by appearing briefly at the podium with George Foreman (it was the year of *When We Were Kings,* a movie about "the rumble in the jungle"), Andrea Bocelli sang with Celine Dion, David Helfgott, the real-life pianist on whom *Shine* (seven Oscars) was based, stumbled gamely through a version of "Flight of the Bumblebee," or Marlee Matlin both spoke and signed her acceptance remarks, all of these stiff gestures essentially torn from the Jerry Lewis playbook. There is no denying that the photos and sound bites made good copy for my lifestyle magazine—we even started a gossip column, the Masked Man, for celebrity sightings and casting news about any film that had a disability hook. With DVDs came the bonus material with sober features on the disability, the state of research, and, sometimes usefully, directions for making a charitable donation.

The catalogue of these Oscar-winning films is long: *Rain Man* (1988) starring Dustin Hoffman as an autistic savant, *Scent of a Woman* (1992) with a "blind" Al Pacino, Tom Hanks playing this card twice with *Philadelphia* (AIDS, 1993) and *Forrest Gump* (retardation, 1994), *Leaving Las Vegas* (1995) with Nicolas Cage as a recovering alcoholic, the relatively unknown Geoffrey Rush struggling with an unidentified psychiatric package of problems in *Shine* (1996), Russell Crowe in *A Beautiful Mind* (2001), Billy Bob Thornton in his own *Sling Blade* (1996), and Cuba Gooding in *Radio* (2003). These megastars took home gold statuettes and arrived on the disability scene with publicity fanfare, which means blockbuster-size audiences spent at least an hour-and-change immersed in the dramas of disability and, one would suppose, absorbed a degree of information and knowledge that might have altered their perception of disability. However, this would be giving Hollywood too much credit. Producers, directors, and writers package disability in such a way as to safely ensure that the audience feels nobly uplifted, even ethically superior, for "supporting" what is in effect a blatantly oversweetened version of life with a disability as concocted by a community that cannot countenance physical imperfection except in certain sanctioned and saccharine forms. The effects are often surreal. The blind star drives a sports car, the autistic or retarded lead utters a Hallmark aphorism that takes on Socratic weight in the nation's op-ed pages for the next two weeks ("Stupid is as stupid does"), the "wheelchair-bound" returning veteran or former athlete finds true love, or at least comes off as a total stud.

The insincerity of Hollywood's actors and filmmakers is essentially the cynical attitude of the exploiter toward the exploited. One of the most horrifying examples of this was the marketing blitz that surrounded *Shine,* which included a concert tour for the real-life pianist, David Helfgott, on whom the film was based. While his avaricious wife, Gillian, monitored the box office, poor Helfgott was skewered by music critics across the country for his amateur renditions of Rachmaninoff and Schumann, which were nowhere near the level of the dubbed versions that musically illiterate movie audiences had heard in the film or the heavily edited triumphs of the digital studio that were released as "his" CDs and immediately soared to the top of the charts, making him the best-selling classical artist for that year. Every morning and evening talk show host wanted a slice of Helfgott, who obliviously smiled his way through the whole sham, hugging anyone he saw with breasts while his handlers raked in millions and the movie grossed $36 million. Where is Helfgott now? Only two years since the movie's release, he is in "semiretirement" according to a long wrap-up newsletter written in 2004 by his wife, and down to well under a dozen recitals a year while splitting his time between homes in Australia and Italy. Dropped by major label BMG, his latest CD was a private-label issue of some sloppy Mozart. His time as freak-of-the-month is up.

While a disability-themed film is in theaters, the brave face remains on, but like most masks it usually slips. After all, these are the people who made the obsession with plastic surgery, the win-at-all-costs war against physical imperfection, a prime-time reality show in itself. Joan Collins once told KABC-TV (in Los Angeles) that she was in awe of Daniel Day Lewis's performance as an artist with cerebral palsy in *My Left Foot,* and in the view of people in the community put her own foot in it, ironically enough because her daughter has a disability, with the memorable comment: "For somebody as good looking as he is to make himself look as ugly as he is in every way is a total art." At least she was sincere. When Charlize Theron was transformed by makeup crews into a murderer for *Monster,* the celebrity press was awestruck at her "courage" to be ugly— "There is nothing extraordinary about Patty Jenkin's debut feature 'Monster' except the transformation of the singularly beautiful (if somehow bland) Charlize Theron into a truly hideous creature"—even though all she had to do was wash her makeup off after the final shoot. When the bar is set that low for the tolerance of anything but the nubile and blemish free, it is nearly impossible for a culture to directly face genuine disability.

Here is the basic plotline: An attractive person is suddenly struck by misfortune and made "tragically" undesirable. He or she struggles gamely to cope and, triumphing, ultimately leads even the most hard-bitten disbelievers with whom he or she has contact to redemption. The optional ending has the character either finding love (*My Left Foot, Coming Home, A Beautiful Mind*) or happily looking on as others do (*Rain Man*). The parabolically if not diabolically symmetrical story lines of disability movies are locked into this pattern from opening shot to final frame, and the standard climactic clips are *Oprah*-ready tearjerkers to stringed accompaniment. As spectacle, this reassuring ritual has a long filmic provenance. According to Liz Greco, an advocate working with the National Federation of the Blind to whom I turned for an article on film and disability for the second issue of the magazine, "Although the American disabled population is estimated at 50 million, there are many moviegoers and moviemakers who, even though they themselves may know a person with a disability, still find the world of people with disabilities somewhat exotic. And what better way to feed the natural curiosity for the unknown, they calculate, than in a darkened movie theater?" Her dim view of the syndrome is shared by a number of others. Jean Vanier, founder of L'Arche, an international network, headquartered in Quebec, of communities for people with so-called mental disabilities, has pointed out that the repulsion society feels for people with disabilities outside the theater "expresses an inner fear of brokenness and fragility. This might partly explain why there is a fascination with disability when viewed from the safety of a picture theatre. It is a detached way of confronting our fears of public shame and inner weakness."

The economics of representing disability on screen involve budgets and revenues vastly greater than those of any other medium. One prime-time television episode of *The West Wing,* with its subplot about multiple sclerosis, pulls a Nielsen rating in the high teens, which translates into over 20 million viewers, roughly 10,000 times more people than any issue of my magazine ever touched. Hollywood's production budgets and advertising revenues make magazine accounts look like a joke. Top-grossing movies multiply all these numbers by a factor of ten. With the stakes that much higher, and the quantitative indexes of the films' reach so superior, the question arises whether the impact of the movies on the lay audience as well as the disability community translates into awareness and change. When autism is on screen, does public sensitivity and support for nonprofits automatically follow, receiving a lift from the film's success? Experts note that the effect of a successful movie on charitable giving is similar to that of a well-publicized disaster such as an earthquake: an upward blip is followed by amnesia. Hollywood is better off just taking the tax deduction and writing the check. George Lucas's Lucasfilms donated the total gate for all eleven preview screenings of *Star Wars* in 2001 to charities including the Joey Fund and the Hospital for Sick Children foundation, saving a section of seats at every show for children with disabilities. Paul Newman's Hole in the Wall Gang (a national charity for children with cancer and blood diseases funded by Newman's own line of foods) is a far more direct and effective way of parlaying fame into funding. Many celebrities turn up at galas where starstruck fans bid feverishly for photo opportunities—it fills the coffers. It also fills their pockets, as personal appearance fees run to $35,000 or more for a meet-and-greet and photo sessions.

The basic equation of reach and attitudinal change, however, gives Hollywood too much credit. Just as celebrity "outing" has marginally altered the public perception of disability—one need only think of the renaming of ALS as "Lou Gehrig's disease" to perceive how—the increase in charitable giving or media coverage accorded to a disability in the aftermath of a blockbuster is far more modest than the audience figures might suggest. Demographics still drive everything from casting to the selection of the disability, the dialogue, and the ever delicate question of medical accuracy. The details can be grim, and even an industry long inured to blowing people's faces off in action flicks or ripping body organs out in science fiction has a hard time with drooling, let alone colostomy bags. A weak stomach for what is real is the prevailing disability in Hollywood, where the low threshold for intelligence is matched by a low tolerance for any kind of disability.

This presents a vivid contrast to the dominant story line accorded to minorities in entertainment. The fear and loathing that were underlying causes of the barriers faced by blacks, Latinos, Asians, gays, and older people both on screen and off have been allayed in part by the familiarity engendered by their rising status in movies and television. By 2004, a gaggle of flamboyantly gay "consultants" could replace the toppled Martha Stewart as home decorating experts on network television while Halle Barry challenged Julia Roberts as a leading lady, Denzel Washington made as much per picture as Tom Cruise, and Jennifer Lopez could outstrip Britney Spears on the pop diva charts, all thanks to the steady erosion of segregationist prohibitions against on-screen interracial romance, heroism, or, to put it bluntly, sheer "normality." In the cases of race and gender, Hollywood and society danced a deft two-step that propelled them toward the acceptance of minorities even as it built audiences in markets (black, Latino, women, and senior) that pushed studios and television networks further into minority programming. Even these minority communities, however, still feel disgruntled about being ghettoized in niche programming or marketing (the old *Shaft* effect, patently obvious in the way movies are sold or, for instance, sitcoms and the local news are directed at African-Americans on such networks as UPN).

As ever, the bottom line is financial. While the music industry has far more blacks and Latinos in executive positions of power because sales support the shift in leadership and it is far cheaper to make a CD demo than a movie, the television and film side of black and Latino programming lag behind mainstream white programming on a relative basis, and far behind them are the disability executives, most of whom keep their disability a secret. The only genuinely powerful person with a disability I ever met in television, for instance, is Phil Beuth, a hard-driving amputee and programming veteran who ran ABC's *Good Morning America* and in 1993 pulled strings to get an AIDS fundraiser prime-time air, to honor a son, Barry, who had died from the disease. That was an exception, and Beuth had to fight his own network to do it again the next year. Media experts point out that Hollywood executives are more insulated from people of color and disability than their counterparts in music. As Todd Boyd, a critical studies professor at the University of Southern California and an expert on the role of blacks in media and pro sports management, observes, "A black face, a Latino face, an Asian-American face are all tied into this country's problematic history. I think it's much easier to deal with that in terms of listening. People say out of sight, out of mind. It's always been easier to pass something off in terms of sound than you would be able to in terms of image." This observation about visibility and the audience's receptivity goes a long way toward explaining the dearth of actors with disabilities on screen as well, and if you think blacks are underrepresented in Hollywood, just consider the opacity of the veil drawn across disability. "Hollywood sees only one color, and that's green," says actor Omar Epps, an African-American. The anomaly here involves the billions that have been made on disability films without the emergence of a similar programming or marketing effort to channel those movies toward audience members with disabilities, including the all-important casting of real people with disabilities in them. Instead, disability movies are made for the temporarily able-bodied, whose dollars support the continued production of the same type of film. If this were true of other minorities, you'd still have minstrel shows and Suzie Wong for the entertainment of white folks.

By contrast, the clumsy shuffle of Hollywood and people with disabilities never moved from a corner of the dance floor where progress can be kept to a minimum, because in the end, as Greco pointed out above, they do not really know one another terribly well and their dancing shows it. Indeed, it would have proven an awkward situation if something like the rapid growth of other minority audiences had occurred and wheelchair users turned out en masse. Until the passage of the ADA, theaters large and small were nightmares of inaccessibility and, in the event of fire, death traps for those with either mobility problems or, in theaters lacking visual fire alarms, those with hearing impairment (although, in the absence of captioning and with the rise of animation, which defies lipreading, there was no great threat of millions of deaf people losing their lives as they simply shunned movie theaters). Perversely enough, just as ramps and elevators became mandatory and doors were widened for wheelchair users, the next big thing in cinematic design was stadium seating—and so wheelchair users in particular found themselves with the Scylla and Charybdis choice of the front row, risking hearing loss and days of cervical stiffness from looking up and being blasted by speakers, or watching from the top tier, where the screen and speakers become an expensive imitation of a decent home television set. It was the architectural version of the message the movie industry had been sending from the screen—that it could care less about the disability market. Whereas the black audience for movies doubled between 1980 and 2004, and ethnic actors took between 12 percent and 14 percent (by 2002) of principal roles, not to mention 14 percent of Oscar nominations, the trend line for people with disabilities was flat, and the number of actors with disabilities in principal roles does not even register on the charts. These figures are tracked by the Screen Actors Guild. For comparison's sake, people of color make up about 28 percent of the American public, including African-Americans, who constitute 13 percent, while people with disabilities count for about 20 percent.

Show Me the Money

In the theaters, the mainstream responds in droves to disability as a theme. The regularity and dearth of originality of these periodic forays into the world of disability confirm at least one fundamental tenet, of moviemaking if not of disability studies: illness is boffo box office. The gross for *Forrest Gump* was a whopping $673 million, while *Rain Man* raked in $412.8 million, *Scent of a Woman* earned $63.9 million, and *A Beautiful Mind* earned $309 million (worldwide). Even the far less cosmetically safe *My Left Foot* rode the Oscar effect to a respectable $14.7 million gross. Responding to marketing imperatives long established, the industry produces movies that touch millions only to leave them as smugly ignorant as ever, reinforcing rather than challenging stereotypes and, by a numbing lack of originality and an infuriating poverty of guts, perpetuating the pity syndrome by seductively re-presenting endless editions of its own static and vacuous, obnoxious, and simplistic versions of people with disabilities that perversely do more damage than the invisibility they purport to combat.

In fact, disability was never invisible in Hollywood. Even the golden age of silent film had an abundance of characters with disabilities. Lon Chaney, for example, the "man with a thousand faces," was also a man with a thousand disabilities, not only the hunched back and facial disfigurement (*Phantom of the Opera,* 1929) for which he is best known; in other movies he is legless, armless, and blind. One would think that in the eight intervening decades some sort of evolutionary development in the representation of disability might have occurred. For people with disabilities who have witnessed the steady progress of other minorities on screen, from African-Americans and Latinos to women and even geriatrics, the static yet enormously lucrative disability ghetto is particularly galling. For some activists, the tasteless and insulting portrayal of people with disabilities as rubes or freaks in comedies, or as bizarre villains, is trivial in its perfidious impact by comparison with the so-called sympathetic representations. In the former category, among the most unconscionable examples are the atrocious insults of the Farrelly brothers, Peter and Bobby, a Rhode Island "gross-out" duo known for such rubbish as *Something about Mary* (which mercilessly lampoons a developmentally disabled character) and more recently *Stuck on You* (starring conjoined twins) and a work in progress that will reportedly enrage wheelchair users in the community even further. Self-appointed arbiters of taste regarding political correctness, they have offended amputees, the blind, the deaf, women, minorities, and even animal lovers. "There's two lines," says Peter Farrelly. "There's a line that the critics will tell you is there. And then there's the real line. And the real line is what we go towards. We never cross that line. Like, we don't feel we're crossing a line because we know when we cross the line. That's when they don't laugh, because the audience won't laugh if it's truly mean-spirited." That is the sort of rationalization that, along with $15 million in receipts each opening week, earns the Farrellys a bye when it comes to the standards of taste or ethics by which less successful creators abide. I nearly had a stroke when the Media Access Office of the state of California gave the Farrelly brothers its Michael Landon Award in 2003 for their contribution to disability culture. Guaranteed a laugh or two from the stutterer or the blind man bumping into the doorframe, and willing to pander to the millions at the expense of a handful of letters or worse, picketers, the beat goes on.

Occasionally one of these jokes slides too far. A version of *Mister Magoo* (actually, a stinker that flopped) drew the ire of the National Federation of the Blind when it was released in 1997. Picketing and boycotting made a dent in its already troubled opening, and there was a sense of victory in the community when it failed to open in a number of theaters where it had been scheduled. A similar outcry had contributed to ABC's canceling a dreadful comedy series called *Good and Evil* (1992) after only seven episodes, and it was again the National Federation of the Blind that protested, saying that a character named George "displays preposterous ineptitude and stupidity." After a letter-writing and picketing campaign against ABC affiliates, the network chiefs pulled the plug. As when the Anti-Defamation League or NAACP pick their targets, this opposition involves a tricky balance between policing and appearing stiffly politically correct, lacking tolerance or humor. Shoot straight and you gain points for the cause. Miss the target and the advocates look like whiners, and the agenda suffers a setback. So far there has not been a Mel Gibson to mobilize a chorus of protest in the disability community.

Even cameo appearances slip into the rut of sentimentality or denigration. As a quick glimpse into the no-man's-land to which secondary characters with a disability are consigned, consider the two scenes in which one of Hugh Grant's friends, Bella, a wheelchair user played by Gina McKee, appears in *Notting Hill* (1990). On the one hand, it is refreshing to see a person with a disability on screen as just one of the gang in a headlining movie, without much ado (although she laments her inability to have children during a postdinner contest to come up with the saddest tale in order to win the final brownie, while the Julia Roberts character complains almost absurdly about enduring cosmetic surgery). Without further ado, the character would be a minor victory in the push for more disability on screen. Once the dinner party ends and Anna (Julia Roberts) and William (Grant) are strolling the street, she has to ask what happened

to Bella—in itself a natural enough segue but on another plane a reversion to a state of mind Liz Greco discussed earlier in this chapter; I ran
into the same problem at *Fortune* magazine with a photo of a plant manager in a wheelchair that my editor wanted "explained." As Richard Cur-
tis's screenplay reads, what seems an innocuous answer to a question in
the audience's mind is actually a throwback to the usual disability routine, which is a play for pity:

> **Anna:** Why is she in a wheelchair?
> **William:** It was an accident—about eighteen months ago.
> **Anna:** And the pregnancy thing—is that to do with the accident?
> **William:** You know, I'm not sure. I don't think they'd tried for kids before,
>   as fate would have it.

All of a sudden we have a tragic heroine ("as fate would have it") on
our hands rather than a member of the comic ensemble. A better film
would have left well enough alone.

Thumbs Up

There are certain movies that are less offensive, at least by degrees. Many
of the best known are in the returning veteran category, led by Jon
Voight's performance in *Coming Home* (1978), in which he plays a paraplegic Vietnam vet (best remembered for his sex scenes with Jane Fonda,
the wife of an uptight captain), and Tom Cruise's similar role a decade
later in *Born on the Fourth of July,* which is (too) loosely based on the
memoirs of activist and Vietnam vet Ron Kovic. In that film, director
Oliver Stone added a scene in a supermarket and another showing the
difficulty of gaining access to buildings (just on the threshold of the
ADA), so there were policy issues flickering briefly across the screen in
what was otherwise a film about the political repercussions of Vietnam
rather than disability. Both films were praised in the mainstream press for
raising consciousness of the plight of veterans with disabilities, but critics
in the community are still grumbling. My favorite comment is from John
Hockenberry's *Moving Violations:* "In the film *Born on the Fourth of
July,* director Oliver Stone is obsessed with penises, and writer Ron Kovic
is obsessed with the war and an idea of America he should never have believed in if he had had half a brain growing up. Only actor Tom Cruise
seems to be interested in the chair itself, but he can walk, so who cares if
he can hop stairs in a wheelchair?"[1] It is difficult to argue with Hockenberry's logic when the camera is pulled back to a sufficient distance for

the frame around the fiction to dissolve and remind us of the distinction between movies and life.

In the returning veteran genre, at least the posttraumatic stress disorder (PTSD) message manages to squeak through. In the wake of 9/11, when children still have nightmares about the burning towers, this issue seems less momentous perhaps or at least less steep a challenge to skeptics, but when *All Quiet on the Western Front* was made in 1930 (directed by Lewis Milstone and based on the novel by Erich Maria Remarque), or *The Best Years of Our Lives* was released in 1946, "shell shock" and the "thousand-yard stare" were vaguely understood and virtually untreatable. By the seventies, the decade of *M*A*S*H* (1970, directed by Robert Altman), *Coming Home,* Michael Cimino's *The Deer Hunter* (1978), and Francis Ford Coppola's *Apocalypse Now* (1979), the gravity of an epidemic was sinking in thanks in part to the stark portrayal of PTSD on screen. With later movies such as *Born on the Fourth of July, Scent of a Woman* (in addition to blindness, Pacino tangos on through flashbacks), *Platoon* (1986, another Stone picture), and even the dreadful *Rambo* series, the diagnostic language was much refined. In the disability community, especially among those who incur their disabilities through accidents, "getting" PTSD can be a subtle marker for understanding and acceptance, and if movies have made this any easier for the public to grasp, then they deserve at least a bit of credit for doing so. It took 9/11 to impress upon many New Yorkers I know the pervasive impact of PTSD even among nonveterans.

Getting the Joke

Even if most directors and studio execs cannot manage to embrace disability for what it is and get past the pablum, certain actors can. Setting aside Reeve, Matlin, Harold Russell, and others with disabilities, and admitting for once that the Method is too shallow to offer a just reflection of the anger of the Vietnam vet in a wheelchair, it is still possible to find a performance that passes muster in the community itself. One of the very few actors capable of rising above the banalities of the screenplays he routinely neglects in favor of improvisation is Robin Williams. Whether he plays a doctor working with "locked in" patients in the influential adaptation of Oliver Sacks's real-life story, *Awakenings* (which grossed $53 million in 1990), or a person with mental disabilities as in *The Fisher King* or the upcoming *First Person Plural* (Disney bought the rights to a book about identity disorder), Williams adds acceptance to pain in a mixture that surpasses Hollywood standards despite the flat performances

with which he is generally surrounded. One theory about how he manages this is that he is himself a person with multiple disabilities, not unlike those faced by his mentor Jonathan Winters, and that the "deep distress that humanized his soul" is his own experience. Having watched
him among people with disabilities at several charitable events, I could
tell that he was far more at home than any other star I had ever seen in
that milieu. He was the first to join Dana Reeve at her husband's bedside
when Christopher was injured, breaking the tension with his own bizarre
hospital humor (see *Patch Adams* for on-screen examples) and bringing
an essential dose of laughter to his old roommate from their Juilliard days
at one of the most difficult moments of Reeve's life. "People were so
solemn. I knew it was not good for Chris, so I dressed up in hospital
scrubs and pretended to be his proctologist. The smile on his face almost
broke my heart. He has told me since that it was at that moment when he
was able to know that he wanted to live." As Reeve recalled, "It was the
first time I laughed since the accident."

A frequent guest at disability events, especially where children are
found, Williams never fails to connect. The one great disability movie
never made, which has been rumored to be in the works for nearly a
decade, is Williams's portrayal of the dissipated and wickedly funny cartoonist John Callahan, for which Williams and his wife Marsha bought
the option, from Callahan, in 1995. As Callahan told me, "Will Robin be
able to hold still long enough to play a paralytic? This won't be Patch
Callahan, believe me, because, you know, Robin Williams has been
through a lot of stuff. When they start filming, with my luck I'll be used
as a stunt quad."[2] I needed to get through a team of lawyers to obtain a
written quote from Williams, and sign an exasperatingly paranoid three-
page contract ("Except as specifically provided herein, no use of Robin
Williams's name, or any use whatsoever of Robin Williams's photographs, voice, performance and/or likeness shall be made . . .") to extract
a written comment from Williams for *WE* magazine's cover story on
Callahan, but it was worth the effort: "Would John Callahan have the
same license to offend if he weren't vertically challenged? I think he would
still unleash lines like, 'Is that a colostomy bag in your pants or are you
just happy to see me?' He just wouldn't be invited to the George Wallace
Memorial Tractor Pull. I've always thought that John would be a great
stand-up comic, except for the standing part. I worship the ground he rolls
on." Perhaps that will be the disability film that leads Hollywood out of
the wilderness, as long as Williams can leave a trail of money behind him.

In the critically acclaimed if not fiscally stupendous film *Sling Blade*
(1996), Billy Bob Thornton, a country-song writer, turned a one-man show
he had revised during eight years of theater performances into a melo-

drama that was panned by some for its glacial pacing but had surprisingly high marks from the picky advocates for people with so-called mental disabilities. During the attendant press blitz for the movie, which rapidly gained critical support and even some thumbs-up in the disability community, Thornton offered a left-handed, quasi-sympathetic compliment to explain why he was so fascinated with disability: "I'm one of those people who just attract weirdos. I always seem to end up, like, in the middle of the desert with some biker, you know, and he's threatening to tie me up or something. I've known a lot of strange people." It would not pass muster in a disability studies program, but at least it indicates more than the usual interest in and confraternity with disability for a moviemaker.

Thornton's main character is Karl, whose retardation has kept him in a state mental hospital for two decades after he murdered his mother and her lover when a teen. The film narrates the unsuccessful transition from the hospital to the outside world. (He murders again, only this time it is an abusive white-trash villain who gets what has been coming to him for most of the film, earning Karl the oddly sympathetic publicity tagline "Sometimes a hero comes from the most unlikely place.") To attain the shuffling gait of his character, Thornton put crushed glass in his shoes, and the dialogue, better than *Rain Man*, is an imitation of Arkansan and the speech of patients in a state hospital. As the critic Roger Ebert remarked in his review for the *Chicago Sun Times*, "If *Forrest Gump* had been written by William Faulkner, the result might have been something like *Sling Blade*." In the opening scene, two student journalists visit the mental hospital to interview Karl for a student project. The doctor in charge is perturbed that the college has sent women, since Karl has little experience interacting with women, and he asks the photographer to wait outside while the writer has her chance to meet Karl. The other restrictions are also interesting. Thornton's script, which won the Oscar that year for best adapted screenplay (from his staged version), uses the warden, Dr. Woolridge, to explain that after twenty-five years in the hospital, never speaking to a woman, isolated from the inquiring eyes of the nondisabled, Karl requires special treatment. There is a lesson here for both journalists and filmmakers. The warden's lines in the opening scene read in part:

> **Woolridge:** Karl's real sensitive about having his picture made. He wouldn't even be on the bulletin board for the Easter Collage. . . . He has problems. You know. With all that. He won't hardly talk to anybody really. Just certain people. He's very troubled.

The admirable sensitivity of Dr. Woolridge in this scene extends to his dialogue with Karl, whose permission for the interview he seeks. In this scene he becomes the intermediary between the person with a disability and the press, and by implication, the audience. He raises the question of whether Karl's story will be "interesting":

> **Woolridge:** Karl, you know, do you remember when I told you about those people from that newspaper? (pause) They want to ask you some questions about your release. They think it would make an interesting story. Will you talk to 'em? Get interviewed. (pause) Now, they're women. I think it might be good for you to. You're gonna be seein' all kinds of people when you go on the outside. This'll help you I believe.

When Woolridge returns to allow the writer (who is frightened) to see Karl, he has two conditions that address genuine human rights concerns for people with mental disabilities: privacy and the etiquette of staring. The movie appeared, incidentally, at a moment in U.S. history when the Supreme Court and the newspapers were taking up the vexed issue of whether death-row convicts with the IQ of children ought to be executed. In addition to being timely from a news perspective, it managed to raise some of the most advanced topics in disability studies, even if by implication it negated the point in that Thornton was obviously offering up his character to be stared at in the darkness of the movie theater. The warden turns back to the journalist with Karl's stipulations: "But, here's the thing. He'll only talk to you. He doesn't want you to ask him anything. And you shouldn't stare at him."

As the shooting script indicates, and the film makes clear, in the very next scene the collegiate reporter sits staring at Karl as he launches into his long narrative, a horrific tale about how he used a "sling blade" to kill his mother and her lover, whom he had caught in flagrante, at the end of which he says that the mental hospital is about to "put him out," and then he adds a brief postscript that is touching in that it expresses his hope that he has not disappointed with his performance. This is a nice slice of irony given that, at the conclusion of Thornton's one-man show or after the movie, what does an actor hope for most but the approval of his or her performance? As with the "drunk-alogue," Karl's yearning for a positive response by providing the expected dramatics shapes the narrative according to the audience's desires and expectations, sometimes at the expense of reality: "Anyhow I reckon that's all you need to know. If you want any more details, I reckon I can tell 'em to you. I don't know if that's enough for your newspaper or not." The movie also has the requisite reminder of the abuse that people with disabilities endure from the ignorant. In this case, the nastiness is embodied in a character named Doyle who receives his due in the end, but not before delivering the kind of vituperation that real Karls have to hear every day. A little more of this in the movie theater, portrayed at its ugliest, would have helped to hold a mirror up to the majority opinion and perhaps made discrimination more disgusting in the eyes of the millions who saw *Sling Blade:*

> **Doyle:** Hey, is this the kind of retard that drools and rubs shit in his hair and all that, 'cause I'm gonna have a hard time eatin' 'round that kind of thing now. Just like I am with antique furniture and midgets. You know that, I can't so much as drink a damn glass of water around a midget or a piece of antique furniture.
> **Linda:** Doyle, you're awful. You shouldn't be that way.
> **Doyle:** I ain't saying it's right, I'm just telling the damn truth. He'll make me sick. I know it.

When it comes to accuracy and understanding the feelings of people with disabilities, the achievement of this film is in part its attention to the feelings of people with disabilities about how they are perceived. As activists such as Rosemarie Garland-Thomson, Paul Longmore, Kenny Fries, and others have pointedly declared in their writings on stigmatization, the rudeness encountered is often unspoken, confined to the stare that isolates. This is one of the few movies (*The Best Years of Our Lives* is another, particularly when the other two vets are in the plane with Russell and intently watching him light his cigarette with his prosthetic hands) to directly address the issue of staring. Thornton pinpoints the confrontation in this exchange between Karl and his doctor:

> **Karl:** I reckon I'm gonna have to get used to looking at pretty people.
> **Woolridge:** Yes you will.
> **Karl:** Reckon I'm gonna have to get used to them looking at me.

Even if the film's grim ending, with Karl reverting to his murderous ways, is a disappointing concession to cinematic convenience and confirmation yet again that people with so-called mental disabilities are bound to be scary types in mass media, the quiet ways in which the film nudges its viewers into walking in Karl's shoes are worth considering. So is the importance of accuracy. Even if these films fail to capture the whole truth of the disability experience, they can offer a measure of truthfulness through detail.

One of the most important films on the basis of *vraisemblance* is *My Left Foot* (1989), which is based on the true story of a cranky and brilliant Irish painter named Christy Brown, played by Daniel Day Lewis.

The real Christy Brown was born in Dublin in 1932, one of thirteen surviving children in his family (nine others died in the squalor). He did
marry a nurse in 1972 and achieved a certain fame as a painter before he
died in 1981. The movie is better than the marketing, which falls into the
old traps. "A film about life, laughter, and the occasional miracle," its tag
declares—somebody call Oprah. Predictably, the trailer plays the supercrip angle, spotlighting what in our terms is a minor moment in the movie
when Christy Brown, who is stuck in goal (lying on the ground) during
an alley soccer match, makes a splendid save by dashing his head to the
ground in front of the ball and then taking fierce punishment while an opponent repeatedly kicks into the ball still lodged against his head. That is
far from the highlight of the movie from a disability perspective, however,
just as Christy's seduction of an attendant he has just met is not the main
point, either. There are a number of finer moments in the script. When
Christy's first art show opens, the dealer pointedly declares, "He is not a
great crippled painter but a great painter." The "warts and all" element,
including the fact that he comes from an impoverished background, is
what makes the film compelling—not like *Rain Man,* with the autistic savant in Armani descending the escalator to win big at Vegas. For instance,
when Christy's mother eavesdrops on his speech therapy (he recites "To
be or not to be"), she comments, after pointing out that she has always
understood him although most find his slurred speech impenetrable:
"There's something in that voice that disturbs me. It's not like him. It has
too much hope." The speech lessons started with a visit from a pretty
young therapist named Sheila, played by Alison Whelan. Christy will not
open the door but insults her through it. She retaliates: "Wouldn't you
like to say 'fuck off' more clearly?" My favorite bit of dialogue returns to
Hamlet. Sheila asks him what he thinks of the Prince of Denmark. "A
cripple. He can't hack it." She says, "He did at the end." Not missing a
beat, he replies, "Too late." This would earn extra credit in either a disability studies course or any Shakespeare class I taught.

The clichés are more Irish than disability-oriented, such as the way the
first word he writes in chalk with his left foot is "mother," and the way
he gives her the proceeds from his first painting, which exceed his father's
annual earnings as a Dublin bricklayer. The staring trope is also reversed,
as Christy returns every gaze and fixes a particularly disturbing look on
that nurse he seduces at the end of the film. Like Stephen Hawking, Christy
is liberated by technology, using his electric typewriter to write his memoirs: "I lay back in my chair and let my own left foot beat time to a new
rhythm." Although he doesn't like appearing in public, he permits himself to be used on occasion by the rehab institute that helped him. "It's a
good cause. For the cripples," he quips, as the audience rises to applaud

him at a benefit dinner. In a fine moment of satire that deftly deflates charity dinners, the nauseating master of ceremonies drones on in clichés about Christy being "quite the bravest man I've ever known" while the subject of this encomium rolls his eyes in disgust.

Once in a while, a film does make a positive difference in the political and social scene. In 1975, the movie version of Ken Kesey's *One Flew Over the Cuckoo's Nest,* filmed at an Oregon state mental hospital, made a deep enough impression on public consciousness to spark wide-ranging investigations into the treatment of mental patients and specifically to question the prevalence of electroshock therapy. On the set, it should be noted, there were also advances. Nearly eighty patients in all were on the film's payroll, many of them with walk-on roles (Jack Nicholson played the lead), and much of the film's validity in the disability community derives from this gesture toward integration on the part of Milos Forman, the director. It was not quite enough for Kesey himself, unfortunately, who distanced himself from the final product because he felt the on-screen character Chief Bromden made so-called mental disabilities too much a matter of rehabilitation. This is rather ironic as Kesey had altered his novel in 1962 after a nurse from the mental hospital where they had both worked threatened to sue him for defamation regarding certain passages, which he deleted.

Don't Call Us

There are other, more important battles to be fought. One of the most significant is the ongoing effort to bring actors with disabilities on screen. As Caroline Parker succinctly puts it, "If you're going to use disability humor in your programs, why not have a performer with a disability in your program? I was watching *Will and Grace* last week, that's a very funny program that's got gay issues in it, and I was amazed to hear that the lead character in it is not actually gay. I don't know if it's okay or not with the gay community, I have no idea. But if it was a deaf character and it was played by a hearer, I think there would be an uproar. People don't black up anymore so why should they gay up or crip up as we call it? And there is no need for that now, there is a lot of talent out there." The principal organization that targets this problem in the United States is the well-regarded Media Access Office, a California state government agency that arranges for actors with disabilities to be included in casting calls for major studios and is a strident voice for inclusion in the industry. The Screen Actors Guild (SAG) Committee of Performers with Disabilities, spearheaded by Tari Susan Hartman, now boasts a roster of six hundred actors with disabilities vying for a handful of roles. Among the success stories are Robert David Hall, a double-leg amputee who sometimes uses a wheelchair and who recently signed a six-year deal to portray Dr. Robbins, the coroner on *CSI,* the number one show on CBS, and the deaf actress Deanne Bray, the first actress to grab a title lead role in a TV series (*Sue Thomas: F. B. Eye,* on PAX), which has always mixed disability with vaguely religious, feel-good themes. By a collective bargaining agreement between SAG and major producers (which actually predates the ADA by a decade) casting is mandated to "accurately portray the American scene." Advocates are quick to point out that we are still a long way from fulfilling the disability-specific aspect of that clause.

The all-time winner in this category of course is the remarkably sophisticated post–World War II classic *The Best Years of Our Lives* (1946), in which the show is stolen by Oscar-winner Harold Russell from the moment he simply handles a match to light his cigarette with his hooks as the three veterans fly to their hometown airfield. With his Boston accent and puppy-dog baleful looks, Russell was a refreshing change from the shallow perfectionism of contemporary Hollywood casting. The movie appeared when wounds from the war were still fresh. Directed by William Wyler, its high-powered casting, including Fredric March, Myrna Loy, and Dana Andrews, guaranteed success. Two of its eight Oscars were won by Russell, who completely tore open the veil of disability in a remarkable scene in which he demonstrates to his loyal fiancée how difficult it is for him to put on his pajamas, and how terrified he is of a fire in the night. It is nearly five decades later, and nothing like that candor or punch has been seen since—just as there has not been an amputee in as prominent a role, which is a remarkable, even infuriating, fact.

Marlee Matlin was the next big hope in *Children of a Lesser God* (1986), in which she reprises the stage role opposite William Hurt, who is a teacher in a private school for the deaf where the plot line revolves about their inescapable romance. "Sex was something I could do just as well as hearing girls," she signs to Hurt, who is determined to make her speak. The fury of Matlin's character, Sarah, pushed the Hollywood envelope for a moment, and Matlin herself, through her association with the Washington-based disability organization VSA (which used to be known as Very Special Arts until "special" took on negative connotations), has been the nation's most visible and adamant champion of sign language.

One of the most famous actors, after Reeve and Paul Newman (who is deaf), to incur disability and use it on screen is Kirk Douglas. In 1999 two movies with characters who had had strokes appeared simultaneously. In *Flawless,* Robert De Niro plays a security guard who has a stroke trying to stop a robbery in his Lower East Side apartment building and who will not undergo standard rehab but consents to taking singing lessons from a neighbor who is a drag queen (played by Philip Seymour Hoffman). Director Joel Schumacher said that the inspiration for the De Niro character was a friend who used singing to regain his speaking, yet the film is as unsatisfying in its caricature of one kind of freak, the drag queen, as it is in attempting to capture the genuine difficulty of poststroke speech. Where imitators have failed, Kirk Douglas at age eighty-three, four years after his own stroke, succeeded. The same year he starred in *Diamonds* as a former welterweight boxing champion who frets over becoming a burden to his family. He sets out on a cross-country road trip to recover diamonds promised to him years before, taking his son (played by Dan Aykroyd) and his teenage grandson. Although the movie ends up mired in sap, it has certain piquant references not only to Douglas's own disability but to his career since he played the title role in *Champion* (clips of that 1949 film are in the movie), and Lauren Bacall, who last played with him in 1950, makes a cameo appearance in *Diamonds* as a madam. All the director, John Asher, had to do was turn the camera on and let the "before" and "after" images accomplish the rest. For fans, it was poignant but also instructive. Before it becomes too painful, of course, the entertainment part kicks in, and the disability is swallowed up in the business of any film, which is diversion. The trouble with a bromide is that it does not improve the patient's condition; it only masks the pain with a palliative that essentially works by dulling the senses.

Even if good taste continues to be a stretch for moviemakers, one would hope that a bit of accuracy is not too much to ask for, particularly given the millions wasted on the historical accuracy of naval uniforms for such extravaganzas as *Master and Commander*. In the case of the movies under consideration in this chapter, I searched the credits in vain for comparable technical advisers on disability, and only *Children of a Lesser God* had sign language coaches. This spectacular lack of curiosity is reflected in the absurdly poor quality of representation, by comparison with other "inner circles" explored by film (the simulated hockey scenes in *Miracle*, released in 2003 about the 1980 Olympic team, took months of preparation involving professionals and Division I collegians paid fairly enormous sums to get it right—all for hockey verisimilitude). One of the many pathetic excuses for the misuse of medical plot points is the reversion to amnesia. As Dr. Yehuda-ben-Yoshay, director of the Brain Injury Day Treatment Program at New York University Hospitals Center, told the *New York Times,* "The typical movie thing where the guy's just fine except that he can't remember who he is, doesn't recognize his wife—that's a fiction, and when I see these movies, I am laughing at the naivete and stupidity of it." He was referring to such inanities as *Nurse Betty* (2003), which starred Rene Zellweger, or *Fifty First Dates* (2003) with Adam Sandler.[3] Other movies that pull this stunt include *Vanilla Sky, Paycheck, Majestic,* and, considered to be better (God alone knows why), *Radio,* starring Cuba Gooding. "Most of what I see in the movies on amnesia is preposterous," comments Dr. David A. Hovda, who is director of UCLA's Brain Injury Research Center, close enough to Hollywood that someone ought to ask his opinion before signing off on a script. At least *Awakenings* hewed closer to the Oliver Sacks text on which it was based, demonstrating, in a way that Montaigne might understand perfectly, that truth can be as dramatic and as riveting as fiction.

Just the Facts

Oscars are also awarded to documentaries, and this is another category in which disability rules. Although it claims a fraction of the reach of mainstream movies, somewhat like specialized print publications, the documentary has so far proven to be far better suited to portraying disability. It is usually backed by public or cable television financing, or by nonprofits themselves. The attention shifts from big-name actors to directors and, most important, the real researchers or personalities with disabilities. One of the big winners in recent years was *King Gimp,* about a painter named Dan Keplinger with cerebral palsy, not unlike Christy Brown, whose career shot off like a rocket when Bill Whiteford made the film about him. As warm and fuzzy as *My Left Foot* may be, there is more to be learned from ten minutes of *King Gimp* than from the entire feature film. Another master documentarian, Jessica Yu, Academy Award–winner, has twice taken on the thorny topic of severe disability and come out with bouquets of roses. She is perhaps best remembered for a humorous moment at the ceremony. During her acceptance speech for her 1997 Oscar for best documentary (*Breathing Lessons,* based on the life of a postpolio poet named Mark O'Brien who lived with an iron lung), swathed in a Mary McFadden gown, she charmed an audience of millions with the line: "You know you've entered new territory when you realize your dress costs more than your film." In 1999 she made her second foray into disability, an eighty-minute film about an arts colony in an unusual setting—deep inside a huge and grim mental asylum—titled *The Living Museum.* Her film touches on two worlds I have lived in—contemporary art and disability—and has the ring of truth on both levels. I grew up near the Creedmor Psychiatric Center, which loomed by the Grand Central Parkway in Queens near the border of the indifferent, idyllic suburbs where its name was spoken as a threat or insult: "You'll end up in Creedmor." Its old-school prisonlike atmosphere was certainly an unexpected setting for what Yu uncovered. The star of the documentary is psychologist and artist Dr. Janos Marton, a real-life Patch Adams (though calmer) who looked at a decrepit dining hall in one of the massive buildings and saw studio space in which born artists could work and find acceptance. The film is peppered with his wisdom: "There are no rules here. Modern art is all about breaking the code, and that is a fertile ground for creating new, interesting and exciting work."

As with her earlier *Breathing Lessons,* Yu knew great material and filmed with sensitivity. "The point is not to do the cripple of the week story. You can't make a film about art if the art is no good, and the art starts with who the person is," Yu told me when the film was first released.[4] While many in the medical community, not to mention editorial writers, were pushing the idea that people with mental disabilities were best served by taking on menial jobs in order to be mainstreamed as much as possible (this was the basis for such organizations as the Marriott family's foundation for the employment of people with disabilities, among many others), Yu considered the possibility that fulfillment could be found inside the walls of the institution in areas other than conventional work. "I don't buy the idea that the ultimate purpose of everyone is to be a productive member of society, get a job at McDonald's, pay taxes. When I hear that they should go out and pull their own weight, I think of all those I know who don't look at all those development executives in Hollywood," she joked.

It is no coincidence that Yu's father is a cancer specialist in Palo Alto, California. Her mother is a fencing instructor, and Yu competed at the world championships in Bulgaria after graduating from Yale with a degree in English. "In fencing and filmmaking you have to find your own style," she says. She lives in Los Angeles with her husband, the novelist Mark Salzman, who starred in the movie version of his *Iron and Silk,* a story about his experiences in China. In the thick of the movie world, Yu was approached by Oliver Stone about turning the O'Brien story into a dramatic feature but decided that it was not a good match. One senses that the run-of-the-mill Hollywood treatment would have been too much of a compromise. "My work is my obsession, and when I'm not researching or editing I spend my time looking for money. But the greatest part of my life is making films about people and their work that I respect." Documentary filmmakers are a bit like organists in the music world, printmakers in the art world, or pastry chefs in cuisine—a subculture enraptured by materials and technique, more interested in cause than effect. Her film, which is generously paced and exquisitely cut, is testimony to that perspective. The paintings, sculpture, drawings, installation pieces, and films produced by the close-knit group of artists she documents in *The Living Museum,* some of them created before the camera, are of astonishingly high quality, and Yu as art critic has a deft touch with the studio visit format, staying out off the field of vision while the artists do their stuff and talk, movingly and profoundly, about what their art means to them. Yu's technique is as subtle as it is penetrating. The camera lingers on the face of the artists after they have spoken, registering those flickers of emotion that unveil more than what can be said. By creating an atmosphere of acceptance and respect, the gentle and enthusiastic Dr. Marton, as much curator as psychotherapist in charge, primed the canvas for art that far outstrips therapy, holding its own in the context of the Soho gallery scene where two of his charges had a show. A memorable scene brings together two artists in a mutual admiration moment in which they realize why each could not do what the other does artistically. Only the sound track tries too hard, tagging artists with anthems ("Sexual Healing" as background anthem to erotically charged paintings, a hard-to-resist pun on the band name Soul Asylum). The link between music and art can be illuminating. Yu draws a close bead on the fugitive, fascinating charcoal drawings being made by one of Marton's artists to the accompaniment of late Beethoven quartets and other works composed after he lost his hearing. This powerful segment would have had more impact without the preceding aural clutter. But that's a minor annoyance in a fascinating and beautifully made film. Of all the movie and television people I spoke with on the topic of the representation of people with disabilities on screen, this (at the time) thirty-three-year-old arrived at the most credible and insightful, not to mention breathtakingly clear, conclusion: "When it comes to disability, people want closure. In a film, the hero with a disability has to either get better or die. The idea of living with a disability is unacceptable. They'd say it's not finished. I resist that notion."[5]

The Boob Tube

The situation on the small screen is no better than in the movie theater, once again with occasional exceptions. Tasteless television representations of disability are more the order of the day. Some of the worst offenders are the daytime talk shows and evening newsmagazines that pump disability for ratings and sympathy. Nothing beats the morbidity and sheer sap of *Oprah* or *Dr. Phil,* whose tearful-to-cheerful profiles of piteous creatures both obscure and famous are almost as ubiquitous as their relentless weight-loss makeover segments, and just as ludicrous from the right distance. Just after *WE* featured Aimee Mullins, an amputee sprinter and fashion model who is one of the community's strongest spokespeople, Oprah had her on for a segment that we all anticipated eagerly (well, we were hoping somebody would mention the magazine). The questions were so inane and solicitous that instead of pride we felt only the kind of disgust that Hockenberrry as well has registered in his Oprah experiences, in terms too profane to cite here. The trouble with Oprah is that she takes the "medical model" to extremes. All her disability programs, in fact, come under the label "medical miracles," which her magazine and publicists tout in breathless terms: "Although scientists and doctors have yet to find a cure for the common cold, recent advances in medical technology are truly amazing. Medical miracles are happening every day. Doctors are finding new ways to save lives, to improve lives and even create lives. Oprah talks with the survivors of risky operations that were never attempted before and the doctors who made them possible." Among the other shows in this category was one about a child named Neal, diagnosed with hydrocephalus (water on the brain) twenty weeks into his mother's pregnancy, who became the first prenatal surgical patient to survive such a tough case. Along those lines, a three-year-old named Mycha, who had been injured by a dog, needed thirty-nine straight hours of facial reconstruction and skin grafts in what was essentially a complete facial reconstruction. Just before Mullins, Oprah interviewed Michael Hill, who had a ten-inch knife removed from his skull in the emergency room. As Oprah's Web site tritely summarizes, "Michael says the experience totally transformed his life, and that he's now more compassionate and giving." That brings us to Mullins, one of the community's major stars. In addition to her successes on the track (she earned a varsity letter in track at Georgetown) she has been a fashion model. One image of her we used featured a bizarre set of wooden prostheses created by the fashion designer Alexander McQueen for a fashion shoot. Mullins was named as one of *People* magazine's fifty most beautiful people of the year in year 1999, a big selling point for Oprah, who used Mullins to harp on her "beauty from within" theme.

The most annoying instance of this kind of sap being taken as serious journalism, however, is presented by Barbara Walters, who takes the prize for persistently crossing the boundaries of propriety when it comes to disability. Her sentimental segments on Reeve and Fox are contemporary television's insipid version of the poster child. The disgustingly manipulative aspect of these broadcasts, including many of daytime's most ridiculous talk shows, is the way they play the emotions of viewers too bored with their own bland lives to resist a candied dose of pity and too stupid to discern the made-for-television tricks by which sentiment is synthesized (the camera work, the music, the rhetoric of each teaser just as the ad rolls on). The most recent affront was a segment on Richard Cohen timed to the release of his memoir, *Blindsided,* about living with both multiple sclerosis (MS), which has affected his voice and his sight, and two bouts of colon cancer. In promos for the show all the usual clichés were trotted out: "Above all, it is a love story about surviving, and rising above fear and anger. . . ." Since Cohen is the husband of Meredith Vieira, who anchors a vapid daytime show called *The View,* and Cohen is a producer who has been behind the cameras for decades, the chatter quickly became hopelessly banal insider gossip about the TV world. Walters used lots of home footage to trace the double-barrel disability situation Cohen faces. As in his self-pitying book, he had plenty of hardship anecdotes and drama, and too much of the segment was devoted to the day he accidentally nearly lost his son on the local train platform when a bout of dizziness hit. It made for "compelling" television, as they say in the trade, but it came at the expense of other less melodramatic but more important facts that had to be left on the cutting room floor. One of the only interesting elements in the piece was its handling of secrecy—the way Cohen's father, who also had MS, kept this information from the family, how Cohen had fooled CBS into hiring him despite his MS and near blindness, and the excruciating decision about how best to tell his own son about his condition. As the description of the show from ABC relates: "Cohen's first glimpse of the storm ahead came when he was 19 years old. His father, a doctor, revealed to him the family secret that he and Cohen's grandmother had MS. A few years later, Cohen was working as a news researcher when suddenly he became disoriented, spilling coffee, slipping on the street, his leg going numb." This plays up the ominous aspect of the disease, which Cohen learned at twenty-five that he had contracted. As she had with the Reeve, twice, Walters knocked hard on the bedroom door. It seems that Vieira had not been up to speed on MS when they started going out: on their second date he broke the news, and when they married they underwent testing to predict whether their children would be affected.

> "He asked me, 'What does MS mean to you?'" Vieira says. "And I said, 'It's a magazine. *MS* magazine.' The worst that I thought was that he could lose his sight. And I was OK with that. . . . Sometimes it's a leap of faith," says Vieira. "I fell in love with this guy with MS. . . . This man's an incredible guy. So anybody that I produce with him, I think would be pretty cool. That was my feeling."

As the promo for the show blathers on, "For the Cohens, illness is a family affair." Vieira said her husband's grace and humor "in the face of adversity" had taught their children profound lessons about life. "Well, I think that he's the greatest teacher they'll ever have," she says. "If they don't already know it, they will. He's teaching them compassion and strength and dignity, bravery." As the interview wore on, I noticed that the camera was lingering more and more on Walters and Vieira—it was their scene. At one point they were discussing Cohen's insistence on using the New York subways to get to work. Vieira: "I hate it. . . . Like I think he sometimes puts his life in danger and it worries me . . . but it makes him feel like 'I'm normal,' you know, 'I'm like everybody else.'" Neither Vieira nor Walters, living in their TV anchor world, could fathom how insulting that "normal" dig can be. Only ten minutes into the program, Walters exhausted her stock repertory of puerile questions and finally in a stage whisper said, "I love you Meredith—you know that." Tears all round while I gag at home.

Fortunately, there were other viewers who were not afraid to call it the way they saw it and express their utter disgust with the way the story was presented. On the show's own heavily edited, glowing Web site, the day after the segment aired a person with a disability let Walters have it on the queasiness she had instigated about Cohen's colostomy bag:

> Do you realize what message this sends to people for whom the "pouch" may be the ONLY solution? There are many thousands of people in the US who LIVE and I emphasize the word LIVE daily with their ostomies. . . . Why is it that always when talking about the bowels, people do not EVER want to hear the reality and the alternatives. This reminds me of people who years ago NEVER wanted to hear about mastectomies for women. Thank God the Breast Cancer movement people finally got it through to Americans that they MUST talk about this, because it will SAVE WOMEN'S LIVES!!! THAT is exactly where we are with colon cancer surgery. It CAN in many cases—SAVE LIVES. In my book, Life is always better than death. I would encourage you to DO some research into ostomates. See WHO we are and how our lives are FULL.

Fortunately, a few weeks after the segment aired, Walters announced her retirement.

Disability and televised comedy are in one of those never-a-dull-moment marriages that include plenty of public squabbling. While the occasional appearances of people with disabilities have helped to leaven the mix somewhat—including guest spots for Marlee Matlin on *Seinfeld* and even a cartoon version of Stephen Hawking on *The Simpsons*—in the standard fare the joke is on the maligned blind guy, the amputee (often a villain), or the developmentally disabled. Take the blind, African-American newsstand operator (cliché) Jake Malinak, played by Alex Desert on the CBS sitcom *Becker*—please. He is the constant butt of disability-related jokes, and usually gives as good as he gets in scripts that, like most sitcoms, are just spitball contests with insults traded for wet paper. The main character, a curmudgeonly doctor named Becker (played by Ted Danson), is an ardent foe of political correctness, and this makes for some blunt moments that often come around like boomerangs to get him in the end but in the meantime can dangle out there as pure insults. Even when he's not mocking the blind guy, he is firing off offensive lines that are meant to be funny but offend: "The only people dumber than talk radio listeners are talk radio callers. It's an entire audience made up of the infirm, the unemployed and the insane." Remarkably, as this book went to press such drivel had managed to squeak through well over a hundred episodes since *Becker's* debut in 1998. Some of the other current sitcoms have brought in characters with a disability, including a refreshingly un-Hallmark version of an asthmatic in *Malcolm in the Middle,* a Fox network success, and a sharp-witted wheelchair-using teen, a former athlete injured in a car accident, on the unexpected CBS hit *Joan of Arcadia,* a rare instance of a character drawn with sufficient complexity to actually surprise the viewer moment to moment.

Most surprises on television are, lamentably, of the type that shock us by demonstrating how far down the scale of taste the producers are willing to descend. My old friend and hockey teammate from our Princeton days, David E. Kelley, had a disability streak running through his hit show *Ally McBeal* during its five-season run starting in 2001, weaving dwarfs and wheelchair users among the other freaks that had viewers tuning in from week to week, wondering what taboos he might challenge next. Although I preferred the inside jokes he made about our old days on the lamentably dreadful Princeton varsity squad, as a disability journalist I could scarcely ignore the uncomfortable jokes at the expense of people with disabilities, including obsessive-compulsive disorder and stuttering, and I watched as, typical of TV writing, Kelley would snatch victory from the jaws of defeat by jamming a little courtroom speech on acceptance, tolerance, and embracing our differences into the final minutes. Sitcom episodes are written by formulas dictated by commercials and industry practice, tailored to ratings success, and, once a show is running, obnoxiously flipping backward to previously successful jokes, all punctuated by the insulting insertion of the laugh track or, in Kelley's case, the often hysterically funny deployment of soul or rock music, just the title of which, or a lyric, would be the punch line. As the show wore on (and out—it was canceled abruptly when ratings plummeted in its fifth season), the freakery took on a darker side that was just plain not funny after a while. It was also clear that some of the disabilities were more actual than fictive, since the cast was riddled with a flurry of medical emergencies including Robert Downey Jr.'s arrest for drug possession (he had been in recovery when Kelley took him on as a love interest for the eponymous lawyer), and the loopy leading character, Calista Flockhart, was herself addled on the set with what the tabloids insisted was anorexia and all its attendant physical and mental complications. Through all this Kelley was tiptoeing along a razor's edge between sophisticated disability awareness and flagrant insults to keep the laughs going. One of the low points was an episode in the third season titled "The Oddball Parade." Ally's eccentric colleagues took on a complaint by four graphic designers suing their company for wrongful termination because they looked different and the firm felt that, in its growth stages, the designers had to come into contact with clients more. One plaintiff was obese, another a transvestite, the third compulsively clapped his hands and had a speech impediment, while the fourth was just "scary" looking. Kelley's sentimental side came out when the episode brought up a parade at the graphic arts firm from which the four oddballs were excluded. After they lost their case—the firm successfully argued that image could be everything—the four along with a large contingent of spectators similarly endowed with tics and oddities held their own parade in the street. Even if it was played for gentle laughs, the episode (like the series) perpetuated the insults by making a comic spectacle of them. In addition, the expectation that a disability would be crucial to the characterization and the plot, and would cost the character either self-respect or happiness, was implicit from the start.

One of the shows that pushed Fox's *Ally McBeal* off the radar was NBC's *The West Wing,* which had its own flirtation with the disability theme. Setting aside the medical melodramas from *Dr. Kildare, Marcus Welby MD, ER,* and soaps like *General Hospital,* which have to put wheelchairs on the screen in every episode, certain TV dramas have done a better job than others in depicting the community. Cleaning up annually at the Emmy Awards for four years, where its gravitas and accuracy make the critics feel good even as it conveniently pulls in the kind of ratings (over 20 million viewers for most episodes) that make the award a no-brainer, *The West Wing* is a long-running melodramatic phenomenon that follows such "classics" as *M*A*S*H.* In the eleventh episode of its first season the creator and main writer, Aaron Sorkin, devised a fascinating subplot for the fictive president Jed Bartlet (played so convincingly by Martin Sheen that his speeches had a more presidential air than those of W, who occupied the office). There is nothing like the dramatic irony of a good secret shared by millions of viewers to boost ratings, so Sorkin gave his president the ambiguous curse-blessing of being diagnosed with multiple sclerosis, a progressive disability that, like an affair with an intern, can be hidden as long as the whole team is either bluffed or in on it. The subplot was crucial to about four episodes, during which the president and his loving staff shielded him from the inquiring eyes of the press and exchanged long sympathetic looks to the accompaniment of stringed instruments. Sorkin spun Clintonesque subplots about snoopy journalists sniffing around the medical records and shady political operatives urging the president not to run for reelection lest he (improbably) become entirely incapacitated in the midst of crisis. Whenever the pressure mounted he was scrutinized for signs of MS symptoms by those in the know.

Then an odd thing happened. The whole MS bit was mentioned ever more sporadically during the second season and, by the twentieth episode, seemed to be forgotten entirely. What happened? Given the nature of the medium, the MS "concept" was probably getting low marks from the ratings police, which monitor, minute by minute, the attention level of test audiences so sensitively that they can tell when a device is flagging long enough in advance to steer the writers to safer ground. In short, the president "had MS," panicked on screen briefly when he thought it would cost him the election, milked it for sympathy, and then forgot about it because the viewers did not care.

In an episode coyly titled "He Shall, From Time to Time . . ." (the MS was relapsing-remitting), the opening scene had Bartlet sweating while working on the State of the Union address, and excusing himself from the bickering of his staff to catch a moment of rest in the Oval Office. When they heard the sound of breaking glass they rushed in to find the president lying on the floor. A doctor examined him, found he had a temperature, and declared that the president had the flu. Meanwhile, the vice president (Leo McGarry, played by John Spencer) addressed the journalists in the Briefing Room to let them known that in June of 1993 he had checked himself into a rehab facility to treat his addiction to alcohol and Valium. Later in the episode, the first lady asks Leo to postpone the Sate of the Union, and Leo is worried because the first lady, played by Stockard Channing, is alarmed.

Leo: This has happened before. (beat) I see you trying to cover the panic. I
    see you prescribing medication. I think you're giving him shots. (pause)
    He wanted to run for President. What does he have he can't tell people?
Abbey: He has the flu, Leo.
Leo: You didn't come back for the flu, Abbey.
Abbey: He fainted. He was running a fever.
Leo: Abbey—
Abbey: He's got multiple sclerosis, Leo.

Leo stares at her in disbelief.
Leo: (pause) Abbey—
Abbey: A fever can be life-threatening.

The president admits that he was diagnosed with relapsing-remitting MS seven years before. He says that he recovers fully after attacks and takes injections of Beta seron, for which his wife, a doctor, illegally writes the prescriptions (another secret the White House can hide for only so long). As Sorkin's commentary runs, "Without thinking, Leo calls him 'Jed,' instead of Mr. President. He asks why Bartlet didn't tell him; he could have been a friend. Bartlet says he wanted to be president, and assures Leo he has been a friend."[6] It is a pity that the masses did not find this more compelling as entertainment, because one of the underexplored dramatic topics in disability is the tricky role of caregiver, caretaker, friend, and family member not just vis-à-vis confidentiality but in terms of the emotional bond that develops. That was not sexy enough to keep the Nielsens up, though.

An interesting parallel subplot of the presidential MS was that the vice president was a recovering alcoholic, also a disability under the ADA, although this potential story point eluded the many legal consultants on the show's writing staff. One day in the office he is confronted by a press secretary, Josh Lyman (Bradley Whitford), just as the White House is in a crucial fight to confirm a new Supreme Court Justice for whom the right to privacy is the major issue of the time. The scene plays out:

Josh: Leo, you know the worst-kept secret in Washington is that you're a recovering alcoholic right?
Leo: (pause) I had a hunch.
Josh: Leo, you're a Boston Irish Catholic and back there and back then a drinking problem wasn't a problem. This isn't what he's going for. Were you into something that maybe wasn't so acceptable?
Leo: (beat) Pills.
Josh: Were you ever in treatment?
Leo: Sierra-Tucson. Six years ago.
Josh: Leo—
Leo: Records kept by these facilities are confidential, Josh.
Josh: He's got 'em.[7]

This is serious business in the recovery community, as well as in Hollywood, where the "right" to anonymity is not always possible to reconcile with the nature of one's career. Sorkin at least deserves credit for keeping it real. When Leo tells the president a journalist is going to out him, the scene unfolds:

Bartlet: Did you have a drink yesterday?

Leo: No, sir.

Bartlet: That's all you ever need to say to me.

Leo: You know it's gonna make things very hard for a while.

Bartlet: You fought in a war, got me elected, and run the country. I think we all owe you one, don't you?[8]

Nor was MS the only disability thread in the tapestry. Marlee Matlin played a feisty consultant named Joey Lucas who showed up in an episode titled "Take This Sabbath Day." She was furious that her candidate for a California House seat position was being starved of funding by the Democratic National Committee and ended up being offered a White House job. Matlin in a sidebar to the official book notes:

> I was a fan of Aaron Sorkin before *The West Wing*. On *Sports Night* he had a character write a letter to his sister who was deaf. I thought to myself, Here's a guy who's not afraid to write in characters who are deaf. So I wrote Aaron a fan letter and told him if he ever planned to bring that woman back, I knew a great Academy Award–winning actress who was deaf who could play the part. We began corresponding by e-mail and the next thing I knew, he asked me if I would like to be on his new show. I didn't have to think twice. Aaron has created one of the most ideal roles that I could have ever hoped for. Joey Lucas is the role that's closest to how I am in every day life. Life for me isn't about being deaf every minute of the day, as some people might think. Aaron has created a smart and witty character who happens to be deaf.[9]

If that sounds too easy, then consider Sorkin's explanation, in the official book about the series, of the MS subplot, which strikes me as completely impromptu if not arbitrary. In his notes to the episode on MS Sorkin wrote: "And then I had this hunch with Stockard. I thought, What if she's a doctor? If she's a doctor, I want there to be a story. I want there to be a reason to make that decision. So, it's not the flu. It's something worse than the flu, but it looks like the flu to everybody else and Abbey has to come back. And all of the sudden, simply for the sake of that episode, I made a decision that was going to affect the series for the life of the series. I did it and there was no turning back once I did it. I said, 'Okay, now this is part of the universe of our story and we're going to be telling stories about this.' That's frequently how decisions are made."[10] On screen, the focus is on secrecy rather than disability rights or President Bartlet's emotional state. If nothing else, this certainly elucidates the privacy versus passing issue of disability awareness.

Not long after, in the fourth season, the president had had enough of the secrecy and was facing serious leaks from his White House staff, so he decided to take matters into his own hands and announce that he had MS. By the spring of 2004, however, the MS subplot had slipped back to the status of a recessive gene in the regular two- or three-story plotlines in each episode. As in many serial comedies or dramas, which echo themselves and reward the loyal viewer with little recollections of previous episodes, *The West Wing* developed its own autoreflective set of in-jokes and coded references. When the president's shy daughter, an AIDS researcher, was "outed" by the press after a Republican congresswoman exposed that her research foundation had received substantial federal funds, the White House press chief confronted the congresswoman to back her off. Her response was that those dollars could have gone into a number of other worthy research areas, including MS. "So you're going to play the MS card, are you?" Toby countered. Raised eyebrows all around (unless of course you just tuned in). Had the fan sites and the Nielsen ratings supported the notion that the MS line was "compelling drama," no doubt Sorkin and his team would have played it up, but the headlines were filled with Mideast catastrophes or gay marriage and, as always, the disability issue took a back seat. Then the MS storyline, latent in the middle seasons, produced its own twist. President Bartlett's exit from office at the end of the fall 2004 season opened the possibility of returning to explore the issues of living with a disability and passing. If the writers demonstrate their usual sensitivity and sophistication, the result will be a closely scrutinized, widely watched addition to the primetime track record of covering disability.

There Will Always Be an England

Not all television has to be this simple-minded. Leave it to the Europeans, with their state subsidies, to have the luxury to be more innovative. On March 12, 1972, Granada TV took a bold step and presented its version of the play *Whose Life Is It Anyway?* Not even PBS could have touched such a live wire in that era, and Granada certainly had its share of publicity fires to put out after the drama aired. It starred Ian McShane in the part played by Tom Conti in London and on Broadway when the play was staged in 1978, and was produced by Peter Eckersley and by Richard Everitt. Untarnished by feeble gestures at making the quadriplegic lead, a young sculptor who has been in a car accident, more lovable, the play (Bryan Clark's debut, incidentally) pits medical technology against the patient's preference to commit suicide through the removal of a catheter, which will allow fatal toxins to build in his blood. In the end, a judge goes to the hospital room to decide on a writ of habeas corpus. En route to that ending, the obnoxious sculptor is alternately witty and hurtful in his bitterness. What makes the script jarring even today is its blunt directness. To a nurse he is throwing out of his room he declares:

> I say something offensive about you and you turn your professional cheek. If you were human, if you were treating me as human, you'd tell me to bugger off. Can't you see that this is why I've decided that life isn't worth living? I am not human and I'm even more convinced of that by your visit than I was before, so how does that grab you? The very exercise of your so-called professionalism makes me want to die.[11]

While the hospital and its lawyers continue to treat the sculptor, and offer the legal argument that his death wish is a transitory result of depression, he takes on such probing issues as man subsumed by machines, the jurisdiction of the state, and the medical ethics of overmedication and extraordinary lifesaving measures. When the judge at the end points out that "many people with appalling physical handicaps have overcome them and lived essentially creative, dignified lives," the sculptor shoots back: "But the dignity starts with their choice. If I choose to live, it would be appalling if society killed me. If I choose to die, it is equally appalling if society keeps me alive."[12] The judge must weigh the patient's rights against the possibility that depression has clouded his judgment. This precise question, which we will take up again in the sixth chapter of this study, rocked the community a decade later when Jack Kevorkian very publicly assisted a series of people with disabilities in their suicides. In the end the judge finds that the sculptor is "brave and clear" in his resolve and orders the doctors to grant his wishes, meaning that within the week, removed from life support, he will die. For many people with disabilities (including Hockenberry, who several times in his memoir fires back against those who insist on discussing suicide with him) the association of suicide and the onset of disability is over the top, but the pointed manner in which Clark thrusts "dignity" into the conversation and focuses the audience's attention on the rights, feelings, and thoughts of the man in the bed instead of the people around him are all first-rate elucidations on screen of a painful reality. Too strong for the contemporary viewer evidently, it has been decades since this was either on a major stage or on screen, although its successors, including a Broadway play by Margaret Edson titled *Wit* that was later made into a movie starring the redoubtable Emma Thompson, have been notably successful.

In 2004 the BBC aired a two-part analytic series attempting to assess the "progress" being made on British television in the portrayal of people with disabilities. The forum made two strong distinctions worth noting in any media discussion of disability. The first was the continuing mistake that TV comedy writers commit by focusing on the medical model of disability rather than the social, which, by turning the tables and making sport of the attitudes or ignorance of nondisabled toward people with disabilities succeeded both comically and "politically." The other clear division was between the taboos faced by nondisabled comedians regarding language and subject matter versus the relative freedom of comedians with disabilities, including the fact that the latter enjoyed open season not only on themselves but on others with disabilities. One of the most provocative questions raised by one of these performers was the appropriateness of a person with one disability playing a character with a different disability, for instance. Among the talking heads were disability studies academic experts as well as actors both able-bodied and disabled who had used disability in their comic routine. Many of their observations would fly right by an American audience, for whom the references would be obscure (despite the long run of Britcoms on PBS), although the "ministry of silly walks" segment from *Monty Python's Flying Circus,* cited as offensive, would probably rouse memories.

Among the comic teams showcased in the second part of the series (which was divided into nondisabled comedians and disabled) was a "disabled comedy trio" called the Nasty Girls. One of them, Mandy Colleran, observed: "I think for me, good comedy like any kind of good performance or even good literature or good art when it's good, is about something that's truthful, about something the people recognize. If a non-disabled comedian in terms of observation has hit upon some kind of truth and so represents disability or talks about disability in a way that kind of has some truth to it then I think the quality of that will probably be okay. I think it's debatable as to, you know, how truthful you can be about an experience that is not yours." Among their sketches was a parody of Julie Andrews in *The Sound of Music:*

> Tiny white tablets and pink fluffy slippers, soggy boiled cabbage and smelly fried kippers, ancient red wheelchairs all mended with string, these are a few of my favorite things. Shiny chrome bedpans and crinkly old zimmers, cold flannel bed baths and starch cotton knickers. Visits from school kids who make us all sick, these are a few of my favorite things. When the nurse shouts, when it's boring, when I'm feeling sad, I simply remember my favorite things and now I feel quite bad!

As one continuous in-joke about the banalities of rehab this has punch and credibility, but one can see how it fits into Cramer's category of disturbing the mainstream, especially the line about the visiting schoolkids. Another sketch that the BBC chose to illustrate the advances made by the community was a controversial piece by Laurence Cramer that gently took the mickey out of Christopher Reeve and the position that a wheelchair user ought to continually "seek to be cured." As Cramer introduced the piece, "It really upset some people because they saw it as returning on my own kind really. It was really an acknowledgement that all disabled people don't agree on everything. Obviously some of us would like to be cured and be 'normal' but a large majority of us wouldn't and I don't see any problem in challenging that view." The reader can judge for himself:

> Ever since his accident several years ago, Christopher Reeve has longed for corrective surgery to make him "normal" again. He's even had to come to the UK for operations, let's face it; you know someone's desperate when they come to our hospitals for help. However, some of the preliminary surgery has gone badly wrong. "The original intention was to use stem-cell technology to reattach the top of Christopher's spine here. However, an unforeseen complication meant that the speech centers of his brain which usually send signals to the voice box here are instead communicating with the base of the spine here." This means that Christopher Reeve now talks out of his arse. For example, he recently wrote, "One of the smartest things we can do about disability is invest in research that will lead to cures, we should be enabling, healing, curing." Therefore the money you give tonight will fund stem-cell surgery to reattach Christopher's brain to his mouth. So please give whatever you can, because otherwise he'll write another book.

At the end of the forum, the performers with disabilities were asked for their wish list. Most focused on the need for greater representation on screen and on stage, the "nothing about us without us" line that seems more utopian in this context than in print media. Cramer's hopes are a useful summary of most of the others on the panel:

> I'd like to see people realizing that disabled people are not a soft option, they're not a cheap laugh, you can't get away with saying things about disabled people that you shouldn't say for example about women, lesbians and gays and all the rest of it, that respect is the order of the day. Secondly I'd like to see more disabled comedians. There's a lot of funny things that happen to disabled people and there's a lot of funny disabled people out there who are very used to using humor, and I'd like to see more of them making a professional living through comedy. Thirdly I mean I don't want it to go too far, I'm worried about what you could call DC instead of PC, Disability Correctness, where everybody has to be obsessed with the right language, you can never make a joke about disabled people, only disabled people can be funny about disability, and so forth and so on. I think that obviously we've got to get rid of the cheap laughs, but I think it's quite possible to have a humorous disabled character in a film or in a comedy rou-

tine as long as we're not laughing at them merely because of their failures, incompetence, or limitations. We have to see them as people to whom funny things happen, not just incompetents at whom we can laugh.

To give credit where it's due, both the Canadian Broadcasting Company and the British Broadcasting Company have made disability efforts, most recently with the announcement by the BBC's director-general that the programmers will, under corporate orders, dramatically increase the number of people with disabilities seen on their programs. The BBC has set such targets as having at least one regular character with a disability in a returning drama series, two out of every hundred extras in drama series, one in every fifty contestants with disabilities on their game shows (*The Weakest Link, Mastermind,* and *National Lottery Jet Set*), two profiles a year of people with disabilities on BBC Four, as well as an initiative to develop new on-screen talent in what is called its "factual output." These are quotas, obviously, but they directly address the problem of not having enough actors with actual disabilities on the screen. Only two years ago, the BBC launched its idiotically named Ouch!, a netcasting outlet and chat room that is part of its formidable Web machine. The television arm of the CBC has sponsored the Disability Network since 1990 out of its Toronto studios. In addition to a *Newsworld* package hosted by Joe Coughlin (who has cerebral palsy), it has twenty-four-hour cable programming. There was a brief foray into the same area by a private Texas company called Kaleidoscope, but its work was so abysmal that it failed within three years. One of the independent media companies devoted to disability (specifically, so-called mental disabilities) is Manhattan-based Lichtenstein Creative Media, which has won Peabody Awards for its long-running weekly radio show *The Infinite Mind* as well as Equality, Dignity, Independence (EDI) awards for its documentaries on mental health and social issues. The radio program is hosted by the former director of the National Institutes of Mental Health, Dr. Fred Goodwin, and often concludes with a star turn by John Hockenberry, whose commentary is worth tuning in for the hour. The program is produced in association with WNYC/NY and airs in two hundred markets across the country including New York, San Francisco, Los Angeles, Atlanta, Washington, D.C., and Boston as well as on the Web.

On the Set

WE magazine made many trips to the movie and television well during its four years, shamelessly flipping the mass-market fascination with on-screen personalities into putative disability awareness (and advertising revenues). After cover stories on Elizabeth Taylor, Paul Newman, Sharon Stone, Michael J. Fox, Christopher Reeve, Robin Williams, Marlee Matlin, and Jerry Lewis, we had accumulated a number of contacts and sources in the entertainment world. I wanted to drill deeper, however, into the problems of the misrepresentation of disability in entertainment. Instead of another puff piece, it was time for the magazine, as it matured, to push for change. In the summer of 2000 I sent Jo-Ann Dean, a high school teacher, advocate for the deaf, and sign language interpreter, to go on location with *The X-Files,* which was then one of the hottest shows on the tube. Her mission was to watch how the writers and director handled the presence of actress Christine Firkins, a deaf seventeen-year-old who did a series of guest spots on the show. She was a part of the huge two-unit cast and crew, a machine of hundreds, at the time, blasting into its ninth season and one of the reasons the Fox network was the surprise ratings winner: the show was pulling phenomenal Nielsen numbers, with nearly 15 million regular viewers.

Dean is an expert, a career and transition teacher of the deaf at Marlton High School in Los Angeles, where she has 350 deaf and hard of hearing students. Her role as a liaison between Hollywood and the deaf community had evolved over fifteen years of advocacy. The story started in July when she got a call from Craig Management, a Hollywood talent agency that had been representing deaf actors for a decade. They were expressly on the lookout for a fifteen-year-old Latino deaf boy to audition for a feature role on *The X-Files.* The show had just come off its best season and a movie spin off—it was the kind of call that agents live for. She pitched a feature to me, and I immediately bit.

It was not by any means the typical Hollywood glamour piece. Dean's students were real people representing one of the most complicated of disability subcultures, and their foray into the surreal world of *The X-Files* made riveting copy. Any minor (under sixteen) working on a show had to be accompanied by a parent or guardian, but most of the parents of Dean's students were not able to take time off, and many did not speak English. She wanted her students to get their shot and took three of them, as many as her Ford could transport, to the Twentieth Century Fox Studios lot. Their first contacts were promising. They were shocked when the greeter, Alicia, finger-spelled her name in sign language, as did Rick Milikan, the casting director for the show, who also took the liberty of asking Dean to read for the part of the teacher in the episode. The next day, Dean flubbed her lines, signing when she was supposed to speak and vice versa, and the boys were deemed too tall. Then the conversation turned to ways in which the show could ensure authenticity in the episode, which would have a scene set in a deaf boarding school. The director wanted to know if flashing lights were used for fire alarms in a dorm. Getting the details right was important. Dean was brought on as the technical consultant and ASL (American Sign Language) tutor for the lead, a returning character named

Gibson Praise, played by Jeff Gulka, who was appearing in his fourth episode. His best friend would be the deaf girl named Thea, played by Firkins. The two actors spent a full day of preparation in the classroom signing. The kids were enchanted, and the conversation shifted from *X-Files* trivia to Play Station games, sports, and skateboarding. Firkins was something of a veteran, having appeared in Fox's film *Speed 2* (which bombed). When she arrived on Stage 5 at the Fox Studios, the playback operator, recognizing her from that gig, hugged her, and others in the crew also recognized her. Dean and Firkins bonded, no doubt in part because of Dean's skill in ASL as well as shared interests in scuba diving. Firkins's sister Katherine, eighteen, also deaf, was also on the set. Chris Carter, the "genius" who had conceived *The X-Files,* greeted Dean and Firkins the first day. He was no stranger to the deaf community; his aunt and uncle are both deaf and have a hearing child. Dean got her requisite celebrity PC quote from him: "Let's see what makes the person tick without the labels. The reality is that there are few roles for deaf actors. The flip side to having deaf characters, I fear, is tokenism, which is opposite to what is fair and equal." In place of the rhetoric, I preferred a longer passage he gave her about working with a deaf actress:

> Christine, I noticed, gets very excited in the creative process. We never spoke about how we would communicate. I just knew I could work with her and she knew it too. It was an unspoken bond. As a director I found it exciting speaking to an actress who has to look at my face in order to communicate. It was easier to direct someone who looks at you with her soul wide open. For a girl with an angelic quality, she made the turn well in her final scene delivering a foreboding look as the possessed bounty hunter. She listened so intensely to what I was saying. Her reach will make her a great actress. I would love to work with her again. I feel her deafness gives her an exceptional quality that is more honest. I never see her acting. It comes from her heart and she is believable. The girl knocked my socks off.

Meanwhile on the set, Dean was in charge of getting the deaf part straight. Fifty child extras were involved in a dorm scene. They were coached by Dean and a staff that included Bob Hiltermann, a hard of hearing actor who had appeared in *A Bridge to Silence* with Marlee Matlin, and Koli Cutler, an interpreter who works with the highly regarded Deaf West Theater and the Little Theatre of the Deaf, and Bryan Buckey, a hard of hearing teacher of the deaf and graduate of the National Theatre of the Deaf's summer program. Most of the technical work involved cuing and polishing the script. One of the problems the coaching staff faced was lack of warm bodies—because there had been such disappointingly low response to the casting call, not all the kids were deaf or hard of hearing. However, at Dean's insistence, director Kim Manners agreed to use only the extras who were deaf for close-ups and signing. This kind of intervention is needed to get us out of the Al Jolson era of fake disability acting.

In the filming of the dorm scene, Dean helped Christine and the other kids to improvise conversations about their day at the fictive school for the deaf, where an alien bounty hunter would assume Agent Scully (played by Gillian Anderson)'s likeness in his search for Gibson Praise, who was hiding in the school. The deaf children became so intrigued by the tight resemblance between Anderson and her double that they flubbed their lines on the first take. Dean's job was to make sure they weren't goofing—signing about the double or, say, the "dead" FBI agent, who was winking and sticking his tongue out between takes.

As I am not a Fox executive or science fiction fan, I can admit that the baffling success of *The X-Files* looks from a distance like a cult phenomenon, complete with its own insider references and quirks that set it apart from the typical television production on both sides of the camera. That makes it difficult to infer from the relatively sensitive, informed, and even earnest handling of deafness in one episode that more widespread changes in the entertainment mentality are afoot. If the main writer and creator of the show has deaf family members, the motivation is personal. As one of the show's coproducers, Timothy Silver, told the magazine: "The trick to good filmmaking is to take advantage of all the opportunities real life presents. *The X-Files* is not a show about the rich and the famous, it's about extraordinary things that happen to ordinary people and the human experience. The key is that they are all there because they are part of life. When someone acts in a certain way they have a certain truth to offer. People enter *The X-Files* from all walks of life and that makes the payoff so much greater, because they become part of the family." Now that is what I call *Access Hollywood!* Dean closed out her article with a deft sketch of the wrap party:

> Just a week before the season began, we all gathered one rainy night at the Academy of Television Arts and Sciences in North Hollywood to screen the first two episodes. Christine drove up in Thea, her new VW bug. Far from a typical LA blowout opening party, most of the crew had worked that day and after one glass of wine during the small cocktail reception they were ready to pack it up and head home. They were already up to episode 11 in the schedule. As I said my goodbyes, I reflected on what had happened on the set. The show is fond of a catch phrase: "The truth is out there." I think the real drama this season on *The X-Files* was not about aliens lurking in desert shadows, but about understanding the often invisible disabilities that are part of the composition of being human.

One of the most important television breakthroughs for the community was *Life Goes On,* an ABC sitcom that starred Christopher Burke, who has Down syndrome and is a major-league advocate for the cause. Although *TV Guide* predicted it would "flop the fastest" of all the series introduced in the fall of 1989, it did go on, for more than a hundred episodes, and with each episode it hit the themes of tolerance and the rights of people with disabilities hard. A timely theme was the progress of Burke's character (Corky Thatcher), the son of a construction worker, from special education to a mainstream high school. Burke is to Down syndrome what Fox is to Parkinson's or Reeve to paralysis, a high-profile, politically active, philanthropic meal ticket who, it is important to remember, never hid his disability or turned his back on the community.

The influence of television on children is one of those hot-button issues that can provoke teachers like me to interminable harangues of alarming vituperation, but certain exceptions can be made, and usually are when *Sesame Street* is mentioned. In the disability community, the show, which tapes in Queens each day, receives thumbs-up all around, and this is due wholly to one splendid lady named Emily Perl Kingsley. Our paths crossed frequently during my tenure at the magazine—we both earned EDIs from Easter Seals and Media Access Awards, small potatoes compared with her dozen Emmys. She is a regular at fundraisers because of her son Jason, who was born with Down syndrome in 1974. For a story we ran about her in the summer of 1999 I followed her around the set during a milestone season, the show's thirtieth anniversary, and despite the massive gap between print and electronic media, the backstage experience was proof yet again that the creative and editorial gatekeepers can, when knowledge and power coincide, vastly upgrade the message and medium. Without addressing the effects of *Sesame Street* on math or verbal skills, a task I leave to the experts, I can say that the disability component of the shows is of such a high standard that it raises one's hopes and expectations for the genre. Kingsley joined the now historic Children's Television Workshop in 1970, just after Big Bird had made the cover of *Time* and the show was winning over the naysayers who could not abide the notion that television could be education. Even before Jason was born, she was inserting disability story lines, encouraged by the PBS support system. She and her husband Charles were urged to institutionalize Jason but decided on bringing him home. Today he works as a coordinator of cultural arts programming at a suburban Association for Retarded Citizens (until 1992, ARC) and lives independently. As a mother and as a media pro Kingsley was positioned to act, but it was never easy. As she told us for a short profile we ran in our July–August issue of that year, "I remember the day after he was born, sitting in bed, looking at magazines and watching television and feeling as if I had fallen off the end of the earth. No one looked like my family. They were all so healthy, so perfect. I felt totally isolated, like I had just disappeared. It was something I wanted to change."

In addition to writing and producing documentaries on the disability experience, her most important work in the field is, I believe, changing the children's TV industry from within. She committed *Sesame Street* to a reality check, bringing guests with disabilities, including Itzhak Perlman and the Little Theater of the Deaf, to do star turns. Casting for diversity, in racial as well as disability terms, brought a regular member of the show, Tarah Schaeffer, who uses a wheelchair due to osteogenesis imperfecta and was in her fifth season on the show that summer. Another cast member was a little rascal in a wheelchair named Italo Alexander Martinez, who was a rookie that year and who had such a wickedly mischievous grin that I handed his parents my card and recruited him to model for a later issue. With seniority and the heft of a dozen Emmy awards behind her, Kingsley could afford to shape the show according to what she felt the audience needed, and the result was pioneering work in the medium that accomplished the one thing that no other show or movies have done: regularly casting people with disabilities to represent themselves and their disabilities instead of watching others' imitations. This is a strategy simple enough to work well for a *Sesame Street* audience, and yet it goes well past the level of sophistication in handling disability of most movies and television. As Kingsley told us, "We include kids with disabilities just as part of the gang. Children in the audience get validation when they see others like themselves. Their siblings receive gratifying reinforcement seeing kids like those in their own families. We take the strangeness out of it. Why should difference be equated with fear?"

CHAPTER FIVE

And Here's the Pitch

How Advertising Uses Disability

A high hope for a low heaven.
—*Longaville, in* Love's Labor's Lost

O f all the cynical branches of the media, the most soulless and ruth-
less is generally considered to be advertising, where anything for
a buck trumps state-mandated "truth in advertising" and the manipulation of mind through image and word descends to subliminal lows.
At least journalism can defend itself by pointing to its lofty muckraking
ideals, filmmaking to the higher calling of the auteur, and the Web to the
utopian connectivity of the New Economy. For advertising, there is no
place to hide from an openly mercenary agenda. Now that the cover of
nonprofits has been blown thanks to scandals at the United Way and Red
Cross, even the "pro bono" or advocacy campaigns (what are called public service announcements or PSAs) are widely perceived to be phony.
How surprising, then, to find that among advocates and disability studies scholars, advertising agencies are considered to be in the forefront of
disability awareness and recognition, out ahead of television and movies
in such critical areas as casting and fidelity to the disability experience. In
a seminal study of disability in the media released in 1994, Jack A. Nelson observed:

> Pardoxically, it is in television commercials, generally regarded as the con-
> servative part of television, that the most progress in showing people with
> disabilities has occurred over the past decade. Until 1983, anyone less than
> perfect was practically invisible on these commercials. It was a case of "only
> the most attractive need apply" as advertisers tried to ally their products to
> the most seductive life-style. In 1982, however, CBS television used for a
> promotion a montage of quick shots showing facets of the new season—
> including a paraplegic wheelchair racer and a deaf couple expressing their
> love in signs. Next, a Levi jeans ad showed a paraplegic doing wheelies on
> the sidewalk with a group of friends without disabilities; a McDonald's
> commercial showed a crowd applauding that included a man on crutches

and a child in a wheelchair; and a Plymouth Voyager ad included a man on crutches explaining the virtues of the vehicle. Since then, a veritable flood of television commercials has shown those with various disabilities carrying out normal activities in happy settings.[1]

Inventing the Poster Child

It was not always so progressive. Before this recent shift in strategy because of economics the principal interaction between advertising and disability was a different matter. Wielding its powers to alter perception in the cause of pity and promotion of "medical miracles," advertising for seven decades had been part of the legacy of paternalism that characterized the broader media industry. From the beginning, the promotional formula for the major national disability charities was created by media businessmen. They were responsible for the marketing strategies still in use today, including print and electronic campaigns to solicit funds, gala dinners and events, and stories fed to the mainstream press. No campaign in history offers a more graphic example of this repressive syndrome than the infamous series of Muscular Dystrophy Association and Easter Seals poster children, a tradition that continues to this day. It has even spawned an addition to American usage, as "poster child" has become a standard way for lawyers to refer, in the context of class-action suits, to a particularly sympathetic class member selected to be presented to the jury as the "poster child" for the other plaintiffs, a way to drum up a higher damages settlement by appealing for sympathy. In the disability community, it is a call to arms. Cheryl Marie Wade, for example, calls her hard-edged performance piece about the disability experience *Sassy Girl: Portrait of a Poster Child Gone Awry.* As Joseph T. Shapiro writes in *No Pity:*

> The poster child is a surefire tug at our hearts. The children picked to represent charity fund-raising drives are brave, determined, and inspirational, the most innocent victims of the cruelest whims of life and health. Yet they smile through their "unlucky" fates—a condition that weakens muscles or cuts life expectancy to a brutish handful of years, a birth "defect" or childhood trauma. No other symbol of disability is more beloved by Americans than the cute and courageous poster child—or more loathed by people with disabilities themselves.[2]

The story of the poster child involves the double history of two of the most prominent nonprofits around today. In 1907 in Elyria, Ohio, Homer Allen, the eighteen-year-old son of Edgar Fiske Allen (a distant relation of mine) was run over by a streetcar. Allen was a prosperous local business-man who chucked his timber business (it had the exclusive cedar log con-tract for the creation of the AT&T telephone network) to devote himself full time to rectifying the lack of adequate medical services that might have saved Homer's life during a double amputation. As he observed the ways that children with disabilities were hidden from public view, he addressed the problem by creating, in 1919, the National Society for Crippled Chil-dren, the first organization of its kind. The birth of Easter "seals" as a de-sign and media campaign came in the spring of 1934, when the organi-zation launched a fund-raising drive. Donors placed the seals (designed by J. H. Donahey, the *Cleveland Plain Dealer* cartoonist) on envelopes and letters. Donahey kept the design basic, because those served by the charity asked "simply for the right to live a normal life." In 1952, the lily (symbolizing spring) was incorporated as the Easter Seals logo, harmo-nizing with the quasi-religious tenor of the institution. By then, it had been running an annual, state-by-state competition for "poster children," one boy and one girl, whose stories were highlighted in ad campaigns and press placements.

The poster-child strategy originated during the Depression when the March of Dimes was created to honor Franklin Delano Roosevelt. By the 1950s, its campaigns were resorting to scare tactics in its public service announcements. As NPR commentator Laurie Block observed in her se-ries *Inventing the Poster Child,* which aired in 1998, "Media campaigns designed to raise funds for services and research have helped shape, over the decades, our common feelings about disability—a compound of pity, fear, and hope which has yet to be untangled." FDR, America's best-known polio "victim," had visited the old spa at Warm Springs, Georgia, prompting his cronies and lobbyists to begin raising funds for rehabilita-tion therapies there. One of them was Carl Byoir, a pioneer in the field of public relations. His brainchild was a series of nationwide President's Birthday Parties, fundraising events for infantile paralysis that featured air shows by Wiley Post and radio addresses by FDR on a nationwide hookup. Byoir unleashed a barrage of cutting-edge promotional tricks, from radio spots to endorsements by movie stars, daredevil stunts, and sentimental stories that had newspaper and magazine readers reaching for the Kleenex. The big graphic guns were enlisted, including Howard Chandler Christy, who had designed the "I-Want-You" Uncle Sam poster, who created one of the first posters of a "crippled" child in 1932. The fundraising balls worked with local groups, who received half the pro-ceeds for their services. Eventually the rapidly growing National Foun-dation for Infantile Paralysis was renamed by singer Eddie Cantor as the "March of Dimes." The success of this new, national, media-driven charity campaign became a model for numerous other fundraisers used not only by the March of Dimes but by Easter Seals, the United Cerebral Palsy Association, the National Federation of the Blind, the American Foundation for the Blind, the National Association of the Deaf, and the Paralyzed Veterans of America.

In the protean world of advertising, it is astonishing to consider how long the poster-child idea has hung on. Eventually, however, the ad agencies caught on to a different trend. Instead of perceiving people with disabilities as recipients of charity, advertisers recognized the potential windfall of focusing on them as consumers. Paternalism gave way to profit, and the nonprofit organizations for whom the agencies were willing to work pro bono had to share their constituencies with major multinationals eager to tap a new market. Even before the other media attained a similar understanding of disability, ad agencies were out front in the representation of people with disabilities as empowered individuals. Some may contend that the astronomically high unemployment rate of people with disabilities does not square with the typical image of a prosperous consumer, but recent polls suggest that nearly a trillion dollars in spending money can be traced to the 54 million Americans with disabilities. It may also be difficult to square this progressive image with the wag-the-dog arrogance and winking rascality of the agency ethic. Yet it is precisely the freedom afforded by that "anything is possible—or real—if I say it is" attitude that gives Madison Avenue its opportunity to be out front on disability. The advertisers were the first to discover the disabled consumer. That alone gives them dibs on a major strategic advance that, for whatever motive, holds out one of the best promises to help reshape the representation of disability.

Church and State

The cause and effect relationships are in at least one sense remarkably clear. Whether you run a large or small media company, you start and end your day concerned about what your advertisers think and feel. Because it's their nickel, they are in control, which is why the budgets for thirty-second spots or print inserts are as monstrous as the combined production costs of the whole magazine or television show in which they are inserted. When ad pages go down, magazines literally shrink by between a third and a half, and editors in chief begin rethinking their story lists to attract new market segments. The primo advertisers get the back cover and best placement in the issue—opening spreads and the coveted right-hand page, with the article on the deferential left hand, wherever edit and ad are paired. During the recent recession, the major advertising shift from travel and luxury goods, including cars, to pharmaceuticals reshaped the entire media landscape, and it was led by the simple reapportionment of emphasis at the major ad agencies responding to a shift in client budgets. The duet of edit and advertising is far more harmonious in real life than the journalism schools or romanticized movies about investigative reporters let on. As an editor in chief, I learned fast that you sell ad space by flaunting your feature stories, which you are glad to divulge months in advance to your ad reps and the agencies even though you are jealously guarding their secrecy among other journalists for fear of being scooped. The goal of the early planning is to match a travel piece to an airline heading in that direction, a design feature to a home-products retailer, and so on, with priority given to the locale or product willing to take out a full page rather than to what the reader may have in mind (a particularly sore point in the disability press, considering the fact that some tourist boards and airlines sell trips that are far from models of accessibility, as I learned when we pitched Florence, Italy). When the ad column in the *Times* or a story in *Advertising Age* announces a new campaign from one of the big agencies, when there is time to design or assign editorial content that will support it, most editors, especially if their contracts include bonuses and profit sharing, will cave in to publisher pressure and give it a shot.

None of this should be a total surprise to those in the print media. Tina Brown infamously collapsed the wall between culture and commerce when she brought her ad-driven editorial philosophy to the *New Yorker* from *Vanity Fair* in 1992. At *Fortune* in the late eighties we jokingly taped a little sign with "Church" and "State" and little arrows pointing to the segregated editorial and ad-sales offices on the fifteenth floor of the Time-Life Building, but when a hit piece titled "The Stumbling Herd" cost us the Merrill Lynch account, the reporters who had worked on it knew to the penny how much it had cost the company in pulled ad pages, because the reps let us know directly. A similar scandal erupted when Lou Gerstner, the chief executive officer of IBM, took exception to one of our stories and pulled all of Big Blue's ads. I then spent five years in art magazines, where it was a given that no show was reviewed unless the gallery took out some kind of ad—in that issue—and you can imagine how rarely a critic would actually be critical. For every Christie's image we used, we made sure we also used a Sotheby's picture, or either of them was bound to pull its advertising, and there were distinct limits to how far an investigative piece could go (even as the two auction houses were colluding on prices, right under our noses) because both had the habit of threatening to cancel pages. Other types of publication are not quite so blatant, although the reader is invited to compare the list of advertisers and that of publishers of books reviewed in the *New York Times Book Review*. These are just the best-known examples of the kowtowing that print editors perform before advertisers, ensuring that in the one-two punch of media exposure, number two is always the editorial side.

If the media lead with ads, then advertisers have both an advantage and a responsibility when it comes to breaking through to new subject matter and attitudes. They have an economic incentive to stay ahead of the game as well, prodded by the deadly danger of "been there done that" in the ad business, where the onus is permanently on coming up with fresh material, quirky angles, and surprises. This helps the disability agenda, because in 1982 a model in a wheelchair had the virtue of novelty. As with the fashion stylists who wrack their brains for some new look and end up with Aimee Mullins in a pair of wooden legs, the appetite for anything eye-catching is immense in advertising. The perpetual movement on to the new new thing offers a motive for broader inclusion and diversification. Once the other minorities have been tapped, it only makes sense for people with disabilities to be up next, especially if casting agencies can uncover the right faces or stories.

The Effects of Cause Marketing

Behind the perpetual creative need for something completely different is a business logic that milks the public's remaining sense of altruism while hopefully skirting its growing alertness to the sophistication of ads as medium. There is a technical term for the strategic deployment of disability in campaigns, as well as for the switch in emphasis toward perceiving people with disabilities less as role models than as the actual consumers and borrowers with enough buying power. Once again following the model of other minorities, disability in the eighties proved a handy instrument in what is called "cause marketing" (more formally, "cause-related marketing"), a branding strategy that counts on the identification of consumers with a particular feel-good crusade on behalf of, to take a few well-known examples, women, blacks, AIDS or cancer patients, the environment, even political affiliations to push product. One of the first historic examples of cause marketing was American Express in 1983 donating a penny to the Statue of Liberty restoration every time the card was used. Among the textbook examples of its effectiveness have been the Absolut vodka campaigns that capitalized on a high-profile outreach effort to gays and the environmentally based sales initiatives of Ben and Jerry's, Patagonia, Home Depot, and The Body Shop. It is a billion-dollar annual chunk of the U.S. economy, ten times more than a decade ago.

Eventually, the strategy advances to the point where the beneficiaries of the cause become the target market itself, shifting from recipients of charity to consumers. The next step is the inclusion of people with disabilities in the company's diversity programs. Hired typically as part of the sales or customer service forces, employees with disabilities attract more customers from the community. Once that step is taken, the tangible benefits of cause marketing are completely realized in the sense that the company not only recognizes people with disabilities as customers but taps the sector for new hires as well, empowering them in the most important possible way. One of the obvious candidates for such a pracitce is McDonald's, which has played this tune twice, first with African-Americans and later with both deafness and developmental disability. To give the company credit, and recognize that some good comes out of cause marketing, the managers do hire people with disabilities (by 1999, a full 70 percent of franchise managers had at least one worker with a disability on board). As Rogercarole Rogers of McDonald's points out, articulating the party line of many companies who have discovered the disability market and talent pool: "We value our customers and workers with disabilities. We have gained from using people with disabilities in our ads, and we are better and stronger for doing so."

It sounds perfect, but before we get ahead of ourselves in praise of corporations who use cause marketing we need to consider the flip side. Experts on ethics are divided on the social cost-benefit analysis of cause marketing. The cycle of cause to consumer has been explored by strategists such as Richard Levy, whose work explores the interaction of the private and public sectors, corporations and nonprofits.[3] He and other ethicists introduce a healthy skepticism regarding the motives and methods of cause marketing. When it induces consumers to let down their guard and buy a product that is not necessarily directly beneficial to the cause, the tactic has drawn heavy fire from promoters of corporate accountability, including S. Prakash Sethi, one of the leading voices in the field and the director of the International Center for Corporate Accountability, who has exposed the use of advocacy advertising as part of whitewashing campaigns to efface corporate misdeeds.[4] The thin line between exploitation and empowerment is defined, I believe, by the adherence to reality. When disability made its debut in cause marketing, a stinging complaint was the justifiable annoyance of actors with disabilities by the fact that the model in the wheelchair was not really disabled but was just playing the role. The situation improved as real-life people with disabilities were cast in these roles. One of the premier examples of a successful ad campaign starring a person with a disability has been six-time Tour de France champion Lance Armstrong's long-term starring role as pitch person for the United

States Postal Service. An amazing 12 million yellow "Live Strong" brace-
lets were sold to benefit Armstrong's foundation, becoming one of the
hottest fashion items in 2004. Further progress was made when, instead
of making gratuitous use of disability to pander to emotions, the ads captured a slice of life and rendered disabilities without the sappy stringed-
instrument accompaniment, recognizing the consumer and treating him
or her with respect by holding up a mirror that accurately reflected the
lifestyle. At this point, we return to the positive side: more actors with disabilities appear in television and print ads to which real people can relate.
Then cause marketing is serving its avowed purpose.

And that is where the Paralympians march in. During my tenure with
WE magazine, a curious employment trend gained momentum. An elite
and attractive group of disabled athletes traced a direct path from the ski
slopes or running tracks to the photo or film studios where ads were shot.
Most of them were amputees or wheelchair users owing to spinal cord injuries. The companies that took them on as spokespeople, however, were
not Quickie and Everest and Jennings, the main wheelchair manufacturers and longtime employers of celebrity spokespeople from the ranks of
elite athletes with disabilities. The new campaigns were on a whole different level in terms of budgets and media exposure. The first company to
put together its team of Paralympians was The Hartford, a massive insurance firm that underwrites hundreds of millions of dollars worth of
group disability policies each year. In 1998, it hired four Paralympians for
a full year of live appearances at conventions and sales events as well as
in a full-scale print campaign. One of them was a recurring star in our
pages, either in the fashion pages, in sports pieces, or as a commentator.
A superb skier and native of Colorado, Chris Waddell became one of the
best-known people with a disability after the surefire stars like Reeve, Ali,
or Fox. He was one of the top earners on the motivational speech and
public appearance circuit after *People* magazine named him to its list of
the fifty most beautiful people in the world in 1997. On the strength of the
press the team received (which amounts to free advertising, because the
company scores editorial hits in tandem with the ad pages it takes out),
the program continued for an extraordinary duration. Another member
of "Team Ability," as The Hartford's overachievers are called, was added
in 2002. Sandy Dukat, a member of the U.S. Disabled Ski Team, was born
and raised in Canton, Ohio, where at age four she had her right foot am-
putated because of a limb deficiency. Introduced to disabled sports through
the Rehabilitation Institute of Chicago (RIC), she competed in the Salt
Lake City Paralympics in 2002 in skiing. In assessing what the team did
for The Hartford, it is easy to point out the first benefit, which was to gain
major points with a large constituency that was already involved in The

Hartford's line of business, people who react as positively as any minority does to seeing one of their own in an ad. Probably as important, however, as the disability market per se was the way the campaign reached decision makers at major corporations, the ones who choose their companies' disability insurance carriers. It was a major step to sway this powerful group with a positive image. No doubt these corporate clients were relieved to find an upside to the customary fear of lawsuits or huge claims that disability insurance generally represents, so that disability made the transition in their minds from a source of risk to reward. As with the deployment of characters with disabilities in the movies or television, then, the inclusion of wheelchair users in these campaigns was aimed at appealing to a nondisabled audience, one of the reasons that the print ads resorted to the "triumphing over adversity" cliché.

To secure a bit of this action for my magazine, I traveled to the offices of The Hartford in the company of my sales representative. We were looking for a simple edit-for-ad barter (The Hartford would pay for a schedule of ad pages, and I would guarantee coverage of its sponsorship of the team in features and news stories). I counted on our accumulated points, having already plugged Waddell a few times in both the sports and fashion slots. I also knew that the upbeat, upscale tenor of the magazine was a super match for the tone of The Hartford's campaign. The meeting in a sunny conference room on the second floor of its deathly quiet suburban offices was civil to the point of boredom, but it was refreshing for all of us in many ways to be on the same page for once. The Hartford's press-office "flaks" were there, looking for a story or "hit," and both sides were essentially preaching to the choir since everybody already knew why it was important for people with disabilities to be featured in the media. I couldn't help noticing how often we all referred to "them" and "they," and that there was nobody with a disability among the eight people at the table. Not surprisingly, both sides got what they wanted that day. We ran a piece on the promotional program, and The Hartford took out a three-issue schedule of ads, at a rate I learned later was much diminished from those listed on our less than ironclad rate card, since The Hartford was better at bargaining than we had anticipated and had no intention of paying the full rate for a page in an obscure two-year-old magazine with suspicious circulation numbers.

The other major American corporation with a team of disabled athletes on the payroll was Chevrolet, which in 1994 inaugurated its "Barrier Breakers" campaign with a slightly more rough-and-ready group of athletes. They were pitching a new pickup and the first round of the SUVs that year, so the emphasis was on ruggedness and durability, represented by the muscular torsos of Mark Wellman, a well-known mountaineer who is a wheelchair user from a spinal cord injury sustained in 1982 on his descent from the Seven Gables in the John Muir Wilderness, Evan Evans, an off-road truck racer who competes in the annual Baja cross-country race (a wheelchair user after a 1989 motorcycle accident), and Sarah Will, the world's top woman mono-skier and Paralympian. Their "inspiring" road show made them stars of a print and television campaign that is still running years later. From a disability studies angle, they would qualify as "supercrips," but from a marketing standpoint they were right on cue as the nation's disaffected youth began to worship snowboarders, rock climbers, skateboarders, and other rebels in the extreme sports category. Wellman spent eleven days climbing to the top of El Capitan, a 3,200-foot sheer rock face in Yosemite National Park, pulling himself up with a rope system (he figured it was the equivalent of executing 10,000 pull-ups on a chin bar, not bad for a thirty-nine-year-old). He and his climbing partner slept on ledges along the way. We devoted a story to the exploit, which was sponsored notably by The Hartford, in our March–April 2000 issue. "I think adventure sports like climbing are really big in mainstream America and I believe the disabled community wants to be a part of that phenomenon" was the mixed message he offered on that occasion. From our point of view, the GM campaign was a boon, not only in terms of a running series of paid ads in our magazine but because we could piggyback on their expensive publicity. One of our first major breaks, for example, was an invitation from the glitzy New York Auto Show to set up a booth (free!) right at the entrance level of the cavernous Javits Center, where we could distribute complimentary copies of the magazine and tout accessibility in cars, with lift-equipped GM vans right beside us. As one of the most heavily attended consumer product shows in the world, not to mention a magnet for the international print and electronic press, this opportunity was worth more to us in circulation, ad dollars, and publicity than we ever could have afforded. We scored with the organizers on the basis that the year before had been the year of the woman and we were the next minority up in the cause-marketing line. Being used never felt so good.

As a rookie editor in chief, I took an anthropological interest in the clash of cultures between Madison Avenue and disability. My debut pitch was at Ogilvy and Mather's crystalline headquarters in midtown. We nervously entered just before nine one morning laden with bagels, muffins, and strong coffee. The pitch to people who are pitchers is a genre of oral presentation all its own. Sitting around the vast conference room, the twentysomething "buyers" of media space for advertisers were dressed to kill and clearly locked into the treadmill between the office and the gym in their quest to be as physically perfect as the models in their ads. They looked bored as they wolfed the bagels. At the end, there were no questions or comments as they scurried back to their cubicles, many of them leaving our magazines and rate cards right on the table. One lingered to talk about some possible health care clients, and it turned out her first cousin had MS. We were a hard sell. Absent the charitable impulse or an economic connection between my constituency and their clients' new consumers, the media buyers could not turn around and present us to their top accounts for the upcoming season.

I took the show on the road to the Fort Lee, New Jersey offices of Carillon Importers, which distributes Absolut, in search of one of the great plums in the print ad garden, the ongoing campaign that had worked its magic in the world of gay publications. The gatekeeper to the Absolut treasure, a gregarious and astute legend in the marketing world named Michel Roux, wasn't biting. He addressed me in no uncertain terms: "Do you know what percentage of spinal cord injuries are due to alcohol-related car accidents?" He did.

I was rapidly learning that advertising people are a breed apart in the media world. What they pay attention to during a television broadcast or when leafing through a magazine is the inverse of what most of us find fascinating. With their own schools, awards (Clios), and trade associations (most powerfully the Ad Council), they cultivate that clubby aura of self-sufficiency that leads to ads commenting on famous ads, little in-jokes that fuel a $100-billion-a-year U.S. industry, according to a recent PricewaterhouseCoopers special report on ad trends. In this arcane and specialized world, disability can seem like cannon fodder rather than a cause. But when they do get on board with a disability ad, their prejudices can rapidly turn around. One veteran copywriter, Brian Keller, now head of his own shop based in Manhattan and Greenport, New York, took time out to explain the appeal of people with disabilities starting in the early eighties. "What we liked about having disability in an ad is that the people are so real. You don't get much of that in our business."[5]

Rolling Out the Disabled Consumer

The history of disability in advertising yields a distinct before-and-after demarcation between the pre- and postdiscovery of the disabled consumer. According to another insider, Thomas Learner, who has nearly two decades in the ad business, the shift from obscurity (or pity) to courtship is relatively recent: "Madison Avenue has always been scared of alienating the largest population in the country and so has always been behind the social times. We were creative in our messages, but we believed our audience was the same—white, able-bodied and perfect. I was on Wall Street accounts during an era when we did not show a black person in an ad. When we did, we sanitized them. To show a disabled person using products went against the mainstream of Madison Avenue's paternalistic view."[6] While some marketers joke that ADA stands for "additional dollars available," the breakthrough campaigns predated the passage of the landmark legislation in 1990. According to a position paper by Beth Haller and Sue Ralph titled "Profitability, Diversity, and Disability Images in Advertising in the United States and Great Britain," the new age of ads using deaf people and wheelchair users started with a 1984 Levi's television ad featuring someone popping a wheelie. In 1986 McDonald's ran a captioned TV spot with deaf students signing to one another in a successful attempt to build "good will" and garner publicity. Haller notes that by 1990 deaf people starred in ads for Crest, Citibank, Levi's, and AT&T, which used Marlee Matlin in its campaign, and that by then two hundred advertisers were using captions for 2,600 TV spots. The wheelchair users were featured in both print and television ads for Citicorp, Apple, Pacific Telesis, Nissan, and Target, which is often cited for its early use (1990 and after) of real people with disabilities in its fliers. Haller and Ralph pinpoint the change: "There is a move from charity advertising of the past to a new awareness of 'handicapitalism.' Businesses are coming to an understanding of the potential power of tapping the disabled market. . . . The better and more prevalent use of disabled people in advertising we believe can be tied to important anti-discrimination legislation in the U.S. and U.K. The ADA kicked off a renewed awareness of disability rights which can be seen in the growing number of disabled people in ads from 1990 on and a better understanding of the disabled consumer market. It can be hoped that the Disability Discrimination Act of 1995 in the U.K. will lead to the same kind of inclusion of diverse disability in British advertising."[7] The authors observe that Britain is a decade behind the United States in this area.

Many of the successful television and print campaigns have unforgettable resonance. In one of the pioneering examples on television, DuPont in 1987 used double amputee Bill Demby (who lost his legs in a rocket attack in Vietnam) on an outdoor basketball court going head to head with his competitors to push the message "Better things for better living." The plastic prostheses he was playing on were made by DuPont. The campaign was greeted with a massive, positive response, including thousands of letters received at the Wilmington headquarters in the first week after it launched, prompting DuPont to pull all the rest of its ads and run the Demby spots exclusively for an entire TV season. Success that spontaneous was all the ad industry needed, with its gold rush mentality, to lure other agencies into the disability theme.

For the summer issue of 1999, I put my Washington correspondent John M. Williams (a stutterer who publishes his own *Assistive Technology News* and has a regular gig with *Business Week*'s online edition covering disability issues in business) on a story about how Madison Avenue discovered "the invisible composer." We wrapped the piece with a two-pager on journalists with disabilities and our top story by John Hockenberry in a cover package on the media. Williams gave the agencies top marks for reaching out to an untapped market with reality-based images that eschewed the usual fashion models or pity approach. He also cannily pointed out that many of the clients were corporations that needed to clean up their own images by at least projecting the appearance that they were more caring and human (and this was three years before we heard of Enron or WorldCom). As Williams wrote:

> What's up in ad land? Agencies are using people with a wide range of disabilities in TV spots, plugging everything from Internet search engines to Oreos. The emotionally charged commercials feature shopping, eating, using assistive technology in the workplace, traveling, playing, skiing, driving, drinking soft drinks, eating snacks, teaching, learning and doing the full range of activities that traditional ads have use. The commercials are running during prime time and top-rated sports events in major markets. They are getting high marks form industry insiders, consumers and advocates in the disability movement for the indelible, positive images of ability they portray and their contribution to the progress of mainstreaming.

When Williams was done, he had put together a formidable roster of major companies that had used disability in recent ads: Saturn, Ford, Chrysler, General Motors, IBM, McDonald's, AT&T, Bell Atlantic, Pacific Bell, Chevron, Campbell's, Target, Gatorade, Nike, VISA, General Mills, Wal-Mart, K-Mart, Coca Cola, Pepsi, Disney, Hallmark, DuPont, JC Penney, Sears, Bank of America, The Gap, Charles Schwab, Starbucks, NationsBank, Unum, and U.S. Robotics.

Assigning credit for the better ads is not always easy. Sometimes the initiative comes from the client, and often it comes right from the top. The now famous Target fliers of the eighties, which showed children with disabilities playing with toys or modeling clothes, were the brainchild of Bob Thacker, a marketing vice president whose daughter has a disability. He was initially worried that the campaign would look exploitative or put off buyers, but the early ads and fliers were greeted with over a thousand positive letters, and Target's marketing department tracked specific upturns in sales of certain items modeled by a person with a disability, making it the most successful campaign ever at the company in terms of consumer response. Consider not only the lucrative results of the program, which has become a seminal case study in disability marketing, but its reach as well: the circulars went to 30 million households in thirty-two states.

Another important client is Charles Schwab, who is dyslexic and a major personal spokesperson for a range of disability causes. It should not be surprising that his brokerage features people with disabilities (notably, one series in which the principal character is blind). Inside major corporations such as IBM and General Motors, marketing executives eager to tap the disability niche are pushing for ads that more directly reach the community. The more powerful the diversity and disability voices inside the company, the more likely this is to happen. At IBM, for example, Paul Luther is a specialist in assistive technology whose lab is based in Austin, Texas, but who finds himself summoned to corporate headquarters in Armonk, New York, to advise the marketing teams on how to reach people with disabilities. The company is a perennial leader in hiring people with disabilities, and after ranking first in my magazine's top ten list of employers it lobbied hard to keep that spot in years to come, in part by spotlighting Luther's work. As he says, the connection is basic: "When we advertise people with disabilities using our products, we sell more of those products." IBM invests in disability-friendly products, gets them to the market, and then uses print campaigns to jump start sales. At a time when growth in nondisabled sales has stalled or gone south, the computer user with a disability is an oasis of fresh possibility. Similarly, GM's mobility program was just a step ahead of those at Ford and Chrysler. As Ken Tregenza, employment relations administrator at GM's headquarters in Detroit, says, "Using people with disabilities in ads is becoming part of our institutionalized thinking at GM and of course we see it at other companies. We now recognize there is a market out there for accessible vans and other products. We recognize them as consumers." GM's ads ran in WE magazine from the first year. Tregenza adds a surprising caveat: "We must develop ads that include disabled people in the mainstream of the community's perception of the abilities a disabled person has. Our ads cannot be so narrow that they only appeal to disabled consumers. The able-bodied population must be able to identify with the product being promoted, too." In addition to appealing strongly to nondisabled consumers who appreciate the company's effort, ads of this kind take us a step further by inching forward the general view of people with disabilities in a more assimilated, less pointedly "minority" context.

The client is not always the one who makes the call on disability—sometimes that idea comes from the agency. During my tenure at the magazine, one of the most successful creative efforts on all levels—commercially and in terms of respecting disability etiquette—was a U.S. Robotics television ad featuring the renowned astrophysicist Stephen Hawking, who has amyotrophic lateral sclerosis and uses a super-duper power wheel-chair with an advanced built-in computer system that makes him one of the most connected users on the planet. Much of the cutting-edge tech-nology, of course, that allows him to use the Web and to communicate through a voice synthesizer was developed for him by U.S. Robotics, which sent a crew to Cambridge University in 1999 to film an ad featur-ing Hawking. The ratings for the ad were nothing less than astronomical. The spot was conceived by a boutique firm called Leap Frog, based in Tampa, Florida. According to Leap Frog, the "pre-post" study to mea-sure the ad's impact showed that over the course of just four months after their debut, the ads pushed brand awareness from 36 to 48 percent, an increase that Michael Dietrich, one of Leap Frog's resident geniuses, called "significant." In the all-important ratings category of "recall," the advance from 52 to 67 percent was even more dramatic, and advertising awareness increased from 19 to 39 percent. Dietrich and his team were ecstatic: "Talk about a breakthrough! These are tremendous gains, par-ticularly in light of the loud 'noise' in the modem category at the time. In short, the results are phenomenal."[8]

The marketing phenomenon I was closest to as a direct observer in-volved Casey Martin, a golfer who in 1998 successfully sued the Profes-sional Golfers Association for the right to use a cart in tournament play. Martin, a stylish golfer who was Tiger Woods's teammate and roommate at Stanford, has a rare circulatory disorder that makes it difficult for him to walk, even stand, for very long, and as he told me the suit was a straight-forward application of the ADA: "My case was about the right to earn a living under the ADA, not the club rules of a golf course."[9] This landmark victory for pro-ADA forces through a series of appeals (the PGA's comi-cally adamant commissioner, Tim Finchem, refused to give in to the opin-ions of either the court or the fans for well over a year) garnered a mile-high stack of press clips all over the world, prime-time coverage on all the networks, and a fan base of thousands for Martin on the Nike Tour (which feeds the PGA tour much as the minor leagues feed baseball).

Nike had played the disability card before the Martin campaign, almost inevitably running the "supercrip" gauntlet simply because the company is perpetually selling the sports fantasy. In an ad titled "Heritage U.S. Up-date," two wheelchair racers (one white and one black) are pumping their racing chairs full out, with the legend "There is no finish line" appearing in the background. Another spot, called "Hope," intercut images of wheelchair races in a montage of athletes and ended with one who pulled up his shirt to show a "Superman" T-shirt below. One series of spots that aired in 1989 featured Craig Blanchette, who was referred to in the ad as an Olympic bronze medalist. In a half-minute spot, we see him for twenty-seven seconds bench-pressing weights, playing competitive basketball and tennis—a driven, all-round amateur athlete. Then the lens turns down to his wheelchair. He says, "So I never quit," turns, and sprints away along a track. The ad was covered in the *Wall Street Journal,* where it was cited as an example of Madison Avenue becoming "increasingly enchanted with the disabled."[10] However imperfect such ads may be in terms of the orthodoxies of disability culture—they harp on the "supercrip" and pity themes—the exposure and industry credibility brought by the fact that they represent Nike, one of the brand behemoths, guarantees that they have the broadest possible impact. Nike did not hit a home run every time up at the plate, however. In 2000 it launched an ad for the Dri-Goat sneaker that was so offensive to the disability community that the uproar and bad press forced Nike to yank the ads within forty-eight hours of their first appearing in print.

Many of the best ads have used sign language, including a very convincing if sentimental television ad for the Internet search engine Snap .com in which a deaf child on a school bus uses ASL and another little boy who wants to be his friend hurries home to his computer to look up signing so he can respond the next day. The story line was concocted by a television scriptwriter for NBC, Mark Bennett, who drew on his experience with an autistic relative to help him stay close to the experience of the deaf boy. NBC's Bertina Ciccerelli was in on the casting, partly because the ad ran during the network's prime-time shows, including *Dateline* and *Law and Order.* Unlike many early disability-themed ads, which used able-bodied actors in wheelchairs or pretending to be deaf, the agency in conjunction with the network went with a deaf actor. Ciccerelli said, "We took the high road. We wanted realism in the ad, and we achieved it." Similarly, a mother and her son enjoying Oreos at a picnic table outside with their two glasses of milk sign the familiar debate over whether or not to twist off the top cookie. David Matthews, a senior manager and affirmative action administrator at Nabisco, commented on the ad: "I think society's attitude toward people with disabilities has changed. The ADA has had impact in this field. We see more people with disabilities in the mainstream, and because we do, they are no longer the invisible consumers." A Nabisco spokesperson, Ann Smith, added, "We use people with disabilities in our Oreo ads because the message has impact. A commercial showing a deaf child signing to his mother communicates the power of the moment. People tell us in their letters they remember our ads with disabled people in them because they show a special bond between the people. Their responses are what we are looking for."

As with a Wal-Mart ad that used both signing and closed-captioning to welcome shoppers, these ads raise the question of the darker meaning of "use" in Smith's commentary. Do they exploit an amplified emotional bass note generated by the child's deafness? It would be ridiculous to ignore the ploy. The magical manipulation of pity to move product is nothing new to Madison Avenue—one has only to recall the funny scene in which Robert De Niro, as a stressed-out mafioso in the movie *Analyze This,* breaks down in tears watching a Merrill Lynch retirement-planning ad on his hotel television to recognize the ploy's effectiveness. This is psychologically even more rudimentary than cause marketing itself, pushing the same buttons that the poster children and Jerry Lewis telethons have counted on for years. It is a particularly low trick when the person in the ad does not actually have a disability, as in the case of the infamous airline spots of the 1970s, which featured wheelchair users who were actors. Even the arbiters of taste in ad land have been known to object to the most blatant of such manipulations. When Dow Chemical used a child with Down Syndrome, recruited with her mother through a local chapter of the National Down Syndrome Congress, for a spot advertising Spray 'N Wash Stain Stick, a writer at *Advertising Age* called the ad "appalling" and "the most crassly contrived slice-of-life in advertising history."[11]

Sometimes, advocates take exception to the upbeat character of ads. As the executive director of a well-known national service organization in the Midwest told Williams when he put together his piece, speaking on condition of anonymity, "There is a problem showing the positive images of disabled people on TV. In raising money, we appeal to the paternalism of the giver. If that paternalism is not there, we have more trouble raising money to find cures." This is an old conundrum for the philanthropic community, and it may be one of the reasons why some of the most backward ads in terms of disability culture are those created for major nonprofits as part of their fundraising efforts. As one British study of the disability advertising phenomenon concluded, "The perceptions and interests of a disability charity are not always synonymous with those of the disabled consumer."[12] There is a practical catch involved here. When a nonprofit is called in by a client or an agency to consult on content and casting, its paternalistic agenda often becomes entangled with the commercial one of the advertiser. Tradition favors paternalism.

Public Disservice

One of the most visible, up-front areas in which advertising and disability intersect involves the making of public service announcements (PSAs), which are often undertaken as pro bono assignments much as attorneys will handle the legal work of a nonprofit and waive their fees. The clients in this case are major nonprofits, many of which rely on extensive national print and television ad campaigns to bolster their fundraising. Unlike straight corporate advertising, the beneficiaries of the ad and the "talent" on screen are the same, ostensibly the community. Disability is a huge component of this sector of the ad industry. When the United Way was riddled in 1994 by the repeated exposure of its mismanagement and internal fraud, it turned to disability as a way to build back its credibility. Spotlighting a number of real-life disability stories that put recipients of United Way philanthropy on screen, the ads were essentially variations on the poster-child theme. Mario Pellegrini of Vital Productions wrote and directed the ads, which also featured football players and ran during breaks in NFL broadcasts as well as in movie theaters. He points to marked increases in donations as well as favorable response to the series indicated by market research. More recently, the United Way has turned to Young & Rubicam, one of the heaviest hitters on Madison Avenue, for a parodic series that plays on its earlier sentimental successes. When PSAs are in production, the ad industry as a whole seems to rediscover its missing heart. Studios and technicians cut their fees to a fraction of the usually outlandish hourlies or per diems, and the "talent" (on-screen faces and voices) customarily accept only expenses. Even the unions look the other way when a PSA is shot, unless it is a big-budget number such as a United Way Super Bowl spot. One of the most notable of the recent PSA campaigns has been launched by Easter Seals to redefine its image and create a parallel message to the poster child—which never stopped, however. The new, restructured messages were created to balance charity and disability awareness. A five-year campaign, incorporating television, radio, and print ads, was designed pro bono by Camphell-Mithun-Esty Advertising, a top-twenty-five agency based in Minneapolis. The campaign is estimated by the agency to be worth $7 million a year and attempts to mix fundraising with public education spots that not only encourage contributions but "reposition the agency as a respected advocate for people with disabilities within the disability rights movement," according to one Easter Seals veteran who helped launch the campaign. In a stunning reversal of its usual condemnation of Easter Seals campaigns, *The Disability Rag,* one of the disability rights movement's most radical publications, featured "The First Step" campaign's posters in its Kudos section.

If the Easter Seals poster child is still the most reviled advertising crime in the disability studies community, other candidates continue to emerge. One of the most insidious is the never-to-be-forgotten disgrace of a 2000 Super Bowl ad using the image of Christopher Reeve "walking." It prompted a chorus of criticism in the disability press starting the day after the game. Responding to the outcry, Reeve told ABC's Diane Sawyer that he was approached by his agent, William Morris, to do the ad and had talks with the chairman of Nuveen, which was pumping one of its dubious funds as well as agency writers before they went ahead and filmed an actor who used to be one of his stunt doubles, walking with Reeve's head superimposed. As he told Sawyer in an interview: "When I saw the ad, I was very impressed by the dignity of it—the quality of the production and the simplicity. Something I insisted on was that I be accompanied by other people who had also recovered, and you see them coming out with me. So it's not just about Christopher Reeve, the celebrity, recovering, but casting myself as a leader of a worldwide movement. I did think the ad was very tastefully done, and I appreciate the fact that Nuveen and the ad agency consulted with me about the commercial at every step of the way." Not everyone in the community agreed.

Put together using computer simulation, it featured a ludicrously fake shot of a man walking with Reeve's head barely affixed digitally to his shoulders (the creators seemed to have forgotten the neck part, and the head was far to small for the proportions of the body). As the figure strolled down a catwalk to the standing ovation of a crowd of extras that looked held over from *The Day of the Dead,* the voice-over intoned some syrupy platitudes about anything being possible. By that time, however, much of America was howling in disgust. Nobody protested louder than people with spinal cord injuries, for whom the trivialization of their medical situation was beyond insulting. Many of them already despised Reeve, who caught more of the grief than he deserved. He had a number of endorsement contracts, which, he openly acknowledged, helped him to pay for a level of care well beyond the means of most quadriplegics. The most compelling reasons behind the outcry are legitimate concerns about the damage the blunder could inflict on legitimate marketing efforts for spinal cord research. This is a time when the challenge is not merely to summon the dollars to keep pace with ballooning budgets but, perhaps more important, to drum up political support for stem cell research. That is not easy when statehouses, judges' chambers, and congressional offices have been perceptibly drifting right, in effect curbing research because it often relies on embryonic tissue. Because it was so fake and so universally despised, and because it sent a macabre message of imminent mobility that was decades down the path from where spinal cord research actually rests even now, the ad militated against philanthropic and political progress for just the causes that Reeve himself espoused. Here you have the most cherished, scrutinized, hyped ad slot in all the media universe—a halftime Super Bowl commercial—and the opportunity for sending an important message on spinal cord research is blown by sheer stupidity. Worse still, Reeve briefly became a laughingstock and sellout, which further set back his important work inside the Beltway.

When major nonprofits in the disability field launch their own campaigns, their medical expertise does not always translate into the deft handling of disability etiquette. One of the most egregious examples of this lack of connection between disability culture and an institution that serves people with disabilities every day is a 2003 radio and print campaign launched by Mount Sinai Medical Center in New York. The battle for the medical consumer in Manhattan has escalated so rapidly that promotional efforts to lure discerning patients to the best doctors, the best operating rooms, best research, and best amenities (all ranked annually in one of the most carefully scrutinized cover stories *New York* magazine publishes) have driven agencies to an all-time low in terms of ethical standards. In the spirit of this bizarre but high-stakes competition, the Manhattan agency Devito/Verdi created a series of dramatic ads that aired on local radio stations and appeared in upscale magazines as well as the *New York Times* touting the geniuses on the Mount Sinai medical faculty even as they scared the living daylights out of hypochondriacs across the city. The "medical miracle" slogan for the series is "Another day, another breakthrough." In addition to elevating hype to sheer hubris, this implies that only by grace of the Mount Sinai doctors will life be worth living. "An aneurysm is a death sentence," proclaims the display type at the center of one print ad. Below it is the reassuring legend: "We have the power to grant you a pardon." A solitary figure surf-casting before a sunset is the only visual image—he is landing porgies instead of meeting his maker, one supposes. In fine print, the Faustian subtext (if you don't get the ambulance to head to Mount Sinai you'll probably end up six feet under) is no less obnoxious:

> Should it rupture, it can cause uncontrollable bleeding. But fortunately, Mount Sinai is the recognized leader in the minimally invasive repair of aortic aneurysms. In fact, our team of specialists train doctors from all over the world to perform this groundbreaking procedure, which enables patients to leave the hospital after only two days. So in addition to saving your life, there's an added bonus: You can get on with it almost immediately.

Even more objectionable ads denigrate living with a disability as a dire consequence of not taking one's case to Mount Sinai. The radio spots use a dual narrative, alternating sentences about the patient who does use Mount Sinai with others about the poor soul who doesn't and ends up depressed, isolated, out of work, "lost." One touts a cochlear implant procedure, another the rehabilitation expertise of the hospital's physical therapists. The print ad for the latter begins, "When Brian Gobbi injured his spinal cord, most hospitals were paralyzed." The mininarrative plays on more cute puns and delivers the miracle line again: "Fortunately, the patient was moved to Mount Sinai Rehabilitation Center. Our physical therapists helped Brian develop and strengthen residual muscles to achieve mobility. While psychologists helped him deal with the emotional trauma. A year after he began treatment, Brian was able to walk again. In fact, he became an occupational therapist. Which some might view as a miracle. But it's really a tribute to a hospital with a pioneering approach to spinal cord injury. And to a patient with backbone." The ad campaign won a prestigious juried Global Award for "excellence in healthcare communications" in the "Communication to the Consumer" category for its creative director, Sal DeVito, copywriter Wayne Winfield, and art director Brad Emmett. Unbelievable.

This kind of trite and demeaning nonsense, along with such lapses in taste as the Reeve debacle, are illustrations of why it would be callow to expect more from advertising than has already been achieved. If disability works in the net equation, it stays in the picture. If it does not produce results or is not cost effective, then it's out. Meanwhile, the paternalism streak hangs in there, even as it denies common humanity to individuals with disability, because the drama and the comfortable redemptive message have their role in keeping the most familiar disability narrative alive. My great fear, having participated in or closely observed only a few years' worth of seasonal cycles, is that disability as a consumer phenomenon has had its spin round the track with advertising and has been let off as passé. It would be silly to accuse the industry of being fickle in turning to another minority—it thrives on using the new new thing and discarding the old. What a disaster it would be if disability, never having cracked the awareness barrier, were to be deemed passé by this monstrously powerful arm of the media.

milestones, Mixed Messages, and Missed Opportunities

The Unfinished Business of the Disability Media

You taught me language, and my profit on it is I know how to curse.
—*Caliban, in* The Tempest

With the mainstream press locked in an echo chamber of clueless sentimentality, and book publishers stuck in a rut of melodramatic memoirs, it is up to the specialized disability press to show the way. During the most promising period in the history of the disability media, those heady years of heightened public awareness and community spirit attending the passage of the ADA, it seemed as though the long-sought "literature of our own" was imminent. A brief efflorescence of new magazines, newspapers, radio and television shows, even a national cable network rode the coattails of the political victory. The grassroots campaign for the ADA had awakened an audience beyond people with disabilities and their caregivers to the presence of a potent if forgotten minority. The moment was ripe for entrepreneurial publishers and producers to fit content to consciousness. This emergence of specialized media companies paralleled other start-up operations—many of them involving fashion or home product design—serving the community. The paradigmatic success story in this sector is still Quickie, the California-based wheelchair company begun by a paraplegic, Mary Hamilton, to challenge the drab hospital supply giants (namely the "invalid care" monopoly of Everest and Jennings) with a lightweight, rainbow-hued product line that answered the needs for style and fun. "If you can't stand up, stand out," Hamilton's tagline went. That was the mantra as well of the new disability press, which hit the newsstands with bright color, bold headlines, and attitude. As with Quickie, the premise of these start-ups was the revolutionary notion that people with disabilities could run their own for-profit companies that, by knowing their market better, could deliver a superior product and make a statement by succeeding.

In the magazine business, this had happened before. Other civil rights movements had supported publications whose pages were filled with images that mirrored their readers' own, and with stories that rang with the authenticity of firsthand experience as well as the urgency of the inside scoop on fresh issues that mattered, leading off the news instead of being buried at the back of a paper. This was the wining formula of *Ms., Ebony, Jet, Black Enterprise, A,* and *Latina.* A slew of gay publications used living with AIDS as the tip of their editorial spears, including *POZ,* which barely preceded the onslaught of disability publications. The business model is enticing: a modest investment in a small editorial staff willing to work for peanuts and the good of the cause who send the production and printing off-site could grow within a few years to a substantial subscriber base and multimillion-dollar ad revenue stream. Many "minority" publications had already been packaged and sold off to huge media concerns, notably *Vibe* and *Ms.,* both of which had garnered substantial returns for the core group of their founding investors. Their business plans spelled out how progress and profit could be compounded.

Nobody is more aware of the business potential as well as the political ramifications than Tari Susan Hartman, who has thirty years of experience on the front lines as a political operative, media executive, and champion of the inclusion of actors with disabilities in Hollywood casting. In this pocket history of the media response to political gains she captures the highs and lows:

> Sitting back on the laurels of our hard-won legislative victories at the south lawn of the White House on a cloud from the ADA victory July 26, 1990, disability pride was in the air, and many of the 2,000 disability rights leaders traveled across country to witness history in the making. We were on top of the world. CNN, AP, all the network and major daily newspapers were there . . . we were finally considered newsworthy! Kick off our shoes and fade out. . . . Circa 1980s: Like other marginalized minority groups, people with disabilities upon realizing independent living issues were not being covered, and/or not covered accurately in mainstream press, set out to form their own specialty media industry and outlets. After all, NPR's Daniel Schorr is right: "If you don't exist in the media, for all practical purposes you don't exist at all." Some reflect the heart and soul of the disability rights movement, and some are still stuck in the medical model hoping for a "cure." Their operating journalistic mandate was "Nothing about us without us," and subscribers are part of the sociopolitical disability rights and independent living movements. Some disability Internet portals came out en masse to cover the tenth anniversary of the signing of the ADA. We were all singing "Kumbaya"—this time with live captioned streaming video. For fifteen minutes of fame, the disability community was sitting pretty, and

each of the sites touted the megabucks to be made by millions of customers
with disabilities who were going to take part in this newfangled e-commerce.
And then the economy tanked, and the casualties of the dot bombs took
the disability portals with them—leaving virtual online ghost towns. Fade
out. . . .[1]

The new disability press delivered coverage that was long overdue in a
tone that was a refreshing mix of pent-up but justifiable anger and celebration without condescension. The voices of "self-advocacy" (a buzz
phrase in the world of developmental disability that originated in Sweden)
overcame the ventriloquists of facilitated communication. Editors and
writers with disabilities were in charge of the copy instead of nondisabled
editorial teams who had for so long relied on a constrained speed-dial
circle of "experts" as sources for the same story over and over. A crop of
star writers rose to the occasion—Kathi Wolfe, Dianne Piastro, Belle Gale
Chevigny, Kenny Fries, George Covington, Paul Longmore, David Mitchell, Mary Johnson among others—and the mere possibility of making a
living as a staffer or freelancer on the disability beat was a sign that the
specialized media had turned the corner. One of the major breakthroughs,
for example, was the syndication of John Callahan's cartoons. Callahan is
based in Portland and associated with the macabre "Northwest school"
that includes Gary Larson and Matt Groening (creator of *The Simpsons*),
and his humor, which often plays on disability themes, is as politically incorrect as it is hilarious. A quadriplegic who cites James Thurber as his
main inspiration, he is not only a nationally known cartoonist but the creator of *Pelswick,* an animated show on Nickelodeon that often features
characters with disabilities, and a sitcom in the works titled *When Quads
Won't Leave,* the promo for which stars Dan Aykroyd. Robin Williams
has long been rumored to be interested in portraying him in a movie.

Once my own magazine was established and I was less worried about
offending readers who might not know about his disability, I gave Callahan the back page for three or four cartoons an issue, and we made him
the cover story for our July–August 2000 edition. As he told me, "I reserve
the right to draw gags about any group or individual, especially about
self-righteous types who presume to defend the disabled. Frankly I don't
care if gags on disability get me run out of town by a mob with pitchforks
and torches, or if they pin a medal on me." The razor's edge Callahan rides
between delivering a strong message and offending even his fellow quads
exemplifies the sharp, clean potential of the disability magazines by contrast with the dull mallet of the mainstream. At its best, the new disability journalism fearlessly cut through the old rhetoric and story formulas
and opened an inner core of highly personal, sensitive issues (community

identity, sex and intimacy, the day-to-day struggle, anxieties and hopes, even physician-assisted suicide) that nondisabled editors or writers had been too timid to approach and generally ill-equipped to understand. That was the editorial promise of the disability magazine boom of the nineties.

Then, as quickly as it had come, it collapsed. By 2001, a dozen magazines had folded, even more Web sites were going without updates for months, freelancers whose bylines were ubiquitous had disappeared, and millions in start-up capital had gone down the tubes. Not coincidentally, the promises of the ADA and independent living, twin pillars of the movement, began to totter under heavy challenges from lobbying groups that had long opposed them. Courts retreated from enforcing the law, schools balked at following through on integration (citing lack of state funds), and federal health care policies shifted away from patients' rights. Today the community once again finds itself facing marginality—most frighteningly through the renewed threat of institutionalization ("warehousing") for people with the most severe disabilities. The demise of so many of the best disability publications, whose success might have signaled changes that in turn could have been solidified through the dissemination of imagery and voices that would have brought about the necessary alterations in attitude, just confirmed what the naysayers had all along predicted, linking disability with inability. Having presided over one of the failed publications, whose rise and demise is examined in detail in the next chapter, I am reluctant to summarily dismiss the failures as the due comeuppance of inept amateurs who had it coming because their product was less than stellar and they could not hold their readers or advertisers. Most of the magazines that went down in flames were actually the best editorial and graphic packages, while the ones with weaker writing, careless editing, and uninspired design (notably *Ability* magazine) survive to this day.

Our own view was that *WE* had to be better than its mainstream competitors to flip the stereotypical assumption that blind, deaf, or developmentally disabled people could not get the job done. What took longer to realize was the fact that it is not just the quality of the writing and the design that determines whether or not a magazine survives. The business logic behind the steep attrition rate in magazine publishing is relatively simple. Blowing a large budget on expensive design and printing, overestimating one's projected revenues, and fudging circulation figures while paying top freelance dollar to writers and photographers is a recipe for failure if the readers fail to materialize. The year my first issue made its debut along with another glossy disability magazine called *Enable,* which lasted less than a year, we joined a staggering 852 other magazine start-ups, all launched in the same speculative fervor and virtually all doomed to almost instant extinction because we were all in hot pursuit of the same tight ad budgets, overcrowded newsstand space, free publicity, and overwhelmed reading public. The afternoon I visited the top magazine buyer in the New York headquarters of Barnes and Noble to explain to him the importance of placing my magazine in a rack within reach of wheelchair users, he smiled and unfurled a banner-length computer printout of the eight thousand or so other titles he had to stock that very month. Ironically, the coup de grâce for *WE* magazine after four years of continuous publishing was a failed trademark-infringement lawsuit brought against Rainbow Media Holdings and Cablevision, which had just launched the We (Women's Entertainment) television network. One minority media company shoved the other out of the way. These niches turn into tight quarters in a recession.

The rise and fall of the disability magazines rode the waves of a larger business trend. The boom coincided with the run-and-gun days of magazine publishing when even the *New Yorker* was losing $12 million a year (but packing up to move into its gleaming, massive new Times Square headquarters). Tina Brown, briefly editor in chief of the *New Yorker,* was the epitome of buzz. As John Seabrook, a *New Yorker* writer who watched her (with trepidation) come and (with relief) go, observed in his critique of the magazine's change from arbiter of culture to "nobrow" marketing machine: "The old distinction between the elite culture of the aristocrats and the commercial culture of the masses was torn down, and in its place was erected a hierarchy of hotness."[2] Disability was hot in 1990. That is why advertisers were jumping onto the bandwagon, Robin Williams's agent was lining up a movie about Callahan, philanthropic dollars were pouring into spinal cord research, and a dozen or so entrepreneurs with little publishing experience could talk their private bankers into opening lines of credit to start disability magazines. Staying hot is the problem, though. Well before September 11, 2001, I would argue, disability had missed its golden opportunity to cash in on the buzz. The movie deals were shelved, the plugs were pulled on magazines and Web sites, the loans were called in. The fickle public that probably was never ready for disability in the first place had returned to its fascination with the body perfect (shows and magazines devoted to plastic surgery). Like the brief flare of the Harlem Renaissance in the twenties that anticipated the rise of Black Power in the sixties, we were all a little ahead of our time, and perhaps it will be decades before a viable disability media will have its next chance, although I fervently hope it will not take that long. The missed opportunity has consequences, because the shrinkage in magazines abrogated the strategic advantage of supporting a disability press that could mount an attack against the political and economic forces holding back the community.

Déjà Vu

It had all happened before. In her provocative article comparing the rise and fall of two early magazines covering the blind community, "The Outlook of *The Problem* and the Problem of the *Outlook*," historian Catherine J. Kudlick describes a polarity between advocacy and service missions that accurately predicts the reigning dichotomy in today's disability publications, some of which emphasize the power of people with disabilities while others implore a nondisabled readership to exercise its power on behalf of people with disabilities. In January of 1900 a new journal called *The Problem* was started in Leavenworth, Kansas, by the American Blind People's Higher Education and General Improvement Association. Its publisher was D. Wallace McGill, a blind professor of music theory and psychology at Kansas Conservatory. The message of *The Problem* was one of inclusion and assimilation. McGill used political coverage to promote suffrage, mainstreaming in schools, and a strong sense of the community's identity. Lasting only three years, the journal nonetheless, according to Kudlick, had a strong impact on the movement to recognize the rights of blind people, largely because it emphasized, for the first time in print, their potential rather than the pathos that generated charitable dollars. Kudlick compares *The Problem* to *The Crisis*, the motivational magazine W. E. B. Dubois edited for the National Association for the Advancement of Colored People.

By 1907, a substantially different magazine, its glossy pages loaded with both photographs and advertisements, made its debut. Called *Outlook*, and edited by Charles F. F. Campbell, an entrepreneur who was the sighted son of a blind educator, it made *The Problem* look sadly amateurish. As Kudlick observes, *The Problem* was designed to appeal to the ear, to be read aloud to blind people, while *Outlook* was for the eye. The former referred to "blind people," the latter to "the blind," emphasizing the difference between what could be done "by" or "for" them in a magazine "about" them. What a difference a preposition can make. Much of *Outlook*'s contents consisted of letters from blind people followed by analyses by sighted professionals, whose crusades against the limitations of blindness were the main agenda. In time, *Outlook* became the house organ and national fundraising weapon for the American Foundation for the Blind, to this day one of the most powerful and effective service organizations. The view of *Outlook*, which was always run by a sighted editor in chief, was that the public perception of blindness had to change before the situation of blind people could improve. In journalistic terms, the magazine leaned heavily on profiles of successful blind people—Helen Keller became a fixture in its pages—going to college, holding jobs, and competing in sports. These were the "supercrips" of their day. Preeminent among them was Keller, a nationally known activist and literary sensation who became the star of the magazine. Her signature was one of the recurring graphic elements reproduced in its pages. Needless to say, *Outlook* long outlasted *The Problem,* which breathed its last after publishing for only three years. Today there are actually three publications called *Outlook:* two are freebies (from the Foundation for the Junior Blind in Los Angeles and the National Eye Institute in Bethesda, Maryland) while the third is the house organ for the Sight-Loss Support Group in State College, Pennsylvania.

Despite their differences, the magazines broke new ground in the field of the media, forcing a new openness on the part of both the blind community and the broader readership they were hoping to address, for the first time using celebrities such as Keller to carve out a public space for others who would be identified as blind. To build the kind of drama that attracted mass audiences, there was an emphasis on performance, with constant variations on the theme of the "miracle of overcoming." The trade-off for creating this spectacle was expanded awareness of all blind people and an opportunity to score gains in such practical matters as getting jobs (still a critical problem) and voting. These magazines helped precipitate considerable signs of progress in an era when the benefits of eugenics were often debated in the press. As Kudlick writes, both publications "assumed blindness would be *the* defining factor in a person's life. For one of the first times in history, these journals argued that this characteristic, always understood as personal and private, might have significant political ramifications. In effect, people like McGill, Campbell, and all those who spoke out in their publications were coming to articulate a reciprocal relationship between a person's sense of self and the wider world of interest groups and experts."[3]

It would be glib but fairly accurate to say that nothing has changed in the century since the glitzy *Outlook* stomped on *The Problem.* Many of the characteristics of today's disability press are found in this anecdote. Eccentric entrepreneurs venture into magazine publishing, sometimes for altruistic reasons, more often to make a killing through circulation and ad revenues if not through an equity sale after building the company. They either take a shot at creating a lavish "book" with high (high-gloss, picture-heavy) production values, or cheap it out with unpaid writers and a physically scruffy print job, paying little attention to graphic design or the "package." Not surprisingly, the glossy attracts major advertisers from the mainstream corporate world, while the advocacy publication chugs along with no ads or modest ones from companies and organizations that serve the community alone. The readership of the latter is tightly bound to the community of that one disability, while the glossy ambitiously targets a broader base. Sometimes this expanded audience is the utopian "pandisability" community of people with all sorts of disabilities, plus their families and friends, and sometimes it is the even vaster sea of non-disabled readers who seek to know more about the experience of living with blindness, hearing loss, mobility impairment, or so-called mental conditions. Editorially, the distinction between these two approaches alters everything from story ideas to language and photo choices. In both cases, however, there is a heavy emphasis on first-person narratives and profiles. The traditional disability-specific magazine concentrates on "service" articles about diagnosis, rehab, and coping with disability along with institutional profiles of the organizations that help out. The dramatis personae of the mass-media publications from issue to issue tend heavily to be the superstars whose performances—athletic, musical, artistic, intellectual—seem miraculous to the mainstream but are not always revered in the community. The most radical publications tend toward political advocacy and the stories of more "typical" people—such as farmers, teachers, midlevel businesspeople—whose modest gains are signs of success for the community and whose frustrations are related to discrimination. Until recently, both types of publications relied heavily on medical stories for content, with the glossies going for the miracle cure stories while the service publications concentrated on devices or procedures that make living with a disability easier, rather than promoting the eradication of the disability. The more advanced publications, in terms of disability ideology, have moved past the medical model and make a point of eschewing research stories because the implication is that disability is a problem to be solved or cured, a no-no in the culture.

The brief life of most independent publications is a given. Those that have the odds most heavily stacked against them are the ones that try to make a commercial go of it. There is far greater security in the other side of the game, where publications devoted to fundraising get ad revenues from major service-providing institutions as well as corporations that toss a few thousand their way out of guilt and the hope for goodwill. Most of the history of disability media has been dominated by the "bom" (benefit of membership), a periodical issued by a nonprofit to stimulate giving. As with "controlled circulation" publications that are distributed free to mailing lists, boms fall into a separate category from the magazines that rely on newsstand sales, subscribers, and advertisers. It is far easier to put out a bom or freebie than it is to make it on the newsstand. In the shake-out after many of the more speculative for-profit magazines of the nineties folded, there was a return to the bom and the newsletter as the dominant bracket of publications. Although many of the boms are nicely produced and promulgate valuable information, they strike me as less viable test cases of the merits of the disability media. Like the "paratransit" systems that run alongside the public transit systems in certain cities, using vans instead of investing in accessible buses and subways, the boms are part of a "paramedia" universe that suspends the rules.

Up Close and Personal

There are certain inherent strengths in the specialty press covering disability. Staying close to your readership is the privilege of a community magazine, whereas losing contact can spell the beginning of the end for publishers just as it does for massive retailers. Most disability-specific publications, shows (notably, *On a Roll Radio,* a syndicated weekly call-in show hosted by Greg Smith), and Web sites are blessed by a high degree of interaction between audience and editor or host. Through letters, pitched stories, or invitations to write, readers often find themselves with bylines inside the magazine or an opportunity to be on air. This intimate bond with the audience has the obvious economic benefit of improving ratings or circulation (a key measure of a magazine's success is the percentage of subscriber's who re-up for another year when their subscription runs out), but it also lends credibility to the copy. A decade before silly "reality" television assailed the airwaves, the disability media provided reality media of a testimonial nature.

For the practice of journalism, this kind of partnership with the community is a mixed blessing. A disability magazine or program has a distinct advantage when reaching out to sources. The point of contact that shared experience affords can narrow the gap between interviewer and source that so often leads to misunderstanding in the mainstream press. But such closeness also raises issues of objectivity, issues that any "alternative" press has to endure. If the accord between sources and writers is too homogenously sympathetic, the effects can be cloying and repetitive. Simply "preaching to the choir" rarely makes for compelling journalism and lacks leverage with the decision makers outside the tight circle of initiates.

The alternative is to attempt to engage what editors call the "neutral" reader who, like a blank page, may not be as well informed on the issue but who presents a greater challenge to the writer. Proximity to sources, on the one hand, yields privileged information, the inside dope, in a conversation between two individuals who know the code and can go directly to matters of urgency and importance. Given the shallowness of most journalism on such significant issues as health care policy, legal rights, and discrimination, this can be a blessing for informed readers who crave more than the fifteen-second quick hit the evening television news tosses their way. Political junkies devour their Sunday morning talk shows, sports fans listen to each other call in on radio shows, hobbyists bookmark their favorite Web sites for that bit of arcane lore or fresh innovation that the abridged news sources are bound to miss. There is an appalling lack of detail in most current news coverage, and specialized publications are the best remedy for the problem. A reporter and a source who both have spinal cord injuries or cochlear implants ideally start from a different point in the conversation and cover the ground on the way to more sophisticated questions and answers far faster. A prime example of this in the disability press is the way in which it assumes everybody is on the same page in viewing the ADA as a civil rights law governing discrimination and not, as many newspapers and television news teams continue to present it, a benefits law making you eligible for Social Security payments or parking spaces. This gives the advantage in political and legal coverage to such publications as *Mouth, The Ragged Edge,* or *New Mobility,* which regularly beat local newspapers or newsmagazines to the best interpretive stories on recent Supreme Court decisions in ADA cases.

On the other hand, snug complicity between writer and source takes the edge off the critical and analytical skills that are also a part of covering a story, which is why a prime criterion of credibility is how close an interviewer and interviewee are. For example, when *Esquire* magazine sent Robert Stone to cover the denouement of the strange pilgrimage of Ken Kesey and his merry pranksters in 1966, the editor ended up killing the story when it was submitted. "They thought I had gone native on the story, and of course I had been pretty native to begin with," Stone recalled later.[4] The responsibility for making the final call on this matter is often the editor's. Stone had dropped too much acid and become part of the story he was supposed to be covering. Even after the New Journalism flagrantly smashed the rules of objective reporting in favor of getting humorous or flashy copy, epitomized by the writing of Hunter S. Thompson, most readers who are outside of the circle rely on the journalist to stand back at some point and balance the story by asking the sources uncomfortable questions. Without pointing fingers, I would say that many of the leading journalists in the community have gone too far in the cozying-up direction for their own good, sacrificing credibility for impact.

The balancing act of traditional reporting brings to mind a cautionary paragraph from Goffman's *Stigma,* as current today as it was in the sixties when it was first published. Focusing on the duality of inside and outside, Goffman reminds us that managing stigma is largely a question of what happens in public. Mass-media vehicles such as magazines are a paradigmatic example of how this plays in the mainstream. Early in the book he spells out the stylistic formula for representing the stigmatized in print. As a cautionary tale, for me as the editor in chief of a magazine that aspired to a general readership, it was like an arrow whizzing by the ear of a deer:

> Often those with a particular stigma sponsor a publication of some kind which gives voice to shared feelings, consolidating and stabilizing for the reader his sense of the realness of "his" group and his attachment to it. Here the ideology of the members is formulated—their complaints, their aspirations, their politics. The names of well-known friends and enemies of the "group" are cited, along with information to confirm the goodness and the badness of these people. Success stories are printed, tales of heroes of assimilation who have penetrated new areas of normal acceptance. Atrocity tales are recorded, recent and historic, of extreme mistreatment by normals. Exemplary moral tales are provided in biographical and autobiographical form illustrating a desirable code of conduct for the stigmatized. The publication also serves as a forum for presenting some division of opinion as to how the situation of the stigmatized person ought best to be handled.[5]

While Goffman's sketch of a disability magazine does not sound all that dreadful, its subtext is a deepening division between the "normals" and the community, spanned by the anomalous but not impossible incidents of assimilation. Clearly not all disability publications hold assimilation as a goal, and many of the most respected, by advocates of disability culture, are vehemently opposed to such a notion. They provide a forum for venting against the "outside," to use Goffman's schema. From the point of view of this study in particular, one of the reasons the disability media are so valuable involves the way they provide a critical perspective on the mainstream media's coverage of community issues. Because no media organization has ever bothered to formally assess its shortcomings in this area (as they often have, conspicuously, with respect to coverage of other minorities), the role of watchdog is especially suited to the disability press, which has approached the task with tenacity and alertness. The terriers in the pack are *Mouth,* a bimonthly with just under seven thousand readers published in Topeka, Kansas, and *Ragged Edge,* a bimonthly that used to be distributed in print to three thousand readers (on disk for blind readers) and now is available only on the Web, reflecting the fiscal exigencies of printing and mailing even a small-circulation publication. *Mouth* was launched in 1990 as "The Voice of the Disability Nation." Its in-your-face credo holds that there is no editorial reason to attempt to catch more flies with honey:

> *Mouth* brings the conversation down to street level, where well-intentioned "special" programs wreak havoc in the lives of ordinary people. People talk about calling a spade a spade. We call Jack Kevorkian a serial killer. And

when maggots outnumber nurses' aides at what others call a "care facility," we call it a hellhole. We say it out loud: If special education is so darned special, every kid in every school ought to have the benefit of it. Some folks call the *Mouth* radical. We think simpleminded is a better epithet. Remember the other George Bush, when he campaigned in a supermarket and discovered that remarkable new checkout scanning technology? The man hadn't been to the grocery store since he was knee-high to a political consultant. Do-gooders are exactly that much out of touch with the helping system that they themselves operate. Ask the next do-gooder you meet: Have you checked yourself into a nursing home lately? Tried to board an "accessible" bus in a wheelchair? Filed an ADA complaint with the U.S. Department of Justice? Asked a charity for actual help?

The older and less successful publication, *Ragged Edge,* started in 1980 as a fiercely independent publication, has as its editor in chief an advocate named Mary Johnson, who is one of the most frequently cited spokespeople for the community (she has had bylines in *USA Today,* the *Nation,* the *New York Times,* and the *Columbia Journalism Review*). If experience in the field is the most important criterion for editorial expertise, then Johnson tops the list of disability editors. She has been in this game for three decades, starting as a researcher with Prime Movers, a Louisville-based nonprofit that specializes in data reports on disability trends. She also helped found Louisville's Center for Accessible Living. She and her writers are unapologetically adversarial toward the government, the mainstream press, and those who just don't get it. The subscriber base may not be large enough to float a print edition any longer, but the readers who check in daily online are staunchly loyal.

From Sex to Suicide

Certain stories are vastly more convincingly and effectively handled by the disability press than by the mainstream. Indeed, a breakthrough in the press coverage of disability came about in the 1990s as the result of a particularly grim sequence of events that was handled with immense capability by the specialized disability media even as the mainstream seesawed between despicable sensationalism and more serious inquiry. Jack Kevorkian's "mercy machine," which he delivered in a Volkswagen van mainly in Michigan, where the courts were less likely to put him in jail, was used to assist eight people with disabilities to die in 1992, and more in 1993. An advocacy group called Not Dead Yet took on Kevorkian in a series of demonstrations that drew national headlines. Even longtime advocates were impressed by the significance not only of the political action, which briefly recalled the fervor over the ADA, but of the response. Evan Kemp Jr., the former U.S. Equal Employment Opportunity Commission chairman, thought the media exposure was significant: "It's the first time that the media took us seriously," he says. "They adequately reported our views; they didn't treat us as children."

Physician-assisted suicide (known in the community as PAS or PAD, for death) is an issue that can spontaneously unite or divide a group, depending heavily on the way in which it is presented. The challenge for writers, editors, and graphic designers who want to hold on to their readership is not simply taking a pro or con position on legality or morality but finding an appropriate tone, dignified and not inflammatory, shaded by nuance, factual without being clinical and callous. The morbid immaturity of the worst print and television stories that chronicled the progression of Kevorkian's assisted suicides across the Midwest in the summer of 1992 was typified by the cartoonlike Doctor Death theme. One exception to this dearth of sensible coverage was a PBS series airing in late 2000, *On Our Own Terms,* hosted by Bill Moyers and featuring interviews with terminally ill patients, their families, and caregivers, many of them facing the crunch between the costs of hospice care and medication and the limits of their health care coverage. Much of Moyers's best work in the four-part series is devoted to palliative care and the management of pain, but the third segment is devoted to physician-assisted suicide, which Moyers gives a surprisingly affirmative spin.

Yet the best coverage given to the issue by far was found in the pages of *New Mobility* magazine. Now the leading magazine in the community by default after so many others have collapsed, it is a monthly published in Santa Monica, California, with an impressive circulation holding steady at twenty-four thousand (down a third from the nineties, despite going after the lists of the departed magazines) and a relatively lengthy track record, having survived since 1989. Devoted since its inception to the needs of wheelchair users, it is not a cross-disability publication. In my view it should be a better magazine overall than it is, but lack of competition and a folksy populism have kept its graphic and writing standards at the same level for nearly two decades. Under pressure from the competition's higher production standards in the midnineties, *New Mobility* lured readers with a distinct upgrade in print and graphic quality, at least on the covers. By that time the publisher, Sam Maddox, and editor in chief, Tim Gilmer, seemed to have two things on their mind: sex and death. Cover after cover was given over to either Eros or Thanatos, and the come-on taglines ("Facilitated Sex") were provocative.

Yet Maddox and Gilmer beat us all hands down in the long series of stories they devoted to suicide. *WE* blinked because the subject was a downer that would have seemed jarring in all our upbeat, can-do stories about visiting Vienna or climbing the corporate ladder. By contrast, *New Mobility* expended tens of thousands of words in its cover package for the April 1997 issue on features, forums, letters and op-eds in what is still the most comprehensive discussion in a magazine of the problem. The scope of this controversy is too complex to be fully laid out in these pages, which will stay closer to the technical aspect of the options that were available to journalists in their coverage. One editorial strategy is the straight-shooting advocacy treatment, picking a side and blasting away in absolutes. As the community position remains essentially one of opposition to physician-assisted suicide on the grounds that it denies value to a life with disability, turning over the pages to an impassioned voice from, for example, the advocacy group Not Dead Yet would have garnered instant applause from the core readership. By contrast, a dispassionate legal, political, or even medical review of the events, rules, and even techniques would have taken opinion out of the mix and delivered the homogeneously factual (if boring) content that many news analysts favor. Each of these strategies offered the easy way out.

To its credit, *New Mobility* opened up more pages than are generally budgeted for such a dark subject, which is difficult not only to illustrate but also to support through related advertising. Rather than turn all that space over to one strident voice or chorus, the editors admirably split the copy, drawing on sources on both sides and, by letting them go at it at length, encouraging them to plumb depths and subtleties that were completely out of the reach of the mainstream press. The highlight of the issue was a long exchange between Paul Longmore, a scholar and heavy hitter in the movement, and Andrew Batavia, a Miami Beach–based attorney and health care policy wonk who favored the legalization of physician-assisted suicide, not just for the terminally ill. Both had disabilities— Longmore had polio and uses a ventilator while Batavia (who has died since) was a high quad (upper-cervical quadriplegic). During a conference call taped for the magazine they held what remains the most interesting and informed debate on the topic, which the *New Mobility* editor, Barry Corbett, had the good sense to run without extensive cutting and with subheads subtly dropped in. Here is a sample of their candid and balanced exchange. The excerpt is taken from midway in the piece, after Longmore and Batavia have traversed the legal territory of some of the recent Supreme Court decisions regarding the right to die as well as the labyrinthine policy restrictions of prevailing medical care systems. All this is material in which one might safely presume Batavia would enjoy a professional edge, yet Longmore more than holds his own, and pushes the envelope to include people with disabilities who are not necessarily terminally ill, a touchy ethical question in the face of the fact that Kevorkian had helped a quadriplegic and a woman with Alzheimer's who were not strictly at the "terminal" stage:

PL: Drew, I'm puzzled by one thing. You started out saying that the issue before the court is physician-assisted suicide for competent, terminally ill people, but what you're now talking about is that same right for people with disabilities as well. Is that your position?

AB: With respect to a constitutional right to physician assistance, I would probably limit it to terminally ill individuals. I do believe that people with disabilities who are not terminally ill should also have that right in states that pass appropriate legislation with adequate safeguards.

PL: Part of the disagreement we have is our analysis of the general situation and condition of people with disabilities. I think that we live in a society that is deeply prejudiced against us, and that we are an oppressed minority.

AB: I have major problems with this notion of societal oppression and how that somehow precludes an individual from making a rational choice. The fact is that there are a multitude of ways in which our society doesn't fully meet the needs of people with disabilities, but I find it extremely dangerous to say that, for that reason, disabled people shouldn't be able to make fundamental choices about their lives. If a state tells me I can't end my life if I'm terminally ill, the state is oppressing me.

PL: It's one thing to make fundamental choices; it's another thing to have the society that's oppressing us set up mechanisms to facilitate our suicides. Any society that would guarantee assistance in committing suicide by an oppressed person is simply indicating just how oppressive and hypocritical it is.

AB: There are some fascists out there, but overall, I don't think that's accurate at all. I believe that we'll end up with a better health care system and a more responsible society if people are given their rights to autonomy over their lives.

PL: I'm not worried about the fascists, I'm worried about a health care system that is profit-driven and is trying to ration health care. And I think it's naive to think that a health care system that is becoming more profit-driven and more unjust is somehow going to become more fair and equitable because the people the system is trying to deny care to are granted the right to end their lives more quickly.

AB: People with terminal illnesses and people with disabilities, once they have this right, are going to shout out loud that this system stinks! And I think the press will pick up on that and ultimately there will be strong political pressures to improve the system.

What makes this chunk of dialogue so interesting is not just the fact that both speakers are people with disabilities who eloquently deliver their convictions and are not afraid to disagree. Look how quickly the point-counterpoint moves past politics and law to embrace sociology, medical ethics, and policy, and even media issues. An editor would be hard-pressed to discover one writer capable of pulling together even a multisource story that has this kind of balance and fairness together with passion. Many magazines would find it tempting to stack the deck in favor of their position, but *New Mobility* uses a hands-off editorial approach that turns out to bolster its antisuicide position by demonstrating editorial fearlessness. More press devoted to disability ought to reach this level of candor and insight, including the humility of Corbett's postscript:

> As abbreviated here, this debate represents a deep ethical and philosophical split within the disability community. If even these two advocates—who have clearly demonstrated their commitment to disability rights for years—can have such contrary perceptions of the disability experience and reach such different conclusions, don't we all need to carefully examine our own opinions? Does the disability community have a consistent party line on assisted suicide? Should it? Are there solutions that would protect the rights of people on both sides? This issue shrugs off easy, packaged answers, and demands that light be shed.

The issue includes several other features, sidebars, and first-person stories on PAS. The best of them is a long feature by the journalist Kathi Wolfe on the Not Dead Yet protests against PAS and Kevorkian in Washington the year before. Wolfe's antisuicide stance is disclosed early in the article, and the slight majority of her sources are in her camp, but she broadened the base of her article to include a number of prosuicide sources as well. In presenting the Not Dead Yet point of view she uses quotes from one of the founders, Diane Coleman, as well as activists such as Longmore, Bob Liston, Carol Gill (a psychologist and well-known voice in the movement), the distinguished Evan Kemp, the former surgeon general C. Everett Koop, and Stephen Gold, another attorney. She gives equal space to dissenters, including one brief (and self-condemning) quote from a court statement by Kevorkian as well as others from Batavia, Bruce Bartlow, and, surprisingly, Hugh Gallagher, author of *By Trust Betrayed,* a book on Nazi euthanasia. Finally Wolfe throws the matter open to the masses, using the results of a survey of *New Mobility* readers conducted by e-mail that narrowly supported her position, by 53 percent to 42. She finds it interesting that 64 percent of respondents worried that assisted suicide would be selectively applied to people with disabilities.

Within the context of an issue of the magazine almost completely devoted to PAS, it is a superbly presented, meticulously researched, and tightly argued piece, a model of journalistic principles.

The *New Mobility* articles are not the final word on this hot-button issue, which has been described as the *Roe v. Wade* of the disability community. In a subsequent issue of *Mouth,* the more radical disability publication, the nondisabled journalist Nat Hentoff expressed his own fear of the coercion of people with disabilities (and parents of children) into physician-assisted suicide, and related it to his pro-life stance: "The ease with which *Roe v. Wade* allows millions of potential human beings to be killed has helped accelerate the culture of death. Once you get used to killing in that way, it's not so difficult to move on, to disrespect human life that's unlike yours or doesn't look like it's going to develop the way you think human life should develop." The disability press was particularly alert to the representation of the community in media coverage of the PAS controversy. In the fall of 2003, *Mouth* took on the Terri Schiavo controversy in Florida (her husband, Michael Schiavo, went to court to have her removed from life support, arguing that it was her wish) and was especially strong on critically monitoring the mainstream press coverage in the Florida papers, the *New York Times,* the Associated Press, and on television ("Media Freakin' on Terri Schiavo"). Mary Johnson launched a scathing series of editorials on the way that the media missed, yet again, the disability rights angle in their coverage of the story.

When the *New York Times Magazine,* earlier that year, put attorney (specializing in Social Security and disability rights cases) Harriet McBryde Johnson's aggressively anti-eugenics article on the cover of its February 16 issue, it prompted *New Mobility* to name Johnson its Person of the Year. During 2003 Johnson actually published two articles in the *New York Times Magazine* (the second, in November, was "The Disablity Gulag," a harrowing look at institutionalization). The first article tracked her Michael Moorish encounter with the controversial Princeton bioethicist Peter Singer, who advocates euthanizing children with severe disabilities (Johnson was born with muscular dystrophy). When it appeared, the nytimes.com message board exploded with more than six hundred responses. The *New Mobility* profile of Johnson that appeared in the May 2004 issue was a solid piece of media criticism. It quoted Carol Gill on the impact of the cover story: "It was a ground-breaking article. It was incredibly reassuring and pride-making to see a really gimped-up woman on the cover of *The New York Times Magazine.* She may not have changed Singer's mind, but she changed a lot of other people's minds." The *New Mobility* piece, written by Mike Ervin, also reached Johnson's editor at the *Times,* Katherine Bouton, who expressed her admiration for Johnson's "total lack of self-pity," and it revealed a fascinating behind-the-byline account of the long evolution of the article. After two civil encounters with Singer, Johnson struggled to write a critical essay focusing on the debate rather than the personal context of her own situation and her feelings about facing Singer's assumption that she was "suffering" and "worse off." That version of the story gobbled up ten thousand words, an exceptional length for any magazine piece. The first editor who saw it was Barry Corbett at *New Mobility*, who turned down her invitation to cut it and make it publishable and also, much to my own surprise, urged her to send it to a mainstream publication. "What I saw was a richly developed story with back stories that were essential to understanding it. Losing the back stories would be losing the story. And I was impressed how generous Harriet was to Singer without giving away the farm. It was such a flawless piece that I saw no reason to mess with it," Corbett told his own writer in a piece about how this landmark article eventually landed in the *New York Times Magazine* (after an "encouraging rejection" from the *Atlantic Monthly*). There is something endearing about a magazine that covers its own willingness to pass up what became a *New York Times Magazine* cover story.

Not all disability magazines are as interesting or admirable as *New Mobility*. If its own circulation figures are to be believed, the 165,000 readers of *Ability* magazine, a bimonthly, for-profit independent published by Chet Cooper out of Irvine, California, is the eight hundred-pound gorilla on the disability shelf. Started in 1991, it was the first in the wave of new magazines to appear in the nineties, all at the same newsstand and subscription prices (around $30 for six issues, $4 on the newsstand) and attracting corporate advertising from, for example, General Motors and Hyatt Hotels. As the only independent disability publication to break the barrier of 100,000 readers and successfully ride out the downturn in ad pages after September 11, 2001, *Ability* deserves some credit for sticking to a successful formula. In terms of journalistic standards, however, and measured against the criteria we have set for the unsentimental depiction of disability culture, it falls far short of the mark that an influential national magazine should reach. The emphasis in *Ability* is on "human potential," and nearly every story has an "overcoming" angle. As my own magazine did, *Ability* leads each issue with a celebrity cover story, including recent pieces on Montel Williams, Donny and Marie Osmond (one cover each), Kirk Douglas, Danny Glover, Christopher and Dana Reeve (one cover each), Camryn Manheim, Naomi Judd, Ray Charles, Gregory Hines, and Elizabeth Taylor. Based near Hollywood, the magazine has a penchant for poolside chats with movie stars that are turned into puff pieces heavy on the "gee whiz you beat the diagnosis" plotline. As with

Andy Warhol's *Interview* magazine, another sappy fanzine, *Ability* leaves the transcripts in question-and-answer format for the cover story, a practice I always felt connoted editorial laziness. Worse still, the soft questions and saccharine, goody-for-you exchanges provide a cloying evasion of the realities of disability. The quality of a journalist's work always comes down to the quality of the questions posed. Flipping through years of *Ability* issues, I never found one hardball question, and only an interview with James Wolfensohn, chairman of the World Bank (a figure I also interviewed) had sufficient substance. To spoon out this sugar at length is to risk diabetic shock, but here is a quick taste from the Naomi Judd cover story. Its author, Jane Rusoff, sets up the interview in this way:

> Five years ago, at the peak of her career, she was forced to retire when she was diagnosed with potentially life-threatening liver disease. But this former registered nurse refused to accept the doctor's prognosis that she would live only three more years: she launched her own health regimen to boost her immune system through the mind-body-spirit connection. Today, physicians are amazed at her remission level.

With that, we are off and running with a "miracle" lesson in the heroic pattern of triumphing over disability interlaced with what disability advocates would call a heavy undertone of the "medical model," a cocktail of two of the most despised tendencies journalism follows when covering disability. This is the signature offering of *Ability,* which serves up hope and inspiration issue after issue:

JR: Naomi, How are you sharing with others the method of self-healing that's helped you?

NJ: I'm on the lecture circuit. I get out and talk to people. I call it The Exquisite Reality. . . . I try to tell them about the spirit-mind-body connection.

JR: What else have you been up to?

NJ: I've been meeting with the most brilliant minds in America in this field. . . . I met with the head of UCLA's Psychoneuroimmunology Program formed by Norman Cousins—he's a close personal friend—Dr. Deepak Chopra, the main doctor in the mind-body field now, or at least the most visible. So I'm hanging out with all these people who are so in tune with the fact that wellness is not a materialistic pursuit; it's a spiritual pursuit.

JR: What's the goal?

NJ: Peace of mind. If a boy comes up to me in the grocery store and says, "I've got AIDS," or if a woman comes up to me in the airport and says,

"I've got metastatic breast cancer," or some other person who has liver disease like I do, I wish that I could bring them home and sit them at my kitchen table and say, "Tell me your whole story." But I don't have that luxury, so what I try to say to them, in 30 seconds, is that peace isn't just the absence of a conflict. Peace is the ability to deal with it. . . . I constantly find myself alone and starting over again. And when I can't change the way things are, I've learned how to change the way I feel about them.

JR: Is there anything special you do to stay so beautiful?

NJ: The only thing I can tell you is that I've never smoked a cigarette, and I've never drunk a beer. I laugh all the time. I have inner peace . . . there's nothing different about me. There is absolutely nothing special about Naomi Judd. . . . I am not a magical being.

A little of this goes a long way, especially by utterly unfair comparison with the deeply intelligent exchange between Longmore and Battavia offered earlier. Just a cursory glance through the questions in the other cover profiles is equally nauseating, and the brief introductions can be insulting vis-à-vis disability etiquette. Here is the setup for an interview with Montel Williams, who has MS: "With his well-conditioned physique and captivating presence, he doesn't look like a person battling a sometimes debilitating illness." Not surprisingly, the copy, which generally should have had at least another editorial pass judging from the errors that riddle it, is heavy on "inspiration." Here is the syrupy lead-in to the Mary Tyler Moore profile: "We spoke to Mary about her work and her passions and in the end found that a lot of what is inside the real Mary Tyler Moore, despite all the challenging times she has had, really is that happy inspiring screen presence we have come to know over the past thirty-five years." I will spare you the drivel that followed. The last laugh, however, is the magazine's—with the access to celebrities that a reputation for softball interviewing guarantees, with 165,000 readers eager to drink this Kool-Aid, and with a willing retinue of A-list advertisers to pay the bill, it has accomplished what no other disability publication has been able to do as a successful business.

The Bom Shelters

Not all magazines have to worry about advertisers and circulation. Each of the massive nonprofits has its in-house media crew turning out Web copy, newsletters, and magazines. Most of these bom (benefit of membership) publications, which often have massive print runs in the tens or hundreds of thousands, making them some of the biggest players in disability publishing by size, are just glorified begging letters, as relentlessly boring as they are paternalistic. There are exceptions, however. Among the major house organs for nonprofits, one of the best in terms of editorial content is *Quest,* a magazine produced bimonthly by the Muscular Dystrophy Association for 115,000 readers who receive it free if they are on the MDA solicitation list. It was launched in 1994 just as many other glossy magazines that were physically similar, including *Deaf Life* and *WE,* were trying out the same recipe of snazzy graphics and expensive paper stock. Paid advertisers help defray the costs of the glossy print job, which, judging from my own experience, has to set them back around a dollar a copy. The editorial policy of *Quest* and other magazines like it (such as the gargantuan *Inside MS,* 700,000 copies of which are printed quarterly for the National MS Society, or the relatively puny *inMotion* for the 35,000 members of the Amputee Coalition of America) has to strike an uneasy balance between service pieces on recent research the organization sponsored and fundraising copy, which has traditionally worked the pity angle. *Quest* may reach 400,000 people (the standard industry rule is to multiply your circulation by four to account for "pass-alongs"), but I doubt that it's read as closely as the tiny advocacy publications.

A more admirable and closely followed bom is *PN/Paraplegia News,* the glossy monthly distributed by the Paralyzed Veterans of America, one of the largest and most politically active nonprofits. Partly because it was a pioneer in the disability media field (founded in 1946) and partly because it is particularly aggressive in its coverage and commentary on policy issues, *PN* is widely respected in the field. Its circulation has dwindled to 24,000 from about three times that figure just a decade ago, but it has a core group of advertisers as well as the massive budget of the PVA to ensure its survival. The PVA also puts out *Sports 'N Spokes,* a bimonthly version of *Sports Illustrated* for wheelchair athletes that reaches 14,000 readers. This spin-off has being going strong since 1975, with steady ad revenues from athletic-gear manufacturers and other equipment sources. As a jock and a fan of wheelchair athletics (I covered the last Paralympics in Sydney), I enjoy this well-written magazine, which diligently collects race and tournament results from across the United States and offers bonus issues on the Paralympics. As a former editor, I also feel that the best place for extended sports coverage is a stand-alone publication such as this, having suffered through the unpleasant experience of watching sports coverage overrun the political, cultural, and service content of the Web site associated with my own magazine. Since *Sports 'N Spokes* has found its wavelength for a core group of subscribers, enough to sustain the publication and satisfy the advertisers, it has proven that there is a viable market for disability sports journalism. However, as I was frequently reminded by advocates and readers, the overwhelming majority of readers with disabilities who read general-interest publications are not attuned to sports, and many find the focus on sports both excessive and uncomfortable, as it quickly drifts toward the "supercrip" stereotype. One of the biggest mistakes my own magazine made, as analyzed further in the next chapter, was to load up on the Paralympic coverage—upbeat, graphically high-impact, and populated by its own cast of heroes, it was too easy to add pages to that section. When you budget a "book" (as an issue is called), whatever you give to one department comes out of another. More sports means less politics, design, community coverage, or arts. Just as in a school budget debate, which ultimately shapes a curriculum, the choices made alter the message.

The deaf community has long been served by a wide range of print publications that has recently been abbreviated in an alarming way because too many of them were poorly managed and lost too much money. The shocker was the demise of *Silent News,* a monthly national newspaper with a circulation last reported to be 12,000. Started by Julius Wiggins in January 1969, it lasted less than a year after his death thirty-three years later. One explanation for its failure was the pressure of the online competition. When *Silent News* was launched, it took on two other newspapers for deaf readers, *DeafNation* and *Newswaves.* Both of them went out of business before *Silent News* did. Heavy on columns and opinion pieces, it was a tough sell for advertisers. Most of the ad revenues were brought in from hearing aid companies, battery manufacturers, and other companies with products for the hard of hearing marketplace. Like so many other small publications, it failed to notify subscribers it was going out of business, simply ceasing publication and closing its doors as rumors of embezzlement swirled in the chat rooms. It was briefly challenged in 1986 by a newcomer, *Deaf Life,* which attempted the slick, glossy lifestyle approach but lasted only three years. Started by a typical speculator, it missed the mark by a mile. Among the survivors after the shakeout are more professional publications, including the 152-year-old *American Annals of the Deaf,* a quarterly produced at Gallaudet University in Washington, D.C. (formerly it was published at the American School for the Deaf in Hartford, Connecticut). There are also academic publications, such as the *Journal of Deaf Studies and Deaf Education,* which promotes sign language, and *Sign Language Studies,* or the *Volta Review,* published by the Alexander Graham Bell Association for the Deaf and Hard of Hearing. For children, the most popular and oldest deaf publication in the United States is *World Around You,* while *Deaf Friends International* is published in Italian, French, German, and Spanish among many other languages. Most of the leading nonprofits have their news-papers, magazines, and online publications, such as *Hearing Loss Journal,* published by the National Association of the Deaf and Self Help for Hard of Hearing People (or SHHH, one of my favorite acronyms if only for its onomatopoeic wit), *Endeavor,* published by the American Society for Deaf Children, *Odyssey,* for educational and rehabilitation profes-sionals, or *Contact,* a quarterly from the Cochlear Implant Association. Although it conforms to the "medical model," one of the most popular is *Hearing Health* magazine, which offers monthly articles on tinnitus, im-plants, hearing loss treatments, and other medical information.

Singing the Body Electric

Print is only part of the disability media picture. There are cable televi-sion shows, radio shows, Web sites, and a network of nearly a hundred "dial-in newspapers" that deliver the contents of the *New York Times, Time* magazine, the *Chicago Tribune,* and other major publications over the phone to blind listeners. One of the most influential operations is *On a Roll,* a weekly two-hour radio talk show that has been broadcast on Sunday evenings since 1991. Syndicated nationally and supported by commercial sponsors, it has studios are Temple Terrace, Florida. Its pro-ducer and host is Greg Smith, a wheelchair user. There are other local radio call-in shows, such as *Disability Rap* in Grass Valley, California, and *Talking Disability* in College Park, Maryland, but Smith's is the long-est running and best known, with a loyal audience he estimates to be in the hundreds of thousands.

The television picture is similar. In New England, a monthly half-hour show called *Ready, Willing, Enable!* originating in Marblehead, Massa-chusetts, and started in 1991, is carried on eighteen cable systems through-out Massachusetts and the southern New Hampshire and Maine mar-kets. It offers interviews and product reviews and is heavy on the service angle, rather than advocacy. My favorite local show is on the City Uni-versity of New York's cable station, which reaches only New York mar-kets. With the unfortunate title of *Special People, Special Issues,* it is pro-duced by Maggie Nieves, the mother of a child with disabilities who has a passionate attachment to the issues and a heart of gold.

When the venerable BBC launched Ouch!, its "revolutionary" new Web site for people with disabilities, I naturally presumed that a mile-stone had been set. Sadly, the opening salvo of features and opinion pieces veered awkwardly from the first-person lane into the shoulder of ques-tionable humor. As with so many other Web sites (as the final chapter of this book will elaborate), its promises of daily updates and coffeehouse-quality conversations in the chat rooms have proven false. What troubles me most about the features, however, is the tone. Humor is never an easy path in publishing, and disability humor is prone to its own particular potholes. Just to offer a quick example of what I mean, here is a first-person piece that takes potshots at the leading British Paralympian, a track-and-field star named Tanni Grey-Thompson, who had recently been honored by having a baby giraffe at the London Zoo named after her, which becomes a recurring joke in the monologue:

Being disabled isn't always totally brilliant. A huge number of people complained when Tanni wasn't able to accept her *Sports Personality of the Year* award from the stage because there was no ramp in the studio. Tanni herself has been quoted as saying: "Hey, it happens. . . . I kind of felt sorry because the BBC are better than that. The coverage they've given to the Paralympics deserves better. I think it was just an oversight." And also: "The look of a ramp did not bother me. I was just thrilled to get an award." Now, that's the kind of noble reaction that wins you *Big Brother*. Let me tell you a story. Last week, I got on a bus. I didn't have my change ready because there was no seat at the bus stop and the logistics of getting my wallet out while standing up were just too complicated. So I ended up in a huge row with the bus driver, who was impatient. During the course of our conversation, a huge number of obscenities expelled from my mouth, and at least three of them were in the top five of naughty words you are not allowed to publish. I'm not necessarily proud of this, but I'm not apologetic either. It was a really embarrassing and frustrating situation, and I was made to feel like I was being deliberately difficult. I reacted naturally. If I were Tanni, I may well have said: "It was an oversight. I don't blame you really. After all, no cripples ever get on your bus, so why would it have occurred to you to treat me with the same courtesy you treat all your other passengers? I'm just thrilled to be on the bus to begin with." Y'know, maybe there's a sloth at the zoo they can name after me. Or a one-legged camel.

The virtues of this excerpt are its candor, its comic flourishes (I concede "sloth" is a funny touch), and its banishment of pity. Like Callahan in his cartoons, the writer, who goes by the nom de plume "Disability Bitch," rides a tidal swell of confessional anger at the crest of which she produces a flash of white wit, the breaking wave of one-liners that cap well-delivered anecdotes. Elsewhere on the site, one finds Lettermanesque top ten lists. One of them, in answer to the (lamentable) query "What happened to you?" (a common question to people with disabilities), offered the following limp excuse for humor:

(1) "I angered a magician."

(2) "My father is also my brother."

(3) "I was born and raised in a laboratory by an evil genetic scientist."

(4) "This is what happens if you spend too much time on your Playstation."

(5) "I was trying to get a kitten down from a tree."

(6) "Sir, you insult me—but thank you for paying attention to me, it means so much."

(7) "Actually there is nothing wrong with me, I'm one of a new emerging species."

I cut off the list at this point out of respect for the venerable BBC and mercy for the people who put the Web site together. When a major media outlet commits this level of resources to a disability media project, one ought not quibble. On the other hand, it is the bloody BBC after all, so why can't they get this right, at least? It is a valid question. It is difficult to think of any other media entity worldwide as vast as the BBC that touches the lives of people with disabilities and that, in the end, might alter the perception of its audience more. This is the same company that recently announced a companywide inclusion effort to give more casting and editorial roles to people with disabilities. If "reach" is the watchword of the media's influence, then surely the BBC exceeds any other outlet for global reach. Yet, what a vastly disappointing culmination the mighty Beeb offered.

Taking the pulse of the disability movement as legal decisions chip away at the ADA and policy decisions regarding benefits are revised is a tricky and important job. Inclusion Daily Express (IDE) is a news service started in December 1999 in Spokane, Washington, to keep advocates, attorneys, professors of disability studies, policymakers and grant writers, and other members of the community informed about articles in the mainstream press affecting the community. For a $20 fee, it e-mails its 1,000 or so subscribers (mainly in the United States but with pockets of interest in Canada, the United Kingdom, Hungary, Pakistan, Malaysia, Australia, and New Zealand as well) the top stories from the mainstream press as well as disability publications, sorted according to beats such as politics, health, and, perhaps most useful, employment opportunities. It is a tiny operation, run by Dave Reynolds, a longtime advocate and professional service provider with a bachelor's degree in human resources who also knows the press. He has written, produced, and directed segments for local television and radio stations in Spokane and edits the daily briefing with a journalist's deft hand. As Reynolds comments, it has been a tough go for the specialized disability media:

I've seen the disability news services DisabilityNews.com, HalfThePlanet
.com (which now has a modest monthly mailing), DisabilityTimes.com,
e-bility.com, spinewire.com, accesslife.com, cando.com and others all come
and go. Even the well-financed, fully staffed icanonline.net gasped its last
breath. I'm not sure why these folded. I think they all had passionate people
involved. I know ican struggled since its founder died three years ago. I had
been told some of the others had dollar signs in their eyes when they started,
or at least had put profits ahead of content, something dubbed "handi-cap-
italism," and that the dot-bomb plunges in 2000 and 2001 dug into their
profit margins too much. I think it's also a fact that, even though one in five
Americans would describe themselves as having a disability, I don't think
most identify themselves as such. It's a fragmented "community," and therefore a niche market. Most people with fibromyalgia may want news and information on fibromyalgia that may impact them directly, but few are concerned with broader disability issues, for example. I decided early on to
make IDE a subscription service, rather than have it be advertising based,
primarily because I didn't want to spend time selling ad space, or become
indebted to advertisers. I also wanted to have it be e-mail based, to give it
a more personal appeal. Even though it still is a struggle (I have to have
part-time work to make the house payment), IDE does plug ahead. It will
probably always have a limited circulation.

Reynolds is a pro. His service is focused as well as timely, and it occasionally branches into other disabilities for certain issues. Unlike some of
the other news services, newsgroups, newsletters, and bulletins, the Inclusion Daily Express stays on top of the news without all the to and fro
of e-mail chain letters or chat room name-calling.

The prognosis for the disability press is mixed. Faced with a recession,
and spooked by the casualties of the media boom still lying about the
battlefield, investors are not rushing in to support another round of specialized press outlets, even though the ad revenues might still be there. According to Tari Susan Hartman, one of the loudest voices crying out in the
wilderness, the situation is in limbo:

> Some disability organizations are now talking about consumerism and
> throwing around marketing terms, but actions speak louder than words,
> and most groups are still knocking on doors with their hand out for dona-
> tions for their annual rubber chicken dinner—and not knowing how to
> make the business case or how to do business with business. We have yet to
> reach out in a systematic way to the mainstream members of the society
> who have functional limitations who are the vast majority, but not the card-
> carrying advocates—that is where our true power base is yet to be real-

ized—for they are the heart and soul of the regular John and Jane on Main Street. Instead of criticizing, it might be more helpful to be observant and learn from their revealing attitudes. Some of us "media advocacy" organizers will continue to hammer away at media to include newsworthy disability issues in their reporting. Constant, vocal positive and negative disability community feedback would help keep the process of fair and accurate coverage moving forward in both the mainstream and disability press.[6]

That is one way of saying that there is much work to be done. Some of the burden will be borne by advocates such as Hartman, but the crucial moves will have to be made by the media corporations themselves, large and small. There is room for another round of start-ups smart enough to follow the road map we drew in the nineties, minus the expensive detours and dead ends. I wish these brave souls luck.

CHAPTER SEVEN

WE

The Short Happy Life of an Independent Magazine

*When a group of individuals becomes a We, a harmonious whole, then the
highest is reached that humans as creatures can reach.*
—*Albert Einstein*

Control over the media qua business is arguably the only means by which people with disabilities can be ensured adequate representation. Although, as we have noted, there are a few outlets that are owned and operated (as well as edited) by people with disabilities, the only organization that managed to produce a glossy lifestyle magazine worthy of comparison with mainstream competitors such as *Vanity Fair* or *Town and Country,* while attracting sufficient coverage of its own to make a dent in the public perception of disability, was an independent publishing company that started out in late 1996 with the promising name of *WE*. At its height three years later, the bimonthly magazine was in the black, all the editors and writers on staff were people with disabilities, and we sent checks to over two hundred more freelancers with a broad spectrum of disabilities, many of whom had never held publishing jobs before or seen their name in print. Even our cartoonist, the notorious rascal John Callahan, whose endpage flirted with the borders of taste and propriety, was a quadriplegic. For four exhilarating and exasperating years, I had the privilege of serving as editor in chief of *WE,* a time when I learned disability on the job interviewing such celebrities as Chuck Close, Robert Rauschenberg, Robin Williams, Paul Newman, Boomer Esiason, Casey Martin, Andrea Bocelli, Marlee Matlin, Stevie Wonder, Muhammad Ali, Stephen Hawking, Christopher and Dana Reeve, James Wolfensohn, Oliver Sacks, Bill Gates, and George Soros, among dozens of others. Because it was a magazine *by* and for people with disabilities, decisions regarding everything from images and language to coverage were made with constant input from staffers and advisers with disabilities. Judging from the wall full of awards from major nonprofits, and the responses still coming in three full years after the magazine ceased publication due to mismanagement and dot-com fever, I would immodestly say we, however briefly, had the formula right for getting disability on the page.

From the outset there were a number of differences between *WE* magazine and our competition in the disability press, as well as between *WE* and any of the previous entrants in the history of the genre. Because we were a for-profit, relying for revenues on the usual split between advertising (75 percent) and circulation (25 percent), our business and editorial plan differed from the extant for-profits (including *New Mobility*, which was not much of a newsstand presence in major markets) or the glossy boms mailed out quarterly by the Muscular Dystrophy Association (MDA), Easter Seals, National MS Society, and other major organizations, whose enormous circulation figures dwarfed our own. Their agenda was to solicit donations, so their content and style never strayed far from the old paternalism. That said, I should admit that we devoured their publications, many of which have very high production standards in terms of graphics and print quality, for story leads and trends. We also distanced ourselves from the for-profit disability press, specifically *New Mobility* and our short-lived imitator *Enable,* by swerving from the "service" function to selling, reflecting our own assertion that it was time people with disabilities were recognized as consumers rather than as patients. While *New Mobility*'s hot column was Dr. Spine (medical model), we gave columns to high-profile, nationally known figures including Tom Whittaker, an amputee who climbed Mount Everest, golfer Casey Martin, whose story had more national television hits than that of any other pro athlete in a solo sport, and, embarrassingly enough in retrospect for her frivolity, Tova Borgnine, the doyenne of Hollywood style and spouse of television idol Ernest Borgnine, who wrote incessantly about "inner beauty." While most of the other disability-specific magazines catered to advertisers of medical equipment (page after page of wheelchairs and hearing aids, bathroom grab bars, and mattress pads), we deliberately courted major brands and urged them not to give us their "disability" ad. We wanted the Cadillac and Jaguar ads that ran in *Fortune* or the *New Yorker,* not the "special mobility" one with the lift to get someone from a wheelchair into the driver's seat.

Going Out in Style

The major choice of creating a lifestyle magazine, along with the myriad smaller options to weigh regarding which product markets to target through our content, was in itself a statement. We recognized—one might even say we were banking on—the transition of the community to social assimilation and a level of economic enfranchisement that had not yet been recognized by even those in the field, who remained divided along the lines that held some people with disabilities were impoverished through discrimination while others were just as prosperous as anybody. Very soon after the magazine was launched critics suggested that we had vastly over-estimated the spending power of the typical American with a disability, particularly given the stubbornly high unemployment level (70 percent at its very best) even during a boom period when most minorities were running at 7 percent unemployed. There is no dishonor in being ahead of one's time with a small business, but mistakes in timing can also cost you the franchise, and one of the circumstantial reasons WE went under may have been the fact it was prematurely launched with respect to the real economic potency of our target market.

The other premise that set us apart from the existing competition was the way we downplayed our advocacy content. As we have seen, with only a few exceptions, most of the established disability print publications leveraged their outspokenness into subscriber loyalty and media exposure. We, early on, wrote off their audience and set our sights on a far different constituency—less angry, less adversarial, more inclined to assimilate and, frankly, to spend freely. It would be facile to couch this in "postdisability" theoretical terms, as though the time for carping had passed and the community was ready for the dawn of consumerism. It was in actuality an economically motivated choice of subject matter. Advertisers would be charmed by the idea of prosperous people with disabilities ready to roll into their showrooms with credit cards at the ready. Even the sunny editors of *Ability* magazine were not ready to bank on this kind of story. In consonance with the carpe diem vitality of our consumer philosophy, we maintained an upbeat, positive spin on all but a few topics. Unlike the memorial pages in all disability magazines, our pages never included an obituary. When we did venture into political or social commentary, we picked our spots carefully, concentrating on such "safe" issues as the international treaty to ban land mines, corporate policies regarding diversity and discrimination, stem-cell research, and the constant battle to make public transportation more accessible. None of these were tough calls to make, obviously, but restraining the urge to lash out as our rivals, notably *Ragged Edge,* constantly did was difficult. They had their agenda, we had ours.

There were inevitable family resemblances between WE and the other disability magazines. Just as the other magazines were independents, we were also the private fiefdom of eccentric entrepreneurs with dollar signs in their eyes and personal connections to the disability world. Our start-up was not fostered by the famous magazine development team at Time-Warner or incubators at similar major media corporations that have launched race- and gender-specific titles. None of the disability media came out of this type of corporate setting, which is one indication of how far the mainstream business centers lag (to this day) in the recognition of the market. The other intersection between the new kid on the block and the established disability press was of course the readership. When we bought our direct mail lists from brokers, we were inevitably treading on their demographic territory (amputees, wheelchair users, deaf and blind readers, the massive pools of multiple sclerosis, muscular dystrophy, cerebral palsy, and postpolio consumers), and that also meant we had to decide on what we could offer that the others did not. When your circulation begins at zero, and your rivals are already cruising at a steady thirty thousand not counting newsstand, you need to start with a game plan for luring away the competition's sales base.

Ours was to address and represent people with disabilities in an entirely different way from the approach of existing magazines, from cover to cover, emphasizing physical beauty, achievement, prosperity, activity, and sophistication. If our circulation figures had built to stronger levels I would be able to claim here that this worked like a charm, but we never actually topped the paid subscriber totals of our older rivals. In this age of revelations regarding false circulation figures (which notably, in the cases of *Newsday* and *Rosie,* have demonstrated the fallacies inherent in the honor code behind the industry-standard Audit Bureau of Circulation), it will come as no surprise that, like many start-ups, we gave our advertisers vastly inflated circulation numbers. Many magazines remained stored at the printer's warehouse after their on-sale dates had passed, in part so we could show printing receipts for 150,000 copies or more when only 5,000 had gone out to paid subscribers.

WE *Meant Business*

One factor began to present itself before our first year was over: unlike the competition, our demographic was almost evenly divided between people with disabilities and their families and friends, who were eager to understand (and cope with) the experience of living with disability. We shifted gears quickly to catch this important wave. The cover line on our first two issues read, "A lifestyle magazine for people with disabilities." For the next issue, we broadened the legend: "The lifestyle magazine for people with disabilities, their families and friends." The gesture beckoned to a different prospective reader. While *New Mobility, Ragged Edge, Mouth,* and the magazines for deaf readers were geared to a core of people with disabilities, we were courting the uninitiated, the newly disabled, and the less angry.

As soon as you change the picture of your reader, you change the way you write and design. From that moment on we were trying to synthesize a message that would appeal to a range of readers, some of whom were in on the code while others needed a glossary. An incentive for spelling out what must have struck many readers with disabilities as basic material was the realization that most of the advertising decision-makers who would be supporting our magazine were also nondisabled. By overcoming their fear of the unknown and their queasiness about disability with a slick magazine featuring attractive people, we were hoping to succeed financially and psychologically where others had turned back. The other change we made at about the same time was to expand our editorial focus from physical disability to the broader and more current (in terms of disability theory) category of so-called mental disability, even though it meant risking the resentment of the "hardcore" of wheelchair users as well as deaf and blind readers who prefer to think of themselves as the real disabled. Our decision was predicated on sheer numbers—the recovery community alone represented tens of millions of potential subscribers.

The magazine started with $600,000 in private capital mainly provided by a crude Manhattan businessman named Raymond T. Coppola and his friends. Putting together the salaries of three editors, the writers' fees, the freelance designer's fee, the prepress costs for scanning and shooting film from which the magazine was printed, and the printing costs, we produced the magazine for around $100,000 an issue (that figure went down as we became better at what we did, because corrections cost money in the production process). Coppola was a former ad space salesman, an obscure specialty in which he acted as middleman between small magazines and advertising agencies, getting a commission from both. This meant he knew the publishing business from the financial side, yet was hopelessly ignorant of the editorial aspects of putting together a magazine as well as disability etiquette.

His sales pitch was nearly irresistible. Coppola vowed to develop a completely unprecedented lifestyle magazine for people with disabilities, touting the pleasures of fine dining, travel, art, music, fashion, architecture and interior design, and financial success. Instead of the usual nonprofit rhetoric handed out too readily in the disability world, or the whining of the disenfranchised, we would find the best and brightest young journalists with disabilities, pay them decently, and prove we could compete on the newsstands and in ad wars with the big boys from Time Inc. or Conde Nast. In his eyes, *WE* the enterprise was plainly and simply a moneymaking venture. The staff viewed it as a cause. Our offices were Coppola's scruffy Upper West Side Manhattan apartment, and to save money we farmed out the design and printing.

To garner credibility in the disability community, Coppola had enlisted an old college friend from St. John's University named Terry Moakley, a quadriplegic (diving accident) and Vietnam veteran, to be the front man near the top of the masthead as editorial director. Moakley stayed with us to the end of the magazine. A former English professor and veteran activist, he was a blessing to me. He would read and vet the copy for disability gaffes and end up catching grammatical errors, and he never steered us wrong. His own reputation was secure in the national disability movement after he had successfully fought New York's Metropolitan Transit Authority and various taxi agencies to make public transportation accessible. When I showed up as the replacement editor in chief, Coppola had already overspent ten grand of his own dough on a glossy prototype with California congresswoman and millionaire paraplegic Michele Alioto on the cover in a sexy pose. Its highlights were the fashion spread and the rate card—the price list for ads, putting first things first. From the start, we were an expensive buy, according to start-up magazine standards, asking $11,000 for a full-page ad with good placement, a bit more for the back cover, all negotiable. Partway to the debut of the first issue, we ditched Alioto as too obscure and too local (scoring high on name recognition in California but not, according to our marketing questionnaires, in the East Coast media centers) and switched to Heather Whitestone, the recently crowned Miss America and a deaf role model.

If you want to learn about the media trade, you should understand how the money flows. The highest-ranking staffer was not the editor in chief but the ad sales representative, a veteran of decades in the business named Bruce Burton, gray haired, spiffily dressed, a ray of bottled salesman's sunshine in the office and a born talker whose smooth technique was instrumental in landing some of our initial sponsors. Our first six-figure, multi-issue sponsors were Citibank, which was counting on a recent effort to make accessible ATMs a success, and Avon, which was charmed by our chutzpah in taking on the fashion frontier and convinced by Burton that women with disabilities would need a salesperson to come to their doors. Burton, veteran of such fabulously lucrative start-ups as *Southern Living* as well as of Fairchild Publications, spent three hours each lunch wringing ads from his old accounts or trying to break new ground with the automotives, drug companies, computer manufacturers, and other likely sectors. It was our beginner's luck to debut in the midst of a gold rush for ad pages in the magazine industry—since that time, the business has suffered double-digit declines annually—and Burton followed his two-page "spreads" from Citibank and Avon with solid single pages from the "mobility" (modified cars for wheelchair users) programs at General Motors and Ford as well as the IBM and Microsoft campaigns for their latest and greatest "software for people with special needs."

On one of the precious few occasions when I ate lunch outside the office,

I tagged along with Burton for a well-earned steak at the theater-district beef palace, Gallagher's, in the company of a major potential client who had known Bruce in the good old days of Fairchild. I was brought for show. Halfway through my third stein of draft beer (Bruce was rounding his second martini and heading into a third, while our prey was hammering back the gin and tonics), I was thoroughly enjoying the ad side of the magazine trade when Bruce launched into one of the riffs we had developed together for the dog and pony presentations we made at all the major Madison Avenue agencies. The refrain was, "*Ms.* magazine did it, *Ebony* did it, *WE* can do it, too." Bored and not buying, that cynical veteran of two decades in the trade stubbed out his Marlboro regular (this was way before Mayor Bloomberg snuffed cigarettes in restaurants) in a half-full ashtray by his untouched side of spinach and wistfully filled one of Bruce's rare pauses for another sip of the silver bullet and a question: "When was the last time a magazine made a difference in America?"

We were all potted by the time we emerged blinking into the mid-afternoon Manhattan sunlight. Bruce and I wandered to Sixth Avenue and hailed a cab to head back up to Ninety-sixth Street and face our ferocious publisher, who rarely let me out of his sight. I knew we would be summoned to Coppola's corner for a thorough grilling the moment the door closed behind us. My nervous staff looked at me with alarm for so flagrantly breaking the habits dictated by my abstemious Protestant work ethic, but I had something in my hip pocket to fend off disaster. I had held tight to that comment of the ad broker, and I launched into what was about to become our fight song. "When was the last time a magazine made a difference in America?" I excitedly and loudly recited. It was soon a mantra in our pages, a staple of our new publicity kit, a punch line in sales presentations, and a slogan emblazoned in blue lettering with our logo on a banner we carted around to nonprofit gatherings and sports events. It may have been a tongue-in-cheek, sardonic aside from the most jaded media veteran I had ever met when first uttered, but in a different tone it was a provocation, a challenge, a motivational instigation that even with my long experience in journalism was a spur to me because I took it personally.

It was intoxicating in those heady start-up days to think our magazine could effect an alteration in the lives of those sitting next to me in the office or at home reading each issue. The "nothing about us without us" policy started in the office—we hired people with disabilities, who had a voice in the strategy and content of the magazine. They were also the public face of what quickly became a cause célèbre in the publishing world, garnering airtime on the local affiliates of CBS, NBC, Fox, and ABC, then broader exposure though CNN and CNNfn as well as the network national news and stories in the *New York Times,* the *Wall Street Journal,* the wire services, and on the radio. Our bike messenger, a strapping Trinidadian above-the-knee amputee named Dexter Benjamin who darted through Manhattan traffic at thirty-five miles per hour using a one-pedal racing bike, was featured on local television and radio. Our press hits were an important weapon in our battle to wrest subscribers away from the competition, to the extent that we hired Howard Rubenstein Associates, one of the premier public relations firms in the nation, at $6,000 a month to plug us. The message was the emergence of the consumer with a disability as a social, economic, and political force. As intermediaries between these consumers and the businesses that were discovering how to pitch their products to them, our success or failure would hinge on the economic viability of an untapped niche. In the thirty seconds we had on television, often as commentators, we could push for progress on vital questions regarding Supreme Court decisions on ADA matters, but to get there we had to concentrate on the upbeat stories and sponsor-friendly pictorials. We used the consumer's spending power as the point of a wedge to drive home recognition of the community. We were not as strident as the established disability media, but we were prettier and more acceptable to the advertisers and television media, so we gained their trust. And that, theoretically at least, enabled us to deliver our stories to a far broader and more powerful audience of decision makers.

We generated resentment from the start among "hard-core" journalists and activists with disabilities who had been on the scene for decades. The major slam on the magazine was that it was "slick" and far too upscale for those living on government checks. As one reader, a hemiplegic after a stroke, wrote three years into our run in a well-argued letter we published in the November–December 1999 issue:

> Although you are making an important contribution to the disability community and filling a niche in the market that would ordinarily be ignored, I am not renewing my subscription for the magazine. You put far too much emphasis on high dollar items. How many of us can travel to Europe or dine in five-star restaurants? In one issue, you showed a home that was designed for a disabled man, but it was about the size of the Taj Mahal. . . . Furthermore, I wouldn't buy most of the clothes you show even if I could afford them, though I do like the fact that you use disabled models. Keep the expensive stuff if you want, but include more that the middle class can afford.

Mike Brannick of London, Arkansas, had a point in this extremely valuable criticism. Our over-ambitious publisher loved to paint a picture of the wheelchair user freely spending his or her multimillion-dollar insurance settlement on first-class plane tickets and hotel suites, but not every person with a disability fits this description. Our fashion, interior design, travel, and restaurant pieces were an affront to the average person with a disability who could not afford the $2,000 Kors ensemble or the $10,000 *Queen Mary II* cruise, who didn't live in the $10-million Virginia estate filled with art or eat at Le Cirque before attending the Itzhak Perlman concert in a box at Carnegie Hall. The anger in the first onslaught of letters to the editor, which also inferred that our fashion models were not disabled, made us wince, and we did start including budget travel tips as well as other concessions to lower income brackets, but we persisted in the high-gloss, high-goals presentation. The reason was not just cosmetic or even financial, although it was clear our advertisers preferred the upscale "aspirational" cast, which connoted spending power. The rationale behind the lavish "package" was as follows: To put the beauty of life with a disability on paper.

If all that sounds normal for the magazine business, there was nothing normal about the atmosphere in the office, where I hammered away at our copy with a managing editor, veteran of three decades in the trade and, as she proudly put it, "four ways ADA," and a deaf intern at three little desks set up along windows overlooking Central Park. Other interns included wheelchair users, amputees, and a number of recovering alcoholics in a local program that was helping them get back into the workforce. It was a far cry from Time Inc. The dining room table was our design and meeting area. I was entrusted with figuring out how on earth we were going to put together the first 116-page issue in time for the scheduled rollout in Times Square, featuring then-mayor Rudolf Giuliani and half the disability leaders in the nation, in March 1997. Between the glossy, hundred-pound coated stock of the covers were profiles, memoirs, paeans, and pans that had been meticulously edited and arranged to confer authenticity on, here comes the hard part, a bunch of newcomers to journalism led by a nondisabled editor in chief. Statistics showed that only one in a hundred magazines that start up ever make it past their first year, and our inexperience as a team worried me. In my days as a reporter for *Fortune* and senior editor of *Art & Auction,* the process of producing a magazine was confined to sitting in front of a computer, cranking out copy a little over the word count stipulated by my editor, then cutting when the paper proofs came back and showed I was long, perhaps weighing in briefly on the choice of pictures and the layout before having all my suggestions overridden by a designer, then going off for a couple of beers and being pleasantly surprised when, a few days later, a nice shiny magazine arrived on my desk, at which point I would flip to see my byline and enjoy the contents in much the same way any other reader would, blissfully unaware of what had actually transpired between my Word document and the final printed version. When you are the editor in chief of a start-up, lacking a "production department," everything from buying paper to printing and binding to mailing, as well as writing, editing, laying out articles, and jostling the placement of ads is within your purview, and I was struggling to learn it all.

Guides to the Labyrinth

I was also in dire need of guidance on disability issues, both as a journalist and as a manager. One of my most reliable advisers, and a frequent contributor to the magazine, was a Washington escapee named George Covington. Considered one of the leading experts on Universal Design and on media issues involving the community, Covington, blind from macular degeneration, was a former White House aide charged with advising Vice President Dan Quayle on community issues. A born comedian and gifted writer, he was (luckily for us) living on the West Side of Manhattan and working on a novel whose autobiographical hero was a blind photographer. Whenever Covington met someone, he took a black-and-white portrait with a small camera that was always round his neck. At home he would blow the image up on his computer screen and learn what the person looked like. His haunting portraits and landscapes, many of which made their way into our magazine, were among the most original artworks we ever published.

But Covington meant much more to us than any mere contributor. He visited or called almost daily, mixing jokes with solid advice, steering us clear of the rocky political and cultural gaffes we headed for occasionally, particularly when it came to taking sides on touchy issues. Although he had been in the battle for decades, and was one of the nation's preeminent advocates for disability rights, he constantly warned us to stick to the consumer track. He also urged us to present our profiles in a three-dimensional, individualized way. "We're not all saints or role models," he'd often say. "We're liars, cheats, and thieves as well, just like anybody else. Don't just paint us pretty." The staff would laugh all morning at his Quayle campaign stories (he would have made an unforgettable character on *The West Wing*) and gratefully followed his guidance.

Anyone who has been on a start-up knows it's a rocky road, fraught with editorial and budget crises that are dramatically different from the complacent cycles of an established magazine. The initial story list for issue one changed dozens of times, and each change cost us time, money, and grief. As word spread about our ambitious plans—even before our first issue, there was an article in the Metro section of the *New York Times,* a quick visit from the local Fox and NBC affiliates, a *Wall Street Journal* piece, and gossip along the disability grapevine—we attracted two types of visitors. First at the door were those who prey on start-up magazines, opportunists from design consultants and freelance journalists to printing and marketing "experts." The others were the people with disabilities who wanted to be a part of what we were doing, including interns who often ended up on the payroll, albeit at ludicrously meager salaries ($18,000 for a reporter, less for an office assistant, no benefits). The prelaunch publicity was good for business, however. After a few more ads came in, including IBM's product launch of a voice-activated software system featuring Curtis Mayfield, a quadriplegic singer, we knew we were on our way. The launch of the magazine was scheduled for March 1997, and nearly two hundred guests turned up at the Marriott in Times Square, where Mayor Giuliani presented a proclamation and activists joined potential investors in a lovefest. Our first cover subject was the first deaf Miss America, Heather Whitestone (who later would undertake a cochlear implant, which would have made a great story). That night she was basically the only celebrity we could muster, although we invited everybody from Christopher Reeve to Itzhak Perlman, who would be later covers.

Culture and Content

Vetting the copy for offensive or "retro" disability blunders was a priority. My managing editor, a marvel of both ingenuity and thoroughness, doubled as copy editor. Every line of every story went through her fine-tooth comb at least twice. In addition to my line-editing (essentially, rewriting) and her copyediting, we had a rigorous system for reading copy in its near final stages that had the benefit, I believe, of an important disability-literate quotient as well as an editorial rationale. When we reached the stage where the articles fit the format of a section and had been laid out, with captions and credits in place, everyone in the newsroom, including interns, was required to stop whatever he or she was doing, leave the phones and computers alone, and read and initial every version until the very last "match prints" (big glossy boards that were used by the printers to match the colors in the images while on press) were finalized. All eyes on the final copy meant typos were caught, of course, but it also allowed everyone from interns to editors to respond to phraseology or photos from the point of view of his or her disability and experience. What was comfortable in the Deaf world, for instance, could cause recovering alcoholics or spinal cord-injured readers to squirm. As we sat

around the dining room table when this reading occurred, usually be-
sieged with dozens of other tasks, the discussions that flared up were, in
my view, wonderful opportunities to air the differences that existed in
what we optimistically called the "community."

The disagreements exposed the sheer difficulty of uniting people of
various disabilities in one common cause. From an idealistic point of view,
inclusion served my overly optimistic agenda of building cross-disability
awareness. On their way to the article about their own experience, the
readers would be exposed to the stories of others, and curiosity would
lead to understanding and the recognition of parallelisms. It was also important to ratify through coverage the efforts of advocates in some of the
more remote areas of the community. Although I could never claim that
the theories one finds in disability studies or even politics were constant
topics in the newsroom—we were there to produce a lifestyle magazine—
a number of the practical decisions we made in those first three months
before anyone ever saw WE were more interesting than many long discussions of more abstract topics because, from a disability rights perspective, the choice between minimally suggesting disability in a fashion
photo—sweeping a model's hair back to show her hearing aid—or revealing an entire prosthetic leg was our opportunity to determine whether
a reader's focus was on the style or the disability, to take one example. If
journalists stopped each day to consider the implications of minor choices
of this kind from an ideological point of view, deadlines would be broken
all over the nation and well-oiled production systems would grind to a
halt. Three years after packing up my desk, I can now consider fully the
strategic ramifications of the way we solved our basic journalistic problems in those days.

Two agendas had to be served: glam and grit, style and service. Our
readers wanted to be entertained and to pick up vital and useful information that would help them cope. The magazine (insiders call the physical
product a "book") was divided into two sections: a front-of-the-book feature well and back-of-the-book "real-life" stories that often came in over
the transom from readers. On either side of this divide, the for-profit context demanded that expenditures and page allocations be justified by the articles' potential for generating revenue. The cover stories were to be sexy
and celebrity-centric to attract newsstand sales, to be a hit in the mailboxes
of those we were soliciting directly, and to wow the ad buyers who were not
disability-literate. That meant no hardcore visible disabilities on that precious, high-gloss, one hundred-pound cover stock. It meant Miss America
in a Donna Karan outfit, arms outspread, silhouetted against a white background with come-on lines like "Miracles in Miami" and "Love, Sex and
Intimacy." The picture was taken during a fashion shoot for which we paid

Heather Whitestone a quick ten grand not including expenses. The message of the cover: sexy, upscale, beautiful, optimistic, mainstream. What was inside had to appeal not only to subscribers as fresh and novel but to ad execs, used to basic magazine formulas, as familiar. Our platform was that 54 million Americans with disabilities had the same appetite for luxury goods and services as anyone reading the *New Yorker.*

We were following the dictates of capitalism down a path that hopefully led to social amelioration. Once the decision to go lifestyle had been made, the models were obvious. *Vanity Fair, Town and Country, Esquire,* and their ilk would be our competition as well as our road map, which sounds like sheer hubris but was marvelous motivational material for all of us. As with any magazine from Condé Nast or Time Inc., big-color and longer stories (including the six- or eight-page cover stories) were placed in a feature "well" at the center of the book, preceded by major ads paying a premium for up-front placement (including spreads), a picture-coded table of contents, and publisher's and editors' letters (important especially in the early issues, spelling out the mission of the publication). To lighten the rhythm of the "mix" we devoted six to eight pages or so to short news items and briskly paced one-page profiles of "People on the Move." Editorial content started with ad bait. The six or eight pages we devoted in each issue to travel, for instance, helped score a Continental Airlines campaign in our first year, although I only learned later that it was a freebie in exchange for carrying the magazine in the departure gate racks at New York's Laguardia Airport and on board each aircraft. We landed a full-page Hertz ad that ran most of the first year because Hertz had recently invested millions in making its airport shuttle buses wheelchair-accessible and was just launching a massive initiative to attract the market of drivers with disabilities. Somehow, despite the Marriott family's massive program for hiring people with disabilities, and a face-to-face meeting with Dick Marriott down in Washington, we missed out on hotel and resort advertising through the entire course of the magazine's history.

Dangling editorial coverage for ad placement was not always a sure bet. Consider these near misses. We had high hopes for our coverage of dining (we struck out on the restaurants, being a national publication, and on the credit cards, which hurt), fashion (we never secured one designer or retail ad), and sports and outdoors (we came close a number of times with Nike and L. L. Bean, but they never came in). At the end of both the travel and dining features, I ran a two-page access guide to the city with detailed notes on the real accessibility problems and features of public transportation, hotels, tourist sites, museums, and other points of interest. Because restaurants and hotels regularly lie about their accessibility, or do not know enough about the ADA to understand the question, we sent out our writers with a checklist we had devised for determining the level of Universal Design features incorporated, including measuring bathroom stalls for wheelchair turnaround or asking for Braille menus and other details. These guides were not by any means the most compelling reading in the magazine, but we learned that travelers would tear them out and take them along because Fodor's simply did not tell them what they needed to know.

Then there was the perpetual question of how much space to devote to health and medicine, which underwent an evolution in our pages that paralleled the departure from the medical model as observed by disability studies theorists. In other words, we hit hard at research and therapy stories in the beginning, paying our top dollar to a genial freelance writer who had been a biologist and researcher in the United Kingdom. We made Dave McMullen our science editor and shamelessly claimed he had been on the team that discovered DNA at Cambridge. He had actually worked in the same lab as Watson in London. This was the beginning of a golden age in pharmaceutical advertising, when, under pressure from generic versions of their most profitable drugs, giants like Pfizer and Merck were pouring billions into print campaigns. Somehow we missed that boom, too, not even grabbing one Viagra ad.

In the pecking order of genres in disability media as a whole, two stand out: the memoir and the column. Many of our competing publications were almost entirely devoted to these two story forms. Both derive their credibility from their "walk in my shoes" (*sic*) premise that the truth of disability is locked in the experience itself. Most of the best material of this kind was placed in its own well. The layout of the book had its own journalistic and policy implications. With the front dedicated to Heroes and Villains (our news shorts on events positive and negative for the community) and op-eds from the chairman, publisher, and editor in chief, we covered our advocacy and news bases.

Eventually these sections were complemented by celebrity columns by Tom Whittaker, a charismatic amputee who had scaled Mount Everest and is a star of the lecture circuit, and Casey Martin, who made national headlines by suing the Professional Golfers Association under the ADA. These were followed by the full-page color spreads and features reserved for such departments as fashion, interiors, design, dining, travel, business, and sports. From the sociological or ethical perspective, what follows may sound dreadful, but it responded to practical rather than theoretical concerns. We invented a back-of-the-book section under the heading of Consumer's Edge that would contain what in-house we referred to as the "hard-core" disability stories, punctuated by the disability-related advertising. This front-back duality might strike some as utterly hypocritical.

Despite our best efforts, the visual quality of the front and the back stood miles apart. We would put Marlee Matlin or Andrea Bocelli (shot by a professional photographer) along with sexy models in the first thirty pages, and use the best of a roll of home snapshots taken with a standard 35-millimeter camera to illustrate our one- or two-page columns offering advice on legal, financial, health, transportation, and small business matters, all written by longtime experts in those fields or first-time writers we commissioned to get the vox populi feeling into our pages. The whole package was introduced each issue by a brief editorial from Terry Moakley, a wheelchair user and nationally known advocate who used his page to bang out some of our strongest editorials on public policy issues of practical urgency, specifically in the field of transportation, his specialty.

I secretly loved the back-of-the-book stories and columns, which were about real people and offered "service" information. My favorite was "First Person," which was the five-hundred-word essay written by an ordinary person with a disability. These pieces highlighted various disabilities and each one essentially opened the eyes of the temporarily able-bodied to what it would be like to live with that disability in their neighborhoods. Another wonderful short feature was initiated by our managing editor, a short we called "History 101," which spotlighted the lives of great figures with disabilities throughout history, including Lord Nelson, Winston Churchill, Frida Kahlo, Beethoven, James Thurber, Louis Braille, and others known to history buffs but not necessarily as people with disabilities. It appealed to the professor in me, and I tried to match writers with historical figures according to disability (although I took all the artsy stories, including van Gogh). We profiled the bond between service animals and their masters in "Animation," which was not just about brilliant German shepherd guide dogs but included as well trained monkeys used by quadriplegics to do all kinds of household chores, as well as the birds, lizards, rabbits, and even Vietnamese potbellied pigs who brought emotional as well as physical strength.

Our cutest and youngest regular contributor was a little girl named Stephanie Hammerman, whom we recruited at least in part (to my publisher's shame) because her father and grandfather were major Wall Street players at Merrill Lynch and he was hoping to hit them up for investments. She had cerebral palsy and started writing for us at the age of seven; we first met at the time when Mattel rolled out its Barbie in a wheelchair. Stephanie and I appeared together on CNN commenting on the doll's sociological significance (she turned monosyllabic just as the lights came on, the only time I ever saw her clam up), and in conjunction with her mother, Robin, we decided it would be a lovely idea if she reviewed toys, books, games, and, most importantly in her father's eyes (with an eye toward her future), computer software. We refashioned an old idea for Editor's Choice, a *New York* magazine–style annotated catalogue intended to drum up product and retail ads, turning it over entirely to Stephanie, who by the age of nine was turning in her bimonthly column like a pro and occasionally coming to town with her mom to attend meetings. This delicate and clever little girl with her winsome smile was a staff favorite who broadened our age demographic and added a whole dimension to our ability to cover disability-friendly design for toys and computer games. Stephanie even received fan mail, such as the letter from Kingstree, South Carolina, from the mother of a six-year-old who wrote to rave about Stephanie's neon pink crutches ("They are perfect!") and asked for information about where to buy a pair for her daughter Erica. That kind of connection was pure gold for us editorially and never hurt in Madison Avenue pitch meetings, either.

On the other end of the spectrum was Tony Coelho, onetime congressman (the original House sponsor of the ADA) from California and, from the inception of the magazine to its end, the chairman of the President's Committee on the Employment of People with Disabilities. We wanted to land a column on employment by this big fish, and we were after the committee's mailing list. But the one person we never managed to find in Washington was Coelho himself. Having disgraced himself in Congress with a fiscal scandal when he failed to disclose his junk-bond holdings just as the ADA was making its way to passage, the White House (Bush the elder) needed to find a place to park him. Since he had epilepsy, the President's Committee seemed a likely spot. His (frankly dull) columns were dutifully ghosted for him by Wilson Hulley, a former public relations executive and firm supporter of the magazine. It became a joke to call the President's Committee and ask for Coelho, because he was inevitably in his New York offices probably making scads of money on a variety of enterprises and investments.

The early trips I took to Washington on the shuttle were also used to line up other major figures in the movement, including Jim Dickson of the National Organization for Disability, Bob Dole, Tom Harkin, Max Cleland, Justin Dart, and the only mainstream journalist at that time getting regular disability issues into a leading magazine, Joseph P. Shapiro of *U.S. News*. Dart was the Martin Luther King Jr. of disability rights, a crusader in a wheelchair who pestered politicians both Republican and Democratic until his death in 2001. The scion of an ultrarich Texas family, Dart was the single most conspicuous figure in the demonstrations that led to the passage of the ADA in 1990, and was the star on any dais when disability rights were being celebrated. Unlike Reeve, Dole, or many another Washington regular, Dart had universal approval in the community. He signed on to serve on our advisory board. Many times over the next four years we went to Dart for quotes, and he gave us an impassioned message on the continuing fight for disability rights for our "millennium" issue (November–December 1999, which also included similar pieces by Bill Gates, Oliver Sacks, Queen Noor of Jordan, James Wolfensohn, head of the World Bank, Kofi Annan of the United Nations and film director George Lucas).

Never a model of publishing efficiency, with only three permanent editorial staffers and no office rent, we ran a tight enough ship to be self-sufficient (sustained by our ad revenues) by the third issue and would have moved well into the black if we hadn't wasted a ton of money on unnecessary editorial changes accommodating our publisher's odd whims. I built a theory, probably more impressive at a dinner party or in a grad seminar than in an editorial setting, that in its early stages the magazine had to lead with an upbeat message. Once it matured and established its readership, we could be more aggressive as investigative reporters, or more balanced in our presentation of the disability experience in its more negative, arguably more real, incarnation. Evolutions of this kind are guided in part by reader response as well as by models, including the feminist, gay, and ethnic magazines that had made it over the years.

A quick example of what I intended to happen is provided by our annual survey of the top ten companies to work for in America, an idea I lifted from *Working Woman* magazine and plugged into our second issue. Over time, I hoped that we would have the guts to list the ten worst as well in a hard-hitting story that would have delivered a one-two punch right where it counts, in the employment and discrimination area. That level of sophistication would have marked a milestone in our evolution. The initial idea was to honor ten major companies for hiring, promoting, and accommodating workers with disabilities, and right from the start it received major air play from CNNfn, the networks, and major print outlets, pumped in part by the publicity departments of the big companies we named in our list. We looked good (especially with all the subscriptions we hoped to bring in from the TV hits), the companies looked good, and, most important, job seekers could be steered to viable human resources contacts at a time when unemployment among people with disabilities was at an alarmingly high level. To avoid the appearance of conflict of interest involving my role as editor in chief (perhaps beholden to our advertisers), I assigned the feature and, most important, the adjudication of the list to a "nationally known" expert in the field of hiring people with disabilities, the author of the only book on the subject. As a former business journalist, I knew exactly what I wanted the writer to turn in: a full-blown report on the employment picture, grim as it was, in counterpoint with success stories from major corporations that included people with disabilities in their diversity programs. This would take a reporter who could bring in the numbers, who knew the human resources field and its lingo, and who had the ADA down pat. Well into the process of putting to bed the article, the longest we ever ran at *WE* at nearly six thousand words, I realized the piece did not measure up, so I intervened and started interviewing human resources managers on my own. Our ever alert ad salesman was in the office one day listening to my conversation as I dangled the prospect of being included in the top ten before the press officers who were the gatekeepers for any high-level corporate sources. They latched onto the story fast, accustomed as they were to fielding questions about their hiring practices that were usually much tougher (it was the beginning of the outsourcing fad, and most business journalists were blasting big American corporations for sending work overseas to underpaid labor). I started receiving unsolicited calls from press offices of major American corporations, such as Caterpillar and Boeing, and my e-mail in box was full of releases from Microsoft and IBM. A devious plan took root inside our office. If they were so eager to be in the article, why not hit them up for ads in the issue?

I walked right into it. We had survived the financial scare of the first issue and had a great second book in the making (cover story on Muhammad Ali, my profile of the artist Chuck Close, a super piece with knockout graphics on amputee skydivers, and an irresistible entertainment feature on movies about disability with an amazingly funny first-person piece by George Covington, our comic star). The issue deserved the best ad support it could get, so I offered my collusion. Snapping up the list of sources, the publisher turned the whole top ten list into a blackmail pitch. Give me an ad, you get on the list. No ad, you're not in the running, and we might even go after you in our villains column. To add an even darker shadow, veiled allusions were made to the protection offered by inclusion on the list against ADA-related lawsuits (even as we went to press I did not realize that AT&T, which ranked third on our inaugural list, was locked in a court battle over discrimination against workers with disabilities). When the issue came out, I made the rounds of the networks, including a long spot on CNNfn, with my fingers crossed that none of the reporters would be bright enough to notice the coincidental relationship between our ads and our ranking, and none of them did. What began as a significant journalistic project, with great potential benefit for people with disabilities on the employment front, ended as a farce and potential source of embarrassment. We ran the top ten list annually after that, and it was amusing to see to what lengths corporate diversity officers would go to promote their companies.

By our third year, we had settled down to making the best magazine on disability ever published. A typical day in the life of a magazine staff is, despite the witty wordplay you see in movies and television, dominated by an endless succession of mechanical problems, each of which consumes more time and money than the relatively straightforward process of writing and editing stories. As a start-up, we farmed out about two-thirds of the writing to freelancers, as often as possible people with disabilities, many of whom were pitching us regularly with story ideas. My staff and I wrote the rest. At least one intern and one reporter were consistently devoted to gathering images and dealing with permission to use them, a reminder that magazine publishing is driven by visual rather than textual forces. As a former writer turned editor in chief, one of the lessons I rapidly ingested, not without resistance, was that the experience of a magazine for most consumers and advertisers is predominantly visual. Reflecting this precedence of graphic over verbal, I spent ten times more money and time per issue on photographers, stylists, and designers than on writers. This even led to a minor breakthrough in graphic design. Frustrated by our lack of a new linguistic label for people with disabilities, we focused on creating a new "emoticon." By 1999, we were using a "no-smoking"–style red circle with a slash through it over the "dis" in "disability" to overcome the linguistic problem with a graphic one (the idea was the publisher's and was rapidly copied by organizations in the field, much to his annoyance, without compensation or credit to us).

I wonder if too much time, and certainly too much money, was thrown away on the fashion shoots, which after all never garnered a penny of ad dollars. They did have an immediate and powerful impact on our readers, the advocacy community, our advertisers, newcomers to disability issues, the models themselves, and the press. Sometimes the benefits cannot be quantified. Just as we started up, a Connecticut-based modeling agency for people with disabilities that called itself The Shot also produced its first book, and we not only gave them their first business but pulled them into the glow of our own publicity on several shoots. Their top earners were some of the athletes with disabilities, such as Chris Waddell, who were also attracting sponsorship funds for their Paralympic bids from companies like The Hartford and Chevrolet that were courting the disability markets. Our fashion photographer was Alberto Rizzo, a Condé Nast and advertising veteran who said he loved shooting our models (usually in his studio in Little Italy) because their genuineness was such a welcome change from the insipid perfection of his usual subjects. Top designers like Kenneth Cole, Donna Karan, Han Feng, and many others were more than generous with clothes, and the pairing of disability and couture became an amusing editorial divertissement for each issue.

Accessible by Design

The articles exploring design (product design, building design, etc.) were the tip of a conceptual spear in our editorial agenda. This emphasis on design ran parallel with our lifestyle slant that optimized possibilities especially for those to whom the doors seemed closed. Within the first six months of magazine design and a redesign, the interior features grew in pages, and ideas about design coverage began spilling from them into other departments, especially the practical or "self-help" ones such as Home Office (another blatant hook for ads) as well as travel and dining. We devised a six-page, thirty-five-point checklist of accessibility criteria for our freelancers to use in evaluating hotels, restaurants, public transportation, museums, and other sightseeing attractions for the access reports we appended to both the dining and travel sections, the former devoted to U.S. cities of note (Reno, Boston, New Orleans, etc.) and the latter to foreign destinations (notably Vietnam, which at the time was receiving a number of veterans).

Another fortuitous conflation of greed and good was the idea to rank the ten best cars for people with disabilities—we had some good luck with the Ford and General Motors "mobility" programs as advertisers, even scoring a Cadillac page, and we wanted to snare not only Chrysler (the new PT Cruiser, for example, turned out to be a wheelchair user's dream because the back seats could be ripped out and the chair rolled right in from the hatchback to the driver's seat) but also Volvo, Saab, and other extremely clever carmakers that pour billions of dollars into new gimmicks every year and were just beginning to discover the profits to be made in catering to older drivers. We never scored those ad pages, but our car guy, a wheelchair user and thoroughly charming Internet wizard named Robert Bennett, came up with some fascinating copy. Many of the carmakers' new devices targeted at the "mature" market proved a boon to people with disabilities. Dashboard displays with big digital readouts were helping drivers with limited vision, while the low placement of the ignition in a Saab was perfect for quadriplegics, who find it difficult to reach around to the key on a steering column, and interior lighting is essential for deaf drivers who need to lip-read passengers offering directions.

This is straight consumer reporting, the popular meat and potatoes of magazines and local news programs on television, and it carries responsibilities with its popularity. The "impartiality" of an outside arbiter such as Bennett is supposed to guarantee that we don't just use the list rankings and evaluations to pump advertisers. Supposed to. As with the top ten companies and top ten colleges list, we'd have sold our souls if the ads had come our way. The technical phrase for this is "selling off" the editorial, a practice that is shamelessly engaged at Condé Nast and rather more discreetly but nonetheless persistently used at more reputable publications like the *New York Times*. The service aspect of this kind of journalism is diminished by the conflict of interest, but the straight volume of information that we included in each issue—especially in those dull but useful access reports that readers often reported clipping and taking with them on trips—represented a step in the right direction. As editor of a consumer magazine, I did feel that balancing our need for ads with our readers' right to know the good and bad aspects of a product should have weighed more heavily in our thinking. We had the chance to be watchdogs, to bark at all the flagrant ADA violators and laggards on the architectural front, but we feared offending.

Led by George Covington, who was cochair of the Universal Design Task Force of the President's Committee, we made a commitment to promoting the principles of Universal Design, a practical movement promoting barrier-free living initiated by Ron Mace in the 1970s at the Center for Accessible Housing at North Carolina State University. As Covington had written, "Most of the elements in our society that define us as 'the disabled' are caused by poor design. If I cannot find a building's address because the numbers are tiny or artistically hidden, I am 'visually impaired.' If a friend of mine in a wheelchair blocks the narrow aisle in a grocery store or cannot get onto a sidewalk because there is no curb cut, my friend is 'mobility impaired.' In the past, designers have failed to realize that when a disability meets a barrier, it creates a handicap."[1] This adherence to a design philosophy involved our responsibility for the magazine itself and the places it went. Thanks to Covington, I was alert to many of the pitfalls of thoughtless design in print. We even reconsidered the "snap-coated" glossy covers and pages because they might prove harder to hold for quadriplegics or those with arthritis—but the appeal to advertisers of the glossy pages, which enhance color effects, was too strong. The rule of thumb in printing is to maximize type size and the contrast between text and background for legibility. The readership to keep in mind is the "low vision" group that includes people with macular degeneration who, with the aid of lenses, have enough sight to discern letters on a page if type and pages are designed in a way that makes that possible. After just one session on this important but neglected subject in book and magazine design, I revamped the fonts and layouts of the next issue, boosting font sizes by two points overall, giving thumbs-down to any fancy headline "display" types that did not have sufficient contrast with their backgrounds to be legible (obviously the maximum contrast is black type on white, so you can imagine how difficult it would be to read a beautiful yellow "script" on a gray background, as one of our features was about to attempt). The "price" we paid was a nominally bigger design bill for one issue and the loss of a few hundred words in the 112-page issue. We never made a big deal out of the change, although it was noted in my front-of-the-book message to readers (the Editor's Desk), yet the redesign struck me as important. It connoted courtesy, on the one hand, and leadership as well. Although there are 7 million potential readers with low vision in the country, the emergence of large-type editions is one of the few accommodations the publishing industry has made to accessibility. By refashioning the look of the magazine to meet their needs, I meant to show how easily the style of thinking of Universal Design could be applied.

The accessibiltiy of our office and the sites where we shot our fashion spreads was also an issue. The 1960s-era apartment building on the Upper West Side where we cranked out the first five issues was utterly inaccessible to wheelchair users, a point that was made by every intern and visitor who showed up at the office. When we finally moved down to Soho, we went about a year before converting the bathroom near the chairman's office to an accessible one with no sill or step and a door wide enough for a wheelchair. Access is not simply a matter of going to the bathroom, however. It embraces the safe and comfortable working area that people with disabilities need. This is called "reasonable accommodation," and it is one of the most vital yet ignored clauses in the ADA. From the beginning of the magazine we were blessed with an intern from New York University who was hard of hearing. She would be able to do phone reporting with a relay phone, which offers a readout in the form of a textual transcription, created by operators at AT&T. The phone cost about $120, and it was my first expenditure on accommodation for the magazine—I can't think of a better $120 we spent in those days of waste and mistakes.

Other than that, as an employer we were so open to an ADA lawsuit it wasn't even funny, since we had so many people with disabilities in and out of a place that was for them a firetrap, and since we made a regular habit of asking people about their disabilities before hiring them (a completely illegal question, but somehow we bracketed ourselves by virtue of our identity politics). We were on a mission to change media. We could break the rules. Accommodation was an important issue, though. In the early days of the publication, when we were spinning our wheels on the layouts especially, we often adjourned at two in the morning, only to answer the bell at eight the next day. This is far from ideal for people in recovery who have a strong need to attend AA meetings, usually in the evenings, and who also hit the coffee and cigarettes hard as the workday stretches. Many had held high-stress jobs in the past—including an executive chef and a fashion editor—that had contributed to their habit, so I had to mete out the long hours judiciously. On the other hand, gritting it out to the bitter end of a production schedule was a point of pride, partic-ularly among my staffers in recovery who ended up making the transition from intern to full-time reporter. They in turn became mentors to the next interns, at which point the anonymity questioned bloomed yet again. We did not run that many stories about alcohol or drug addiction, and in one profile of an artist, Robert Rauschenberg, I muddied the waters sufficiently regarding the reason he was in a disability magazine to make it look as though his dyslexia was as much the reason as his being in recovery.

Identity as Point of View

The general, unstated policy of the magazine was that anybody could write or assign stories, but I had dibs on art, interiors, and business be-cause of my experience and my position. I wrote about two-thirds of our cover stories, too, and assigned a number of the rest to freelancers who had access (to Ali, or Sharon Stone, or Elizabeth Taylor), generally pay-ing a meager two thousand or so for the story and shelling out another thousand to agencies for a good-quality cover photo and a few quarter-page photos on the inside. As often as possible of course we cheaped it out by using publicity shots and party pictures provided by nonprofits that loved us. In others words, if someone on my staff wanted to write, that person could propose and usually get the assignment.

This poses interesting questions—did the deaf writers want to work on deaf stories, the people recovering from alcohol addiction on recovery stories? Not by any means. When I assigned reporting or research, did I match the disability of my editorial staffer to the disability of the person being covered? If so, did a staffer in recovery, say, disclose this fact to the source, establishing a bond, or should the reporter keep quiet and en-courage trust by other means. The reader will have long ago noticed, for instance, that television producers inevitably send out a woman reporter to interview rape victims, or African-Americans are sent to cover civil rights demonstrations, and of course, after the murder of Daniel Pearl by Islamic fundamentalists as well as 9/11, all the contortions made by major news organizations to assign Jewish or Islamic reporters to appropriate (even safe) locales and sources. Without compromising the anonymity principles we championed, I did want to make the most of the reporters' knowledge, as it is clear to me that one of the major shortcomings of media in general is a lack of expertise in complex areas on the part of the reporter. The medical, legal, ethical, and political questions that surround addiction and recovery are dense enough to limit the circle of experts to a very small group. People who have been through a twelve-step program and can string together enough sentences to make a feature constitute a small circle. As the editor in chief of a magazine that aimed at making headway in this challenging area, I wanted my "experts" to step out of the shadow and take on these assignments, but could not ask them to do so.

We were willing to use the growing popularity of disability studies to sway ad agencies, but for practical reasons there was precious little of this material in the magazine, even in the think pieces and book reviews, and the stars of disability theory, including historian Paul Longmore, aesthetics professor Rosemarie Garland Thomson, sociologist Henri-Jacques Stiker, activists Gary Karp and Kenny Fries, appeared in our pages only in the context of book reviews or the occasional lifted quotation. The language of the typical book or article in the field did not mesh with the pace and diction of a lifestyle magazine. Probably because I was so tightly bound to the office and the issue-to-issue problems of simply meeting our print deadlines, I did not spend a great deal of time in university libraries with the new collections of essays in disability theory, or with the *Disability Studies Quarterly,* which is the main refereed academic journal devoted to the specialty. There is a fundamental difference between covering a community and theorizing, summarized in the old journalism-school chestnut "Show, don't tell." Our goal was to present the success stories and the possibilities, the issues and the advances, as "straight" reportage with as little commentary as possible. We were out to make disability history, not write it.

Under the Microscope

One of the most prominent disability scholars, Rosemarie Garland Thomson, actually contacted us and showed up in our offices twice to greet the staff, look over layouts for a coming issue, and share a cup of coffee and a long, extremely interesting conversation in my publisher's empty office (must have been a slow day, as I rarely had anything more than half an hour to devote to any drop-ins) during which we discussed the mission of the magazine and the fashion spreads. Curiously enough, our talk ended up as part of one of her most often reproduced and cited articles. Having earned a doctorate in English from the Graduate Center of City University of New York in the early 1980s—where theory ruled in the era of deconstruction—I could keep up with her that day when she pressed the unavoidable conversational buttons such as Foucault, "the gaze," representation and its discontents, marginality. It was a crash course for me in current disability theory, a welcome link between my past scholarly life and my current media existence. I did not realize I was being interviewed, and was surprised three years later (the pace of academic publishing being what it is) to see my own magazine's fashion layouts reproduced and dissected in a remarkably clear, thoughtful, and wide-ranging article, "Seeing the Disabled," that was included in a collection curiously and somewhat misleadingly titled *The New Disability History.* She offered an anatomy of modes by which disability is represented in photography. Many of her points are useful to our understanding, too, including the importance of moving past medicalization, the discomfort caused by people staring, and the rhetorical manipulation of public opinion through visual imagery or, as she puts it, the way "popular photography has calcified the interpretations of disability embedded in the images."[2]

Garland Thomson's point about staring is worth noting: "Staring is the social relationship that constitutes disability identity and gives meaning to impairment by marking it as aberrant. Even if a disability is not apparent, the threat of its erupting in some visual form is perpetually present. Disability is always ready to disclose itself, to emerge as some visually recognizable stigmata, however subtle, that will disrupt social order by its presence. . . . Disabled people have variously been objects of awe, scorn, terror, delight, inspiration, pity, laughter, and fascination—but we have always been stared at."[3]

After a terrific and opinionated history of photography and disability, she enumerates four options: the wondrous (supercrip), the sentimental ("the stigmata of suffering"), the exotic (freak), and the realistic (the close-up). Having once wowed our readers with spectacular shots from a skydiving club called Pieces of Eight, which is completely made up of amputees, including one unforgettable sunset view of a man with a peg leg dropping in silhouette from the sky, I expected the magazine to be consigned to the "wondrous" category. As Garland Thomson explains it, "The picture operates similarly to the figurative pedestal on which women have been placed so as to keep them out of circulation in the mundane world of political and economic power. By positioning the disabled figure as the exception to human capability rather than the rule, the wondrous estranges viewer from viewed, attenuating the correspondence that equality requires."[4] That certainly sounds like many of our features, including a fashion piece I showed Garland Thomson that day featuring the Paralympic sprint champion and double amputee Aimee Mullins. Garland Thomson tees up on those images:

> As a gorgeous amputee, Mullins becomes an embodied contradiction. Her prosthetic legs parody—indeed, proudly mock—the very idea of the perfect body that has been the mark of fashion until today, even as the rest of her body conforms precisely to fashion's impossible standards. Rather than concealing, normalizing, or erasing disability, these photos use the sensationalism and stigma traditionally associated with disability to quench postmodernity's perpetual search for the new and arresting image.[5]

One of the pitfalls of publishing stories about athletes or celebrities such as Mullins is that a magazine promotes the "supercrip" at the expense of reality. As Garland Thomson points out, "Images of disability as a familiar, even mundane, experience in the lives of seemingly successful, happy, well-adjusted people can reduce the identifying against oneself that is the overwhelming effect of oppressive and discriminatory attitudes toward people with disabilities."[6]

Then Garland Thomson turns to my magazine, reproducing a page from one of our controversial fashion spreads as an example, thank goodness, of a "form of realism" that "constitutes a rhetoric of equality, radical in its refusal to foreground disability as difference." She writes, "Such ads reimagine disability by casting what had been culturally invisible—the disabled body—in the context of what is culturally hyper-visible—the fashion model. . . . Although this ad panders to the conspicuous consumption that all advertising does, what makes the image radical is that it does not appeal to the conspicuous contribution associated with charity photography. In other words, the conjunction of the visual discourse of high fashion, which has traditionally trafficked exclusively in standardized, stylized bodies, with the visual discourse of disability, which has traditionally traded in the pathetic, earnest or sensational, creates a visual disjuncture that calls previous cultural images of disability into question."[7]

I am thoroughly in agreement with her on the conclusion: "Understanding how images create and recreate disability as a system of exclusions and prejudices moves us toward the process of dismantling the institutional, attitudinal, legislative, and architectural barriers that keep people with disabilities from full participation in society."[8]

Fine-Tuning to the Wavelength

Marketing and sociological trends were converging, and WE became a nexus that, by putting those on paper, could amplify and extend them. Those were heady days for all of us on staff, particularly those of us who were taking our first lap as disability advocates and did not realize that many of these trends had come and gone before, along with the political and corporate promises that gave us more fuel for optimism. Inexperienced as I was (my first day on the job I had misspelled spinal cord as "chord" in a piece on rehabilitation), as editor in chief I found myself in television studios commenting on disability issues involving politics, business, and society—and plugging our 800 number—sincerely promulgating the sunny side of disability as captured in our pages, the travel and dining options, the astounding performance of athletes and entertainers, the economic progress as exemplified by our own success. My staff was a happy crew of accomplished and fulfilled people with disabilities, and the subjects I interviewed each week or the story ideas that were pitched to me were, almost by definition, success stories. Like a politician who hears only from the yes-men around him, I began to believe. Most journalists are cynical by nature. Cultivating an ironic disdain for one's material is one way to nurture the vigilance good journalism requires, questioning rather than agreeing, exposing instead of accepting. Advocacy journalism, which in a subtle way I was practicing under the guise of consumer and lifestyle reporting, dulls that edge. Simply put, I probably liked the people in my articles too much, just as I probably liked my staff too much, too, to be an efficient manager. As superior as I was in straight journalistic skills, I deferred to disability experience and secretly remained in awe of what for many of my sources and staffers was rather ordinary stuff. This naïveté may have cost us. One of the earliest and yet permanent cavils the experienced readers with disabilities expressed regarding our publication was that it was "too positive." True, there were far more heroes than villains, winners than losers, people on the move, world-record athletic performances, entertainers reaching the top of the charts, and smiling bosses who "got it." That's what made us an easier buy for the ad agencies, where fresh-faced recent college grads far removed from our world wanted to hear about how cool disability could be. But the veteran activists and media voices, with the exception of Justin Dart, were keeping their distance.

So many targets, so little courage. We fluffed it too often. Given another four years, having established both our circulation and our longstanding ad accounts, we could have gone further into the negative territory especially with our Heroes and Villains spread, in which news briefs about progress being made on the political or economic front faced off against setbacks, generally from misguided airlines, idiot talk show hosts (David Letterman was an easy target, and I always regretted not nailing Howard Stern), and, almost like shooting fish in a barrel, the U.S. government. In the Villains column, we did score one or two solid hits in what proved to be our strongest advocacy moment in each issue. There were also the low points. The publisher wanted to cut a deal with Jerry Lewis for the magazine to be featured on the annual Muscular Dystrophy Association telethon, so we told Lewis we'd put him on the cover. When I ran the idea by Covington, he howled and threatened to resign from our board. I incorporated, as a concession, a few paragraphs in the story on the controversy surrounding Lewis in the community, but the cover story made us lose points with the community. As Hockenberry wryly notes,

"Much of Jerry's money goes into investigating genetic screening to prevent people with MD from even coming into the world. Jerry's kids are people in wheelchairs on television raising money to find a way to prevent their ever having been born."[9]

In many ways, our editorial dilemma of using beauty to garner power mirrored that of the philanthropic machine we were attempting to circumvent. The rights of the "last minority" are sometimes better served by honey than vinegar, and the nonprofit machines that I have seen in action are far more successful when they accentuate the positive—formal galas at the Waldorf—than when they go for the jugular. There is no equivalent of the NAACP or NOW for people with disabilities that has any clout. The closest you come are the National Council on Disability and the National Organization for Disability, both Washington-based service organizations, and the various legal teams that make a specialty of ADA cases, most notably the legal stars of the Berkeley-based nonprofit Disability Rights Education and Defense Fund (DREDF), which was often the source of my stories in Heroes and Villains. As welcome guests in both political parties, despite the longtime association of disability rights with the Democrats, and as a "lifestyle" category publication rather than an advocacy one, we had entrée. Playing the pleasant guest, we parlayed one celebrity profile into the introduction to another, and the major organizations, such as Easter Seals, the Muscular Dystrophy Association, and United Cerebral Palsy, advanced our cause by mentioning us in their newsletters or letting us dump thousands of magazines in the goody bags for their events or their mailings. A magazine's ability to promote change depends on reach, and with every handshake and photo opportunity I managed to set up for my publisher with a senator or chairperson of a multibillion-dollar foundation I was extending our penetration into the circles of influence that were also our target market.

Up Close and Personal

The best thing that could happen, and often did, was for readers to turn up at our door. Occasionally the representatives of lesser-known disabilities came forward, either in the form of letters to the editor or in person, literally arriving at the offices. This sounds like an immensely awkward situation but in most cases turned out to be absolutely revelatory. By the time the editorial staff was one hundred percent composed of people with disabilities, which was in our second year, it was a point of pride to bring readers into the odd little newsroom where we all sat facing one another and introduce each of the players. Then we would sit wherever we could find room, usually a couch out in a hallway near the office, and I would listen and learn.

One of the most difficult aspects of being a journalist in the mainstream is gauging reader response. Through a sophisticated series of subscriber surveys, major news organizations like Time Inc. and the *Times* can paint a remarkably precise portrait of the average reader and his or her interests, from age and education right down to the car he or she drives, the Scotch or wine enjoyed, holiday plans, and on-the-job responsibilities. All these demographic tidbits are vital to the wooing of advertisers, of course, but we journalists use it to fine-tune our copy according to the profile of the reader. In a smaller outfit, however, direct contact through the phone, e-mails, letters, events, and casual encounters with readers is vital. We answered our own 1-800 number for new subscribers from the time it was instituted in our first months, and informally chatted them up about their responses to specific stories or their hopes for upcoming stories. Like other disability magazines and radio programs, we counted on daily interaction with our readers and often recruited them to be writers.

As an editor and writer, I found that these direct encounters were a boon to my ability to shape the subjects we covered and the way we covered them, and I have to admit that, as a rank amateur in the disability field, they were eye-openers as well, from which I came away with a vastly expanded sense of why I was doing the magazine, and for whom.

The most profound of the many deeply moving visits we had came one afternoon right in the middle of one of the worst deadline crunches I can remember. I could tell from the tone of the receptionist that "the young lady who would like to see the editor" was not to be denied. I emerged from our frantic offices, closing the door on the expletives and ringing phones, to find a small woman my own age leaning on a cane, looking at the framed covers we kept on the wall, and, it seemed to me, conducting with her free hand an unseen symphony she was hearing in her head. I introduced myself, and she murmured something about the pictures. Seeing that mobility was a challenge, I invited her to sit on the couch nearby, where she tucked herself into a corner, her cane demurely parked by the armrest, her eyes wonderfully bright and alert to everyone who passed by, to whom she smiled. The amateur Marcus Welby in me kicked in, and I started weighing the symptoms to decide whether she had cerebral palsy or muscular dystrophy. In the meantime, I wondered aloud whether she would like coffee or a soda. She chose ginger ale, and I returned with an open can and a straw, acting on a great tip from a cerebral palsy interview I once did. She reached into her knapsack and retrieved a handwritten letter a friend had helped her write that she wanted published in the magazine.

The smile and glittering eyes were one thing, but the letter was another. It blasted us for ignoring an important disability for the past two years, Huntington's chorea, and challenged us to include an article soon to address the needs of the 2 million Americans who lived with Huntington's, as did Marisa Yudkin, the undersigned and my guest. Chastened and intrigued, I settled in for the twenty-minute crash course in a rapidly moving degenerative disease of the neurological system that is hereditary (her father had recently died from its effects, and when Marisa was born she had a fifty-fifty chance of contracting it).

Marisa, a dancer who was my age, used the constant motion of Huntington's as a starting point for her choreography (in my nerdy way I became all the more intrigued by the etymological link between dance and *chorea*, the name for the disease). She often danced in recitals and workshops up and down the East Coast, and lived on her own in Brooklyn. Her speech was difficult but not impossible to grasp, and with about the same effort as it takes to understand a speaker with advanced cerebral palsy, I ostentatiously filled a couple of notebook pages with her story and accepted the atmospheric (that is, blurred) photo of her on stage as a possible graphic for a later issue. Meanwhile, I was feeling guilty about leaving my troops in the lurch, especially after the office door opened a crack and my managing editor shot me a "what's up?" look. I began making my excuses, and Marisa graciously accompanied me to the elevator where I pushed the button and hastily left her to get back to writing captions for the travel piece in the issue, which had to get out the door to the prepress house by that absolute, fixed chronological point of every small business day, FedEx pickup hour (the independent media world lives according to Memphis Mean Time). It was a notoriously slow elevator, and I don't know why but I turned as I reached the door and looked down the hall to make sure she was all right. The view was suddenly and inexplicably ravishing in its beauty. Marisa stood back from the elevator doors with her whole body, head through shoulders down to hips and knees, waving to and fro in a slow but absolute tempo. I froze until the doors opened and she disappeared, then rushed in to open a new document in Word and type the best lede (opening sentence) of my life: "Have you ever seen a willow sway in June?" It was one of those spontaneous verbal responses to stimulus. "We're putting the People on the Move dame on hold," I abruptly announced, using the terminology we had coined for the one-page, front-of-the-book profiles, one male one female, that constituted two of the too few pages in the issue we had already completely written, edited, copyedited, captioned, and signed off on as complete. There was a groan from the staff—I was no autocrat except insofar as being a stickler for deadlines, and this was no way to run a magazine, I knew, but in silence for the next twenty minutes or so I wrote a prose poem to or for

Marisa, and Huntington's got its coverage in WE. A month later I was with my kid sister, an orthopedic surgeon and this book's dedicatee for her extraordinary powers of diagnosis and empathy, and when I asked her about Huntington's the quick intake of breath with which she prefaced her own experiences in that area told me everything. Marisa did not have a chance. She was so thrilled when the magazine came out that her friend came by to take a box of issues to her next concert. It was the last I heard from her. Huntington's usually proves fatal by fifty. I did not have the heart to find out how she was doing as I prepared this book. To me, she will always be dancing by the elevator door to a music that is timeless.

There were many lessons learned over those years. One of the most practical was the importance of good design. Because I'd written on architecture in the past in some of my books, and because it saved on fees, I wrote nearly every one of the interiors features and delighted in turning up such gems as a Rem Koolhaas home in Bordeaux created for a wheelchair user, the ingeniously renovated headquarters for two of the most important organizations for the blind in Manhattan, and, to my utter fascination, gardens and extended care residences specifically created to provide a therapeutic setting for Alzheimer's patients, both safe and stimulating. As I interviewed architects, industrial designers, psychologists, and therapists about the devices and design solutions that remedied particular problems—among my favorites, the textured floor at Visions headquarters what was part of a "way-finding" strategy for cane users—the grab bag of tricks I accumulated turned into a modest set of insights into the ever more perceptible ways in which the buildings and products that surround us when poorly designed place inordinate restrictions on all of us, but particularly on people of varying abilities, impediments that are inherently discriminatory. These flawed environments restrict such rights as the ability to get to work, to travel, to vote, to enjoy an education, not to mention all those pleasures that fit into the "lifestyle" equation the magazine was pumping. Although legislation could never reengineer attitudes, it could more effectively address the design issues that reflect the general indifference of corporations, universities, governments, and, even under Clinton, the attitude of the people. The more attuned I became to the flaws of even the most recent buildings and products (I need look no further than the spanking new "vertical campus" of the college where I teach, completed just a year ago, at a staggering cost of $400 million, and one of the most disability-unfriendly places I've ever seen, despite the longstanding efforts of CUNY to serve the community), the more I believed that people with disabilities were far from paranoid in sensing sheer animosity all around them in the ways that people expected them to steer through minefields of design barriers from their homes to their offices.

In the interiors features, we placed an emphasis on beauty while using both photos and text to discreetly but pointedly subordinate the accessibility features (such as grab bars of lifting devices) to a background role. In addition, the particulars of the disability for which the household was designed were minimally described, simply because it was plain that my readership did not need as much instruction in the disability as in the design. For example, the house that Koolhaas had done in Bordeaux for an unnamed client was reportedly designed for a rich businessman who'd smashed up his sports car. I saw no reason to report any of that classic juice because it struck me as beside the point in a celebration of what was genuinely a triumph of design. Its focal point—and this to me is still as astonishing as it was when I first saw the images—is a ten-foot by ten-foot "room" in the center of the Minimalist house that is essentially an open elevator. This whole room descends to the wine cellar when the owner wants to fetch a fine bordeaux. It reappears as the dining room on the first floor when he is entertaining and then ascends to the second-floor library when he is not entertaining. When the room's floor is not there, at a particular level, there is a huge gap in the house. I still relish the sheer irony of where I first found the plan and images, in a superb Museum of Modern Art exhibition in New York titled *The Un-Private House* for the ability of someone outside to see into the living space.

The formula of an interiors feature was basic: big, beautiful pictures—generally an opening spread and at least two following full-page full-bleed images with pull quotes—dominated the layout, with extended captions that attributed all the fabrics, art, and accessibility features (bathrooms were big) in the style of shelter rags such as *Architectural Digest* and *Elle Decor*. We were, after all, dying to steal their ad clients. The 1,200- to 1,500-word story opened with the "ooh-ah" or "drop-dead" highlights of the house—Koolhaas's outrageously large and open elevator, a disappearing wheelchair ramp from one floor to another in a Cambridge, Massachusetts townhouse, a fireplace built into a massive curving picture window overlooking a California canyon, to name a few examples. This is no deviation from the typical house-tour routine of capturing the visitor's fancy with some ridiculously expensive engineering gimmick or material, the old $10,000 granite countertop trick that lingers in the mind long after the visit is over. The less this had to do with disability the happier I would be, in that it hammered home the point that an accessible home need not look like a hospital interior, all chrome-finished grab bars and severe contraptions for lifting patients from bed to bath. If the architect was a known star in his or her own right, a potted biography and review of earlier masterpieces came next (certainly this was the case for Koolhaas, for Samuel Mockbee, a Macarthur-genius grant winner, and for FDR, whose fascinating sketch for an accessible cottage in Hyde Park we unearthed for one story about the building's restoration).

A Near Miss

It all sounds like a recipe for success, but one thing eluded us: the circulation figures we needed to bolster our ad rate. The magic number for the lifestyle category to court the type of advertisers we wanted (American Express, Nike, BMW, Mercedes, Absolut, and the like) is 300,000 readers, and we frequently mentioned we had met that figure, but only orally. On paper we claimed we had 150,000 readers by the end of the first year, and we once actually printed that many copies, when the first anniversary issue came around and we had an advertorial insert in collaboration with my old employer *Fortune*. Both magazines were set to run a sixteen-page section on including people with disabilities in corporate diversity programs. In addition to raking in tens of thousands in ad revenues for us, it meant a big-time collaboration and handily served our efforts to push for the employment of people with disabilities. It was a major coup for us.

In truth, our paid circulation hovered around 3,000 throughout the entire run of WE magazine, a shameful, baffling, paltry figure that represented the actual number of people who were paid subscribers. Even after the earnest efforts of two newsstand brokers, paid up front to get our magazine into airports and other prime locales, our single-copy sales were similarly disastrous, never exceeding 1,000 copies. The rest were given away, dumped at charity events, drop-shipped at the merest request, stuffed into closets, and basically wasted in an effort to retain our third-class postage rates, which depended on our ability to show that the magazines had been "requested" and were not being direct-mailed without the recipient's previous consent. This was a matter of both price (several thousands in mailing costs per month) and pride. All magazines start at zero, but after expensive direct-mail campaigns, television and print coverage announcing our 800 number, and the old favorite, word of mouth, one expects results, and we were beside ourselves by the second year when we were turning out a super magazine, right on time (we never missed our print deadline), receiving rave reviews from both the community and the media alike, yet never reaching even the crucial level in circulation that whole time. Our ad revenues of about $700,000 were above our costs, which I had learned to keep down by eliminating the repetition and corrections that our designers, prepress house, and printers made the most money on, and bargaining like hell with writers and photographers.

Through three years of consistent improvement, the magazine had reached the stage where we were not floundering in mistakes or casting about for innovations. The formula for the issue was in place, from feature placement to departments, and our deadlines were being met with far greater ease than before. By that time, we had developed a reliable roster of writers with disabilities to cover major topics and turn in the annual special reports on business, cars, design, movies, education, and other issues. We had arrived at the point where we were steadily refining stylistic details involving design and editing.

A journalist on a beat inevitably develops a proprietary attitude regarding day-to-day experiences or observations that seem linked to anything within that sphere of reporting. A Wall Street reporter keeps a peripheral eye on the ticker. This habit in me rose to new heights when the magazine was my own and the beat was a community. "He's one of mine," I'd think as I followed a person with a different gait or white cane in midtown Manhattan. At shopping centers and arenas I scanned the "handicapped" parking zones and put free copies of our early issues under windshield wipers. I found myself devoting unprecedented attention to the spinal cord and orthopedic wings of the hospitals where my sister, a surgeon in Vermont, and my mother, a volunteer in New Hampshire, worked. One's perception can be entirely redirected by a journalistic agenda. Suddenly I was scanning the headlines for "ADA" and "stem cell," bookmarking support groups and nonprofits on my Internet browser, collecting gallery invitations to openings for artists with any known disabilities as well as any labeled "outsider" or Art Brut. I spent far too much time watching *Access Hollywood* to see who was checking in or checking out of the revolving door between back lots and recovery clinics, practically the entire cast of *Ally McBeal* or *Friends*. A stutter on the radio or on the phone, asymmetry in the smile at a bookstore reading (stroke?), all were fair game for interview requests. I could spot a hearing aid a hundred feet away, and identify its manufacturer at fifty.

A Matter of Privacy

Well before I became editor in chief of a disability magazine, I ran into thorny issues such as passing while I was in the "mainstream" journalistic world of Time Inc. For one *Fortune* magazine piece about government-supported entrepreneurial "incubators" mainly located in the Midwest, I interviewed a factory manager who was in charge of a team of thirty workers in what we deemed an exemplary use of the government subsidies and small-business acumen. When the photographs for the piece came in, the reporter (that's me), writer, editor, and managing editor convened for a twenty-minute session with the art department in a little room off the main conference area of the editorial offices. It was a quick slide show of last-round cuts for the final article, and as three or four of the shots of the manager on the factory floor came up on screen, it was clear he was a wheelchair user. "Why is he in a wheelchair?" the managing editor asked.

I did not know, so I did what any reporter would, scribbled the query in my notebook and headed back to the phone to repeat it to a source. The manager in Wichita was busy, so an assistant took the call. I cringed to hear him shout the question over the din of the machines, and could quite distinctly here the reply: "None of his fucking business." That put me in a pickle. Before the end of the editing process, I had repeated the relay of managing editor and editor to factory twice, and still the manager in Wichita resolutely refused to say why he was in the wheelchair. As much as I admired him, I found it annoying at the time.

Now I recognize that factory manager as an early advocate of privacy, and *Fortune* as an early instance of a mainstream publication that didn't get it. My curiosity was not always welcome even on behalf of *WE,* and many times on a bus or subway I was snubbed when I offered a free copy of the magazine. There were latent problems about which we were in cheerful denial. Long after we were finished publishing, a new biography of John F. Kennedy raised the issue of his ability to discharge his duties in the face of his medical problems. The book itself would have made fodder for an editorial in *WE.* Not only does it impugn Kennedy's leadership and qualifications on the sole basis of his medical condition, but it also weighs his sex life and his pills in the same scales, coming down on the side of the medication in terms of being more scandalous. It is a good way to sell books, of course, but both medical and sexual matters are touchstones of privacy issues. With Kennedy's medical records exposed, a similar rending of the curtain opened other politicians' health to scrutiny, and one of the first names to pop up in the ensuing media hubbub was that of Tom Eagleton, a martyr to the cause of mental health patients' rights whose vice presidential candidacy was snuffed by a leak that he had undergone psychoanalytic treatment for depression. These are some of the most dramatic examples of medical privacy being violated, but in the wake of serious new rules at hospitals and in doctors' offices nationwide regarding privacy, I feel that the magazine may have been on the brink of compromising a serious boundary involving its readers, its sources and subjects, its staff, and its very premise. We were celebrating in public a private matter. Perhaps we were bound to falter. Was it our Achilles' heel? I was captivated one day by an extraordinarily candid essay on this issue by Franklin D. Reeve, poet, translator, and father of Christopher, who began the piece with a complaint about all the strangers who endlessly bothered him for medical details on "Superman's" brave fight to walk again. He nailed the paradox of "private grief for public ends" in this passage:

> The more Christopher appears on television, the more frequently they approach, assuming that I can give them some bit of inside information that will bring them into the exalted family circle. If I so much as touch upon the realities of Christopher's situation, they look puzzled—even betrayed. So I have learned to give them a "hot tip" on the date of his next important TV appearance, and they leave, somehow assured that by seeing me they are involved in the good fight and are cheering the underdog. For me, it's an unrewarding charade, made all the more painful by the realities of the situation. People who support the "good fight" have no idea how they're discriminating against—that is, denying individual identity to—an individual father and son struggling to maintain a difficult relationship in the face of differing values and overwhelming physical problems. In Christopher's case, the role of "handicapped Superman" has taken the place of reality. If I refuse to be de-individualized, or if I insist on mentioning the misery and hardship that my son feels daily—he who can never be alone, who must be wakened and turned every couple of hours during the night—I become a nay-sayer to the image of which he has become custodian.[10]

These days, with the collapse of the magazine behind me, I wonder if we missed an inherent flaw, so eloquently and movingly exposed in this confession, in the very premise of our effort to glorify in public what is legally or ethically better left private.

Nobody had ever heard of protected health information (PHI) when we started the magazine. By 2004, as this book was being completed, it was a hot topic in hospitals and among health care policymakers. PHI now comprises such a broad spectrum of situations that even the volunteers at hospitals are drilled on the subject. In 1996 the rules were relatively clear when it came to AIDS and mental health treatment (including recovery from alcohol and drugs). Then came genetic testing and the controversy over disclosure of "de-identified" information that was used in research (de-identified after personal identifiers linking the data to the patient had been removed). A magazine that takes an aggressive pro-research stance, as we did, can find itself on the wrong side of the privacy issue in that even data collected on multiple patients, and reported only as group statistics, are protected health information, especially in the case of deceased patients. This runs directly parallel with the public-private dilemma faced by the hospitals, which are required by law to report to their state and federal oversight agencies anything deemed to be in the public interest, and at the same time to maintain personal privacy rights. Although most institutions would avow that the public interest comes first (one thinks of communicable diseases such as SARS in China and the suppression of information there), fear of lawsuits has certainly advanced the cause of privacy. By April of 2003, when the new Federal Privacy Rule's rights became effective, the classes of protected information had been extended to all types of treatment, payment, and care.

The new law cast unexpected light not only on patients' rights but on the vulnerability of certain information. By enumerating the vast circles of formerly nameless flunkies who can view your records, it suddenly reminded us that the curtain had been pulled back a long way on our naked medical profiles. In a teaching hospital, for example, even under the new PHI laws, a patient's cirrhosis treatment would be known by the doctor, consulting specialists, nurses, outreach workers, secretaries, therapists, dietitians, technicians, pharmacists, administrators, payment coders, record clerks, managers, billing managers, bill collection agencies, quality assurance reviewers, credentialing committees, lawyers, accountants, patient representative, publicists, medical students, residents, nursing students, therapists in training, faculty, researchers, research coordinators, and epidemiologists, not to mention the nosy but well-meaning volunteers. That list alone would make a healthy start for a magazine's circulation.

When I was still embroiled in the struggle to keep the magazine going, I had precious little time to ask deep questions about what philosophical and ethical principles were wearing down our prospects for success. The obvious quantitative problems were staring us in the face, including our circulation woes and the concomitant ad revenue compromises we were forced to make because, according to industry standards, we could not justify our page rates without an audited circulation statement showing that we actually had the readership we claimed we did (we were never even close). Our direct-mail recipients who were sent free magazines would occasionally send them back with angry notes about how we had intruded on their privacy, as though we ought to have bagged them in opaque covers as some AIDS publications do. The mystery of our low circulation could be explained in part by this sensitivity. In other ways, we remained baffled. Our overtures to major disability organizations had been rebuffed, perhaps in part out of their suspicion that we were trying to turn a fast buck, including appeals to distribute the magazine through the Muscular Dystrophy Association, Easter Seals, the Shriners hospitals, and, even after a super and lengthy cover package devoted to the theme, the Disabled American Veterans and their 2 million-plus members. We were retaining our core subscribers but not making inroads anywhere, and it was driving us all nuts because the magazine was coming along well, the diversity of disabilities in our pages was far more sophisticated than it had been, and the critics were conceding the fact that we had the lifestyle formula down pat. In our frustration, we thought we had run into the indifference of society. In our more perverse moments, we blamed people with disabilities themselves, who were used to receiving magazines and other perks for free and therefore reluctant to fork over twenty bucks for a subscription.

It was only much later, in the quiet of long Friday afternoon sunsets accorded to academics who no longer have to meet printers' deadlines, that some of the underlying causes of our demise began to assert themselves. We were pushing the public envelope on disability as an identity-shaping, community-defining, life-altering badge of honor. Passing was not in the conversation, but should have been. In analogous dialogues about race, for instance, the most sophisticated media would take on the issue of passing directly. I would bristle when a celebrity turned my interview request down on the grounds that he refused to be typecast as a person with a disability—notably, the great German singer Thomas Quasthoff, who even told a *Wall Street Journal* reporter, a week after I had called him, that he had shot me down as a way of driving home his point that he would not be pigeonholed in that way. His refusal of my interview request made it into the *Journal,* much to my chagrin.

We missed the ethical and political story about the new protections provided to patients by privacy laws, which would have made good think pieces, but more importantly we missed the way in which the assertion of privacy rights unexpectedly undermined the standard civil rights model we had been counting on to bring us success along the lines of the pattern set by *Ms., Ebony,* or the many gay publications, for which "outing" was not only part of the drama, a story line, but a mass-market force in sustaining the magazines. One of the major civil rights victories of people with disabilities, the ADA, had a potent privacy component—the employee's guarantee that details of his or her disability need never be divulged. In the most basic terms, two of the most promising legislative breakthroughs of our time for people with disabilities were at cross-purposes, and as a media organization depending for our survival on the impulse to "go public" we were caught in the middle. In the meantime, we were battling knuckleheads in the mainstream, such as John Stossel of ABC's *20/20,* who were maliciously targeting the ADA week after week ("Over the years, I have interviewed two dozen people who say they have multiple chemical sensitivity, and it strikes me that their lives revolve around being sick. It's as if being a victim is what gives them purpose.")[11] By the beginning of 2001, it was dawning on us that the whole disability rights movement was making a subtle turn, and that our agenda might no longer be on course anymore.

I will put the history of *WE* on pause here—the final chapter, in which I expose the false promises of the Internet miracle for people with disabilities, will make clear how a steadily growing media company with a healthy magazine can be scuttled in months by a bunch of adolescent Web fanatics. The lessons learned in putting together *WE* every other month sharpened my critical faculties for what other media organizations, including advertisers and filmmakers, were doing with disability, and I certainly did not like what I was seeing.

CHAPTER EIGHT

"on the web we're all equal"

And Other Myths about Disability and Multimedia

If thou wilt needs damn thyself, do it a more delicate way than drowning.
Make all the money thou canst.
—Iago, in Othello

Between editorial takes at the magazine, I would wander in Soho, generally stopping in at art galleries to recharge my visual and intellectual batteries for the next round of deadlines. One hot summer afternoon in 1999, when dot-com fever was at its height in New York, I turned up at the blue door of a gallery I had never visited and, after one look at the invitation card taped by the buzzer, which read *Prosthetic*, headed straight up the dirty, dark stairs to a big, brightly lit gallery space on the second floor.

I was fleeing the wide-eyed hype of callow Web fanatics who saw nothing but Net in those days and who had taken over my magazine. Imagine my disdain, then, upon finding an "information installation" that combined my two worst art nightmares, conceptualism and the Web. Somewhere in its elaborate tangle of headphones, monitors, and turning wheels of photographs the slippery texts promised a glimpse of a person with disabilities who had been injured in a car accident and, one presumed from the title, used a prosthesis. The gallery show was the front for an elaborate Web site, one of the earliest of many exhibitions that relied heavily on the Internet. I was prying, but the crummy sixties-era photos of stunned children and insipidly grinning aunts and uncles set against hideous wallpaper returned a confusing mix of signals from happy times in what seemed a typical suburban family, all pulling faces and wearing polyester. After my second or third lap around the gallery, my patience fraying, I headed toward the desk where the boyishly handsome art dealer had just clicked shut his cell phone after lining up guests for a rooftop party with what I immediately assumed would be the coolest art types and beautiful people. Asked for the lowdown, he smiled and began the patter. The artist, William Scarbrough, was only thirty-one and had already been featured in such unartsy mainstream media as *Penthouse, Details, New York,*

Harper's, Artbyte, a Dave Barry column, the page 6 gossip column of the *New York Post.* The kid had even appeared on the *Jerry Springer Show*—how hot is that?

Spare me. I just wanted to know about Stuart Tiros, the person with a disability whose life story was the narrative basis of the exhibition, and what he thought about the show. My editor's instincts had already kicked in. Would he be available for an interview? The dealer's grin broadened. "There is no Stuart. It's all a fiction."

The floor spun, and a wave of embarrassed fury reddened my cheeks. I returned to the exhibition, which reeked of authenticity and the banality of those nickel-a-bushel personal Web sites that keep millions of egos puffed up on a daily basis, the blogs where "picture whores" vamp for their digital cameras and whimper about their boyfriends. The hoax had immediately gotten under my skin, and I wanted to meet the rascal who concocted it. Curiosity breeds perverse hungers, so I set up a lunch date with the artist at a trendy garden bistro in the same Soho neighborhood. A week later I was sipping a decent white burgundy under a leafy trellis contemplating the way I might still incorporate *Prosthesis* in the magazine. William Scarbrough, the artist, turned up in rumpled white T-shirt, jeans, and work boots, looking as if he had just come off the morning shift on a construction site—which he had, because that is one way for an artist who does not sell much of his work to support his expensive computer habits (he was also moonlighting as a designer for NBC's Web site). With his Fu Manchu and wayward black hair he looked like a holdover from the Philadelphia Flyers of the 1970s, the sort of guy you don't want to see in your rearview mirror behind the wheel of an old Buick creeping up on your bumper.

It turned out Scarbrough was a true ironist. While his exhibition pushed many of the buttons of art du jour—installation based, Web intoxicated, pathetically confessional, all served with a dab of political correctness thanks to the disability angle—he maintained a firm satiric handle on these gestures. The formula was enough to get many fashionable artists into the Whitney Biennial, but Scarbrough had embedded stronger meanings that foretold the downward corkscrew turns my own enterprise was about to take. Like Lauren Slater's faux memoir, Scarbrough's big idea was to use the Web format to cultivate *im*personality: "I get to express my inner voice, but it goes out completely veiled. What if it were the exact same physical installation, but it was my life, me, my world, no disability? You'd be gone." I nodded in agreement. Still smarting from my misreading of the exhibition, I pushed him for the inside scoop. Back came an answer that was more than metaphor. It was insight: "The Web is the prosthesis. That's how we use it."

When I took that line back to the office, the publisher, cranking up our own Web site and looking forward to the hundreds of millions in instant wealth he projected for himself through an initial public offering, started using "the ultimate prosthesis" at once in marketing and investment bank presentations. Little did he know that the "ultimate prosthesis" he was touting was, in the eyes of the artist who coined the term, the Web as dildo.

The Dot Con

Scarbrough's elaborate deception was part of my rude awakening to the New Economy. Completely behind my back, the "revolution" in the company had been taking place for months down in Manhattan's financial district, where the mayor's office had rolled back corporate taxes to create a "Silicon Alley" along William Street. The chairman and publisher signed a lease on twenty thousand square feet of space on the sixth and seventh floors of an old social services building and cranked up a dot-com within a couple of months, replete with banks of cubicles, massive glass-enclosed offices and conference rooms with massive leather chairs, state-of-the art workstations, towering stacks of servers, and the obligatory windowless "war room" in which the highest of the high-tech strategies were mapped on whiteboards while pizzas and joints were consumed. The budget for all this was astronomical by comparison with the shoe-string the magazine had been on. Those leather chairs were $600 each. I was there when an IBM team came in to look around, and in the elevator, not knowing who I was, one commented, "They overspent by a factor of ten." Lunch meetings at the trendy Balthazar in Soho would run up $3,000 tabs while the chauffeured black Land Cruisers waited outside. Over a hundred dot-commers who looked and acted like central casting's epitome of the computer geek were hired at double the salary of any of my editors with scarcely any background checks and, most important, no training or interest in disability. It was a shot at the Internet jackpot pure and simple, funded by a $15-million cash infusion squeezed from our investors in return for the lure of the typical New Economy stock option package. To get in on the trend, which only lasted months, we rapidly needed to put up the facade of a successful Internet start-up. One day it was announced the magazine would be called *WeMedia*. The comic parade of Silicon Valley–style marketers and strategists began snaking through our one-room office on their way to meet the chairman. They represented all the archetypes of the boom—the slick, fast-talking, twenty-something salesmen who promoted the Internet as the savior of American capitalism and would line the coffers with gold from banner advertisements (we never made a penny on them). We had our guru, the unkempt, tattooed "convergence" genius whose too-cool-for-school Web tricks would win awards and amaze millions of online "community members" (they never logged on, much less registered and surrendered their personal information). According to a business plan, the Web convergence master, whom I referred to as Meatloaf because he resembled the rock star, was pulling down $210,000 a year (exceeding the sum of the salaries of the magazine staff) with further thousands' worth of stock options and a massive expense account. In back offices lurked the grizzled veteran opportunists from broadcasting who were there to cash in quick on hideously expensive simulcasting projects mainly involving disabled sports. The Gen X nincompoops playing Frisbee in the hall were supposed to "code" all day long when they weren't riding their Razor scooters, blogging and instant-messaging each other across the vast space of our Web "laboratory," which had become one of thousands of such asylums across the United States devoted to a crazed scam that, we now realize, vacuumed up billions of dollars from legitimate enterprises. It was insane.

On top of the conventional dot-com rhetoric touting lateral management and the triumph of creativity, we had another layer of oratory promising great advances for people with disabilities. The site would offer business and educational opportunities to the "home-bound," as the dot-commers insisted on calling them, for example, along with lucrative shopping services. The Internet would eradicate the loneliness of being disabled because everybody would be connected, and nobody could see or hear your disability online, eliminating stigma and discrimination. Virtual reality would turn everybody into the gymnast, ballet dancer, or sex god he or she longed to be. Passing would be the game. The Web geniuses cooked up a personals ad section and dating service (nobody signed up). A massive political operation was promised that would enroll hundreds of thousands of new online voters and activists who would propel Al Gore to office in the next election (didn't happen). A real estate shopping mart would match accessible homes on one coast with buyers in wheelchairs on the other (another company beat us to this rather clever idea). The Web would revolutionize disability culture! Nor were the hucksters at WeMedia the only ones pumping the extraordinary changes the computer could bring to the community. It is almost cruel to quote some of the early cheerleaders ex post facto. Here is Jack Nelson, one of the leading writers on media and disability, extolling in 1994 the virtues of virtual reality:

> The virtual environment allows everyone—regardless of their physical abilities—to move about, to fly through the air, to turn somersaults, or perform other feats—regardless of the physical constraints of the human body. When

one can maneuver through a virtual environment by hand motions or even voice control, it makes no difference if the user is sitting in a chair or in a wheelchair. Through virtual reality those whose mobility is limited in the real world will be able to attend virtual conferences or visit exotic places in virtual travel.[1]

In the clear light of the morning after, sobered by losses on the stock market and painful memories of the naïveté with which we embraced the dot-conners, a far different view of the impact of the Internet on disability has been disclosed. Is it possible to turn this around and consider the ways in which computers exacerbate or cause conditions that are disabling? The alarming rise in carpal tunnel syndrome cases certainly offers statistical substance to the detrimental effects of overuse. A heavy toll has also been levied on our eyesight by long hours in front of the screen. A nation already plagued by ADD and ADHD is enticed by the "hyper" in HTML. It is more difficult to cite diagnostic figures for the various types of addiction the Web fosters, but nothing is more annoying than the temporary paralysis induced by video games on a slack-jawed, zombie-eyed eleven-year-old consumed with a passion for rolling over stolen cars and lopping off the heads of prostitutes. As addictions are part of the disability definition, we should also consider the wicked waste of time and energy lavished on online gambling, pornography, blogging, and deal-making on eBay. I am not a licensed therapist by any means, but personal acquaintance and much of the research I have done has led me to believe that one of the great enemies to mental well-being among people with disabilities is the tremendous loneliness many face day to day, and I think the isolation of cyberspace far outweighs the much touted "connectivity" of chat rooms and e-mail, particularly as the identities of so many bizarre users out there are false and their own scams are so insidiously widespread. Starting around 1998, we fielded too many stories for our Villains column about people with disabilities being cheated by Internet crooks peddling everything from equipment to insurance. It is a web of deceit as much as it is a network of support.

Meanwhile, on the ground in those frantic days we still ran a legitimate magazine with a staff of four editors, and it baffled and annoyed us that the kids produced a Web site promising all this pie in the sky and at the same time using none of our content whatsoever. The Web text was backsliding into the language of pity we had studiously exiled from our pages. The content veered toward the medical and finally ended up with sports and entertainment. All this missed the tone and balance we had carefully achieved in print. I had to have two or three pieces edited or removed for inappropriate language ("wheelchair-bound" showed up, for example), but the part that was killing me was that as with everything else in those days people went to the Web site first and it misrepresented the magazine. It was illiterate, naive, unsophisticated, and at times silly. Technically it was also a disaster. The site was always either crashing or a crashing bore. Most disastrously, however, it was not disability-friendly, a technical miscalculation that would prove its undoing.

Yet all around us we were watching millions being made on dot-com start-ups that successfully launched their initial public offerings. I will not pretend I was completely immune from the fever. As I watched all the money being chucked around on custom-tailored suits and limos that shuttled the little WeMedia executives around Manhattan, I became jealous. I had been granted 100,000 options, which I could exercise as soon as the stock was issued, as I had number one seniority in the company (the first ever hired), and the estimate we all heard of the opening price was $12, so I bragged to my wife we had at least $1.2 million coming to us on the launch of the stock (when I planned to immediately cash in). I made sure each of the editors received options, too, so we were all in on the deal. Notoriously cheap, I astonished my hockey teammates after a couple of Thursday night skates by buying rounds, and you can imagine the lotto-style fantasies I indulged. I started mimicking the spendthrift ways of the dot-commers downtown. Nearly every afternoon I treated my whole staff to ice cream or cappuccinos at the café in our building, or started taking them out for lunches. The staff would join me at the orgiastic dot-com parties at watering holes in Battery Park or Tribeca, where all the little paper millionaires congratulated one another ad nauseam at an open bar and proclaimed the transformation of American capitalism by the wonders of the Internet.

The Great Inaccessible Disability Web Disaster

But there was trouble from the start. Once the Web site was up and running (having missed every deadline set for it during the past three months), launched in a Times Square hotel ballroom by Walter Cronkite while our $75,000 promotional film was being shown on the Jumbotron at $5,000 a minute, it became quickly apparent that it was not ready for prime time in terms of disability protocol. On the technical side, it was inaccessible for users with disabilities. Inaccessibility stems from overreliance on design features that cannot be used by blind, deaf, or mobility-impaired patrons. As soon as it was up and running, I put the site through a quick and simple audit created by programmers at MIT and administered by the World Wide Web Consortium. It failed miserably. You would have to be Sherlock Holmes to find the all-important "text only" button on the gateway. The hideous graphics danced and fluttered incessantly, a nightmare for low-vision users. The designers had failed to include descriptive text captions (so-called alternate text tags) for the graphics, especially the photos. Flash technology, which is murder on deaf as well as blind users, was used all over the site. The audio and mpeg (movie) clips had no closed-captioning for deaf users. The complexity of the home page defied the mouse skills of a person with limited mobility. The litany of ills went on for more than a dozen pages in the printed report that I started furiously waving around the office. Having just run a story in our Heroes and Villains column on the need for greater regulatory scrutiny regarding Web access, this fault in our own now-conspicuous public face was mortifying. I shot off pointed but civil memos to Meatloaf and his minions, and you can imagine the sarcasm with which they were received: "Dude, take it easy. The site's so cool."

For the next four months, absolutely no steps were taken to make the site accessible, even as the Flash and other "cool" features that made it more inaccessible were being piled on. It was also overreaching itself in many areas. As we had fluffed our circulation figures, the Web meisters were ridiculously inflating their hit counts as they scrambled to put together numbers that would appeal to Wall Street—at one point we were even instructed at the magazine to enter the chat rooms, where hits were always supposed to be generated but where there never was anybody at all even though we had heard so much about how "home-bound" people with disabilities would embrace the Web chat room as a way to socialize. An audit prepared weekly by Web Trends showed that we were barely getting seven hundred real users a week, probably half of them concocted by the cheaters downtown. The chairman approved a massive, $250,000 print campaign that put full-page ads in the *Wall Street Journal, New York Times,* and *Washington Post* to drive traffic to the site. Billboards were rented, and we blew tens of thousands every weekend sponsoring sports events from sailing off Newport (our logo emblazoned on our boat's spinnaker) to skiing to mountain biking. We were hemorrhaging money on promotion. None of the ads mentioned the magazine or the 1-800 number for subscriptions—had we plugged the magazine that lavishly we could have doubled our circulation in a week. Then came the radio ads on New York's top news station in drive time—I nearly ran off the road the first time I heard my own company's spot. We still weren't getting traffic. Meanwhile the Web staff kept growing, especially on the marketing end. Increasingly I was feeling like Danny DeVito in the silly movie *Twins,* who discovers that his twin brother is the monster Arnold Schwarzenegger. Unlike the comedic *Twins,* however, the magazine would be killed by its Web site. Even after pulling off the near impossible and bringing a start-up magazine into the black, we would be destroyed by our own mismanagement and overweening greed.

The beginning of the end came when I learned that a team of fifty Web "geniuses" was heading to Sydney, Australia, in September 2000 to simulcast the Paralympics on our site, using the Los Angeles TV anchor Bree Walker Lampley (wife of a major sportscaster and a one of the most famous on-screen personalities with a disability) and renting the network facilities left behind by the NBC Olympics team. We packaged and paid for an hour on CBS on New Year's Day for a highlights program from the Paralympics, hosted by Bree and plugging the Web site. It pulled miserable Nielsen ratings. This twenty-day debacle cost us $7 million, enough for me to run the magazine for a decade. We had paid the international Paralympic committee for our sponsorship rights in addition to footing the bill for coders, cameramen, editors, and hangers-on to live in Sydney for nearly three weeks. Up until the last minute, they were struggling to make it to the deadline of a live feed, and yet later it would turn out to be immaterial because nobody at all was watching, anywhere, because the Flash technology took too much memory to load and, of course, for most of the target audience back in the United States a live broadcast from Sydney came in the middle of the night. One of the signals that a Web site is inaccessible is its reliance on Flash. The gallows humor started at the Paralympic Games. "When Pierre goes down, Pierre goes down in flames," our chairman shouted to the publisher during the fireworks at the end of the opening ceremonies. We had blown big bucks on a long shot that would spell the demise of the magazine. From a hockey buddy at Donaldson, Lufkin and Jenrette I already knew they and the rest of Wall Street had passed on the initial public offering, laughing at the business plan, which even by dot-com fever standards was ludicrously overstated, so I quit to return to teaching. Defectors started renouncing their stock options and joining other Web ventures while a sudden move was made, too late, to tighten belts around the company and wait for the next investment bank to show up with an offer to underwrite our stock. It never did.

The Site Crashes

I applied myself to finding a new editor in chief with a disability for the magazine and arranged for Ted Kennedy Jr., an amputee who had a slight reputation in disability circles and an interest in journalism, to visit the Web site. He had a useful celebrity cachet and would be great for ad dollars even if he did not apply himself to the copy as I had—my staff could manage that. He toured the Web cubicles with a blank look on his face, sniffed the problems, and never returned. After I left, the magazine missed its next deadline by five months and then reappeared, rife with errors of fact and grammar and almost totally devoted to sports and entertainment, following the lead of the Web site. The investors took one look and lost confidence, vetoing any further expenditures. A cable television network called Women's Entertainment started advertising itself as WE, the name we had abandoned, and a futile effort was made by WeMedia to sue the new WE, even as the whole staff was laid off. More than two years later, mainly out of curiosity but also to see what in the files could be salvaged for future study, I revisited the Web offices just as workers were packing up the last of the expensive coffeemakers and mugs, the souvenir hats, key chains, and other swag we gave out like every other dot-com of the time. The cubicles were all empty, wires like viscera poking out from cabinets that had held all the best computer equipment money could buy (it had all fetched a paltry sum at auction months before). In a corner, boxes of the magazine had tumbled into a heap—the Sharon Stone cover on top. The empty desks were coated with a fine gray dust in the middle of the vast, cold, silent space. I secured a shopping bag full of old magazines that I still wanted to give to people who had been in the articles, and turned the lights out on the rest.

Autopsies of mismanaged dot-coms are fairly common in contemporary business literature, but what made this tragicomedy different was the suicidal way in which a media enterprise turned its back on its own audience. There may be organizational and financial explanations for the death of WeMedia, but I would argue that the Web site did not deserve to succeed, because it made the mistake of rejecting the importance of accessibility. We should have created a showcase for Web design ideas, not an impenetrable maze of well-known barriers for users who are blind, deaf, dyslexic, or mobility impaired. Web accessibility is far from being my field of expertise, but even as an occasional Web user I can attest to the difference between accessible design and design that rejects users with disabilities. This ironic tale should become an object lesson in accommodation for all media companies. Until the laws governing this aspect of disability rights are more tightly enforced, and the attitude of Web designers changes, people with disabilities will have to endure even more of this discrimination. It is beyond belief that they had to face it when they tried to log on to a site purporting to serve them.

Web Accessibility and the Law

Lost in the dot-com euphoria was the basic inequity of the Internet services, which instantly transformed the lives of those who could afford and use them. The others, however, were sidelined, and that included many people with visual, aural, and mobility limitations for which all the earliest Web sites were woefully unprepared, not to mention those who were too poor, too old, or too physically remote even to try their hand. As with most media and telecommunications technology, there were laws on the books that were applicable, even if they were rarely enforced. We can trace their antecedents back to the Telecommunications Accessibility Enhancement Act and Hearing Aid Compatibility Act, both of 1988, and Title IV of the ADA, which set up a nationwide relay service (up and running three years later in July 1993) along with the Television Decoder Circuitry Act of 1990. All this legislation was for the benefit of the deaf and hard of hearing, as well as for those with speech disabilities, for whom the existing telephone and television systems were a nightmare of inaccessibility. It is easy to overlook the telecommunications components of the ADA, too, which many people view as specifically focused on architectural barriers, but public accommodation included telecommunications services and hardware, which had to be hearing-aid compatible and have volume control just as buildings and other public works had to be wheelchair accessible. In 1996, Congress enacted Section 255 of the Telecommunications Act, considered by many advocates to be a significant extension into cyberspace of the ADA's provisions because it forces telecommunications service providers and equipment manufacturers to ensure accessibility while empowering the FCC as well as the Architectural and Transportation Barrier Compliance Board (the "Access Board," or federal agency that reviews accessibility complaints) to levy fines when codes are not met. Congress also tacked Section 508 onto the Rehabilitation Act to use federal procurement contracts as a cudgel in forcing corporations to make their Web sites, software, and equipment accessible, because no federal funds can be spent on noncompliant contractors. Section 508 also requires that people with disabilities seeking information or services from a federal agency, such as the IRS, have access to all the same data provided to the public—it took effect in August 2000.

It is criminal that so many Web sites governed by Section 508 remain inaccessible and apparently blissfully unaware that they can be sued and lose their federal funding under Section 508. One of the first groups to take notice of the problem was the National Council on Disability (NCD), which issued a policy brief in 2000 that circulated and was ignored during both political parties' national conventions that summer. It deemed the laws adequate but raised concerns about their enforcement, calling for research into Section 508 and Section 255 compliance. The policy paper stated, "the Federal Government's strong enforcement of laws, reinforcement of research in universal design in information technology and telecommunications systems and products, and use of its huge purchasing power in accessible electronic and information technology will determine, to a large extent, whether or not progress is made in this increasingly important area of American life."[2] Advocacy groups such as the National Organization on Disability and NCD have had some success in pushing for both regulatory change and government assistance packages. The Web has so far defied extensive regulatory control, although antispam legislation and the protection of privacy, especially under the onslaught of identity theft, seem poised to break that hands-off streak no matter who controls Congress and the White House in the coming years. Government spending is one way to promote accessibility, so that the $120 million in low-interest, long-term loans for people with disabilities who purchase assistive technology, the $20 million in funding for "telework" purchases for qualified people with disabilities, or the expanded Department of Defense contracts in its Computer/Electronic Accommodations Program (CAP), or the $3.7 billion in additional funding authorized by the White House for state grants to implement the Individuals with Disabilities Education Act Part B (bringing the total expenditure to $10.1 billion in fiscal 2004) are major additions to the economic incentive for private companies to push for more advanced assistive technology. The community has never been a big fan of the Republicans, but all these measures are part of a presidential New Freedom Initiative announced in March 2004 for people with disabilities that is heavy on the assistive technology theme, including $15 million to promote accessible voting systems. There is even expanded tax relief for businesses that buy computers, software, and other equipment that aids telecommuters as well as long-overdue breaks for those who want to work and not lose their Social Security and Supplemental Security Income benefits.

Sometimes new laws are not enough, particularly if they are shunned. In November 2003 a federal appeals court in Miami heard from ten of the top national disability rights groups, who filed a friend of the court brief urging U.S. District Court Judge Patricia Seitz to overturn her ruling in favor of Southwest Airlines, which had successfully fought an ADA-based complaint about its disability-unfriendly Web site. As Judge Seitz wrote in her decision, the ADA does not apply to online services such as airline reservations. "To expand the ADA to cover 'virtual' spaces would be to create new rights without well-defined standards." The appeal was denied by a three-judge appellate panel. As the amicus brief stated, "Making the Web accessible to people with disabilities is not difficult, and includes such things as designing and generating Web pages so that information is available to a wide range of people, including those who may be unable to hear audible content; who may be unable to use a mouse because of a physical impairment; or who access the Web using software that reads the content of a Web page out loud to persons who cannot see the screen content." Landmark cases against major corporations or government bodies are still pending as of this writing.

Ramping Up the Information Superhighway

The inaccessibility of the Internet is the most pressing civil rights problem facing people with disabilities today. The architectural analogy, grounded in such synonyms for thresholds as portals, gateways, and interfaces, provides a suitably graphic introduction to the crisis. In the same shamefully prevalent fashion as insensitive architecture of the pre-ADA era shut out people with disabilities, the vast majority of sites bar users who rely on a select and simple repertoire of accommodations that have been around as long as the Web itself but have been shunned by designers and overlooked by their clients too intent on cool effects and extreme gestures, promulgated to generate traffic, to attend to the basic courtesy of ensuring that people with impairments of various kinds can easily navigate their sites. To their detriment, most accessibility tools depend on text, making them old-fashioned, uncool, and doubtless a challenge for many semiliterate software designers. For all the New Age, woo woo rhetoric of dot-com promoters, even through the recent "alternative" initial public offering of Google, with its friendly claims to break through to a more altruistic "alternative" corporate model, the track record of Silicon Valley with regard to disability is pathetic and hypocritical. The self-declared social consciousness of such pretentious corporate cultures as Google, Amazon, Netscape, and thousands of lesser enterprises, along with old-economy companies including most of the major media outlets (ABC, NBC, CBS, and CNN foremost among them), is belied by the fact that their sites are blatantly inaccessible to millions of users. The outlook for the immediate future is bleak, judging by the absence of disability awareness on the curriculum for the next generation of Web designers. Unlike the major architecture schools, which have courses in ADA compliance built into the curriculum, no Web designer or programmer I have interviewed for this book has ever had a minute of instruction on accessibility features as part of either an undergraduate or graduate course in HTML (the programming language) or Web graphics.

As a ramp is an inexpensive, easily configured and built inclined plane, so too the essential components of Web accessibility are almost insultingly basic and low-tech. Even the higher-end, state-of-the-art accessibility options (such as American Sign Language schematics) fall far short of the fanciest multimedia tools around today. Most Web design principles for accessible navigation are as basic as any graphic tools for easier visibility, including building in ways to boost on-screen text size, enhance contrast between words and background, and clarify the placement of information on a screen for those who have difficulty either seeing or processing. Once the main obstacles are identified—graphics without captions, mov-

ing images, frames, tiny type in pale colors (remember that 20 million
Americans are color-blind)—the challenge is to find ways around them
using a forgotten array of tools that Microsoft, IBM, Dell, Apple, and all
major manufacturers have installed in their products. These are the most
underused accessories in the computer industry today, judging by the
problems reported.

Even though cyberspace was touted as the be-all and end-all for people
with disabilities, it took a smart, brave organization to show that the
Web is as barrier-ridden as any other marketplace. Based in Cambridge,
Massachusetts, the nonprofit Center for Applied Special Technology
(CAST) devised a simple (and free) battery of tests for Web accessibility.
As many as 3 million sites are evaluated monthly using its criteria, which
regularly prove that many of the most elaborate and popular sites are
virtually inaccessible, not just to blind users (as is sometimes assumed),
but to a wide cross section of the disability community. CAST's Michael
Cooper points out that the multimedia-heavy entertainment sites, for example, rely too heavily on complex graphics provided through Shock-
wave and Java script. These are a labyrinth for the blind and those who
have difficulty maneuvering the standard mouse. Major offenders, identified by CAST and by my own spot-checking, include Barnes and Noble,
Yahoo, most media outlets including nytimes.com, most movie promotional sites from the major studios, and a shocking number of nonprofits
in the disability field. Although lawsuits so far are rare, the failure to
meet CAST standards has been used as evidence in Section 508 complaints.

How can you tell if a Web site is accessible? One quick way is to look
for the Bobby insignia originally conferred by CAST on accessible sites
the automatic programs have checked. The Bobby technology developed
by CAST was recently acquired by Watchfire, a for-profit business software firm that sells the Bobby re-design package for $299 and maintains
the free testing service. If the vetted site's designers have gone to that
trouble, and passed the test, that already means that organizations's Web
team is sufficiently aware of disability issues to bother. The criteria start
with the availability of a text-only version of the site that can be used with
voice-activated software. That would mean that someone who is blind or
partially sighted, or someone who has a reading disability that is aided by
a vocal version of the text, can easily navigate the site. He or she uses the
text-only button to convert the contents, including pictures, which should
be descriptively captioned, into a document that can be converted by even
the most basic text-to-speech software into a synthesized voice for the
user. That is only step number one.

At CAST's Web site (www.cast.org) professional Web designers and others learn how to analyze their sites for accessibility problems. The basic lessons are not all that complicated, even for the layman, and involve principles that have guided the Universal Design movement since its inception nearly four decades ago. The CAST suggestions, in part, stipulate that good Web design ought to be:

- *Perceivable.* Ensure that all content can be presented in form(s) that can be perceived by any user—except those aspects of the content that cannot be expressed in words.

- *Operable.* Ensure that the interface elements in the content are operable by any user.

- *Understandable.* Make it as easy as possible to understand the content and controls.

- *Robust.* Use Web technologies that maximize the ability of the content to work with current and future accessibility technologies and user agents.[3]

This list makes such sense beyond the disability application that it highlights one of the logical justifications for reconsidering how Web sites are put together. The great ripple effect of Universal Design has always been the way it benefits a variety of people, not just people with disabilities. In the physical world, ramps are used by bicyclists, people pushing strollers, and wheelchair users. In just this way, accessible Web content is a blessing for people with and without disabilities. One of the favorite examples is the computer user who is in a noisy environment and needs captioning, or who is visually distracted while driving, for example, and needs text-to-speech. Where the eyes or ears are otherwise occupied, or overwhelmed by ambient distractions, many of the accessibility features first developed for people with disabilities are welcomed by all, much as the garage door opener, created for the mobility impaired, has become one of the most beloved household gadgets around. Captioning alone has proven an invaluable aid to search engines, because it makes finding a famous movie quote or character that much faster. The list of these ancillary benefits goes on and on. The mechanisms by which they work can be boiled down to a few simple precepts:

- Someone who cannot hear will want to see the information normally presented via sound.

- Someone who cannot see will want to hear or read through Braille information that is usually presented visually.

- Someone who does not have the strength to move quickly or easily will want to use as little movement as possible and have as much time as they need when operating Web interfaces.

- Someone who does not read well may want to hear the information read aloud.

These are such simple and sensible statements that it is remarkable how many Web designers choose to ignore them. Yet, after all the hype, almost three-quarters of Americans who report having a disability also do not use the Internet, according to a recent study from the Pew Internet and American Life Project. Over a quarter of respondents say their disabilities make it difficult or impossible to go online. "Currently, the disabled are less connected than many other groups of Americans," the report claims. "Just 38 percent of disabled Americans use the Internet. This compares to the 58 percent of all Americans who use the Internet." Another study, by researchers Colin Keane and Joel Macht of the Neil Squire Foundation, points out that many people lack access to adaptive technologies that would help them use computers and retrieve information from Web sites. This goes back to an old problem—gaining access to wired rooms and buildings, access to computers with enough memory to support some of the more elaborate screen magnifiers and readers, and finding a workstation that is the right height for a wheelchair user (my own local public library had five computers up and running for a year before it had an accessible one). As with other minorities, the income level and unemployment level of people with disabilities as a sector means that access to these tools and services is a chronic problem. Some of the obstacles are psychological as well as economic and social: "Thus, it is likely that some individuals (especially those who have little knowledge of the Internet and computers) believe their disability impairs Internet use when in fact it does not. There are social and psychological explanations why some Americans do not use the Internet. A person's sense of personal empowerment can make a difference in her decision to go online or not. Those who feel less in control of their lives are less likely to go online."[4]

Time to Sue

Setting aside the hubris of the utopian "New Economy," which turns out to be as elitist and exclusive as the old one, the sheer illegality of Web inaccessibility is an overlooked front on the political battlefield. The gap between mainstream Web users and those with disabilities is too wide, and they are drifting apart rapidly. Closing that gap is going to take legal and political action. To be specific, if a site is in any way linked to an institution receiving federal funding—as many educational and health care sites are—then it must provide accessible features according to Section 508 of the Rehabilitation Act of the federal code. This means, just to pick an embarrassing example close at hand, that my own college's Web site is breaking federal laws. As I pointed out to the administration and the Web meisters fully four years ago, the portal of the Baruch College Web site has no text-only button whatsoever (never mind one that is easily found, usually on the top left corner of the gateway). That is the leadoff violation in a string of other gaffes reported by a repeated Bobby scan that found none of the material on the site fully accessible and essentially gave the whole site failing grades. The fiscal risk is posed by the loss of future federal grants-in-aid and line-item budget funding, which at my college would amount to thousands of dollars a year. Even as administrators urge those of us on faculty to put more and more of our course materials online using an extraordinarily maladroit private-sector system called Blackboard—whose contract with CUNY amounted to a hefty $400,000, including $43,915 from my campus each year—as a professor with an interest in disability rights and a rudimentary understanding of Web design garnered mainly as a user, I have become more and more uncomfortable with the level of resistance to basic accessibility principles presented by the system. When one of my undergraduate business communications students, who is blind, tried to use the site he was flummoxed from the start. I put as much of the course materials as I had prepared on disk into basic Word format so that his digital reader could produce an audio version. A pleasant Ukrainian fellow student assisted him in enjoying some of the handouts, and I summarily gave up on the college's discriminatory and illegal online system as of that semester. There is no point in becoming an accomplice to anything that excludes students in a public university, the very premise of which is access and serving the disenfranchised.

The risks posed by litigation are usually sufficient to urge companies to make progress on an issue like making their Web sites accessible. The prospect of attracting new business and making customers happy adds to the incentive. Finally, there is the vast market for assistive technology, one of the undervalued sectors in the overanalyzed technology market. Even for stock analysts who have picked apart the computer racket from hardware to software, storage to silicon chips, broadband to wireless, the assistive technology area is virgin territory. While the numbers may be low as of this writing, it is inevitably going to be more significant as the rest of tech becomes boringly familiar.

The Way Ahead

As rudimentary as the basic accessibility features are, it is infuriating to realize that the research arms of many major computer companies and universities are at work on assistive technology so advanced that it could profoundly alter the experience of the Web for people with disabilities, if only they could get to it. There is good news in computer technology beyond the amazing advances in free online gambling and porn. The once awe-inspiring innovations of Stephen Hawking's custom-made joystick and modem in 1999 are now ho-hum, standard-issue peripherals (it is amusing to think of the way he apologized for the flat American accent of his voice synthesizer). Voice-activated software for word processing and spreadsheets has advanced tremendously in the past decade, a boon to quadriplegics and anyone for whom the standard mouse and keyboard require too much dexterity and strength. The convenience of voice-activated technology extends well beyond the media, to the interior design breakthroughs that make a home more secure, comfortable, and accessible. Screen magnifiers and text-to-speech programs using the improved sound systems of PCs are fast taking the place of Braille for blind readers and writers, and offering therapy addressed to a wide range of learning disabilities including dyslexia. Speech-to-text software and captioning help deaf computer users, and even Deaf proponents of ASL have something to cheer about with the inclusion of a sign interpreter in a pop-up window on some of the more advanced sites. When one of my editors had a cochlear implant, the speech therapist used a fascinating therapeutic program created by IBM that permitted her to see an immediate chart of her pronunciation next to a chart of the proper sound, which she would then try to match. It offered a specificity and visual guide that no previous technique had afforded. With Alzheimer's reaching epidemic proportions and projected to become all the more prevalent as the baby boomers age, significant progress is being made on programs and peripherals that anticipate the mental processing problems that dementia precipitates.

Engineers at IBM and Microsoft in particular, in well-funded programs that are clearly motivated by the profits promised by vast markets, have created state-of-the-art screen magnification, voice-activated controls, and easy-to-use hardware that vastly expand the basic accessibility package offered by off-the-shelf computers or software. As in the ad game, the watershed in computer business strategy came when major players stopped viewing people with disabilities as "patients" in rehabilitation and started targeting them as customers. Some of the economics of this shift are still, as in the medical technology field, a gray area, because major institutions offering services, including not only hospitals but universities, libraries, and nonprofits with specific disability constituencies, are the "customer" for the higher-end multimedia tools. As with many other minorities, people with disabilities and the institutions that serve them also receive federal and state tax breaks and incentives for their technology purchases. All this high-tech gadgetry takes money. For those who struggle to pay for some of the latest and greatest, the Technology Related Assistance for Individuals with Disabilities Act, which advocates fought to pass in 1988, has provisions for assistive technology that often make up the difference between what a user has available and needs to spend, and state offices of technology assessment are charged with matching computer hardware or software with individual needs. In some states, such as New Hampshire, low-interest loan programs and alternative financing, refurbished hardware, and free training are all offered, on the state. Admirable as this is from a social support perspective, it effectively promotes higher pricing and holds the market back from being completely "free" and consumer driven. Vestiges of paternalism are permitted to linger in a system in which an $800 software package designed to help dyslexic students costs only $40 after incentives. Economists and policy wonks can debate the merits of this system all they want, but the manufacturers will view people with disabilities as consumers, pure and simple, only when the playing field is level. The same skewed relationships are observable in such industries as wheelchair and hearing-aid manufacturing. Even under mitigated competitive circumstances, advances in assistive technology continue to astound.

One of the major advertisers in *WE* magazine, and a perennial presence on the Top 10 Companies list, was Microsoft, which has a vast team at work on assistive technology. Bill Gates was fond of telling people he had a permanent disability: his eyesight. Referring to glasses as an "accessibility aid," along the lines of a wheelchair, he once wrote in answer to one of my queries on the topic for our cover story on the end of the millennium:

> Any tool that lets a person who has a disability gain better access to the world is an accessibility aid. . . . Helping accommodate people with disabilities makes sense. Just imagine how much worse off society and millions of individuals like me would be if eyeglasses had never been invented. When ways are found to keep people productive, everybody benefits—not just the individuals, but their friends, relatives, employers and the whole economy. Anyone with limited mobility can appreciate how the Internet and electronic databases have opened vast amounts of information to easy access. The PC is one of the greatest accessibility aids ever but people who are blind

have actually lost ground in recent years. Today's more powerful PCs and software, which use graphics heavily to communicate large amounts of information to the sighted person, have proven problematic for people who don't have eyesight. As the Internet becomes more graphical for people with sight, its content threatens to become less accessible to the blind than it is today. Fortunately, a growing number of computer and hardware and software innovations are being developed specifically for people with disabilities, including blindness. We'll get there. I can see the day coming, even with my glasses off.

Many of the most advanced innovations come from two particularly disability-friendly technology labs housed at prestigious universities: MIT and the Georgia Institute of Technology. The wonders of the MIT Media Lab have been extolled in rhapsodic features in *Wired,* the *New York Times,* and my own magazine, including the sexy consumer-products stuff such as smart clothing or appliances, which anticipate by a decade or so the expensive toys one finds at The Sharper Image or in the Hammacher-Schlemmer catalogue. A more serious and useful research line is devoted to an array of disabilities, including programs for dysgraphia and dyslexia developed by a stunningly prolific inventor named Ray Kurzweil. His name is already familiar to those in the blind community as the inventor, three decades ago, of the Kurzweil Reader, one of the first digital reading systems. He is most famous for his collaborations with Stevie Wonder, who not only uses the Reader in its latest incarnation but Kurzweil's electronic keyboards. When Wonder wanted advice on whether or not to try a radically experimental implant technology that, by use of a camera and digital hookup similar to a cochlear implant might allow him to see again, he turned to Kurzweil for advice. For over two decades, the two had collaborated in computer technology. Kurzweil invented and developed the world's first "omni-font" reader for the blind and went on to develop the most advanced software in the fields of voice recognition and palm-size listening devices for the deaf and dyslexic, his current passion. His interest in the field began in 1974 when he sat next to a blind man on a plane: "He explained to me that the only real handicap that he experiences was his inability to read ordinary printed material. So I had found the problem we were searching for."

Right after the Reader made its debut on the *Today Show,* Wonder checked it out for himself. "Our receptionist was skeptical that the person on the other end of the line was really the legendary singer, but she put the call through to me, anyway. I invited him over, and he tried out the machine," Kurzweil recalls. Wonder wanted one right away. "So we turned the factory upside down to hurriedly finish up our first production unit. We showed Stevie how to use it, and off he went in a taxi with his new reading machine by his side." Kurzweil and Wonder teamed up again in 1982 after a studio session during which they lamented the sad state of electronic instruments, which at the time failed to mimic the timbre and tonality of a real Steinway. The two founded Kurzweil Music Systems, and if you pay attention to what instruments are used at rock concerts in particular you will note that most of the top acts use Kurzweil.

The move from hardware to software followed the trend in the computer industry, and Kurzweil's voice-activated software products, now marketed by Lernout and Hauspie, became essential for blind and deaf users and are used extensively in therapy and schools. After the voice-activated break-through, Kurzweil turned his attention of the needs of the deaf community and developed a palm-held continuous speech translator fast enough to display a text message in real time. Revisiting the idea of the Reader, he recognized the need for an advanced software solution for learning and reading disabilities, and the Kurzweil 3000 was born. It scans a document (whether in print or on screen), displays the page including pictures, then reads it out loud while highlighting the image in print as it is being read. It is content-independent, so teachers on all levels from elementary through college can use it to improve speed and comprehension. The device combines visual and auditory feedback to teach critical independent study skills supported by audible spell-checking, word prediction, dictionary, thesaurus, e-mail, and browsing tools and even test-taking applications. As a writing teacher, I was most impressed to see that as a student types, the software speaks (in a clear, humanlike voice, not the usual creepy synthesized one) each letter or word, so the student can quickly recognize and correct mistakes. The combination of motion, colors, and highlighting helps stimulate the brain directly and counter the effects of dyslexia.

Kurzweil is a tireless writer, too. Back in 1990, his *Age of Intelligent Machines* was a cult classic among brainiacs. It included a chapter (unfortunately titled "The Handicapped") that predicted a new age of portable scanners that would instantly translate not only text but signs and symbols into a medium that could be apprehended by the user, whether artificial speech or text, with access to online and multilingual information. Such "seeing" machines, which would take the place of companions who describe, will be miniaturized, he believes, to the point that they can be built into glasses, making one's vision sharp enough, especially with regard to peripheral vision, that we all might want to use them. In the same book he was remarkably prescient about the most subtle and insidious of barriers: prejudice. To his credit, he included this passage, which fourteen years later remains an optimistic vision for the future:

A not unimportant side benefit of intelligent technology for the handicapped should be a substantial alteration of these negative perceptions. If the handicaps resulting from disabilities are significantly reduced, if blind people can read and navigate with ease, if deaf persons can hold normal conversations on the phone, then we can expect public perceptions to change as well. When blind, deaf, and other disabled persons take their place beside us in schools and the workplace and perform with the same effectiveness as their nondisabled peers, we shall begin to see these disabilities as mere inconveniences, as problems no more difficult to overcome than poor handwriting or fear of public speaking or any of the other minor challenges that we all face.[5]

The language of this passage is not exactly politically correct, and many disability studies classes could go to town on his use of "overcome" or the implication that the development of suitable electronic gizmos would eradicate disability and thereby also wipe out disability culture. But the endgame that Kurzweil is describing here, which is the triumph of the prosthesis, is a familiar theme in the tech sector devoted to disability. For Kurzweil blindness, deafness, dyslexia are problems to be beaten, like having a bad Japanese accent and finding a speech therapist or technical aid. He tempers his predictions with an understanding of the limits of the machines: "We're not creating cybernetic geniuses today—not yet. The intelligence of our present-day computers is narrow, which can provide effective solutions for the narrow defects of most disabilities."[6] By 2009, he predicts that print-to-speech devices and navigation systems like high-tech guide dogs will assist the blind, portable speech-to-test listening machines will be ready for the hard of hearing, and computer-controlled orthotic devices, "walking machines," will enable paraplegics to stroll and climb stairs. There is a synesthetic logic to much of this thinking, which finds ways to translate information from one form available to one sense into another—sight to hearing, hearing to touch or sight.

The giddy temptation to speculate about the toys of the near future leads quickly to scenarios that border on science fiction. The enhancement of life with a disability through virtual reality is an important subtheme, which in many ways is a media story as well. As Thomas Furniss has claimed, "Right now, we can build virtual worlds for quadriplegics in which they can move and behave just as well as if they weren't handicapped. We can imitate whatever movement they have—finger movement, even eye movement—to give them full physical mobility control in a virtual environment."[7] What sounds like a ride at an amusement park could also end up being big business, of course, just as home entertainment systems are, much to the amazement of those of us who would never dream of building one, a major sector of the interior design economy. These technological wonders are linked to the media and electronics industries. "Content is king" was the mantra of the dot-commers, even as they focused on building bigger and faster networks and tinkered with Flash to make it faster but let their content fall to slipshod levels. Just as book and movie executives have acceded to the grim fact that their total business is now dwarfed by the monstrosity of video games and have sought ways to get in on the profits through becoming content providers, so too the development of virtual reality as assistive technology will entail content issues as yet unaddressed.

Perhaps this is the area over which disability scholars decades from now will continue to argue—the ways in which imagery, symbols, text, and other media content have been used to either benefit or denigrate the community. Setting aside the obvious defaults—porn and violence—it is likely that virtual reality will find some educational and vocational avenues in which Kurzweil's sunny predictions may turn out to be true. A quadriplegic with use of his or her sip-and-puff device could control an elaborate virtual reality simulation of, just to fantasize here, an organic chemistry laboratory where a difficult titration is in progress. For the student to control the environment, albeit a virtual one, is empowering. The titration completed, a lab report is submitted to the crime scene investigator (or professor) just as reports are turned in by the other forensic scientists or students. That would be an advance over today's exclusive lab setups. But the more typical pattern of high-tech innovation, which leans more toward passive consumption than enabling or empowering activity, leads us to picture a different outcome. If virtual reality technology serves only as a fancy form of entertainment, is this any more than an opiate? There is something faintly sadistic about simulating ordinary sensation and movement for a brief period and then returning the person with a disability to reality after the machine shuts down.

Speculating further, the nature of the content is still subject to many of the criteria we have used throughout this study. Assuming that it is created by researchers and media experts familiar at close hand with disability culture, its sensitivity to disability issues has a better chance. However, if this is an in-house project at Google on which young engineers not plugged into disability issues are joyfully at play, more of the same condescending or cliché-ridden materials will be presented. Garbage in, garbage out. Technology remains at least on that level just another media recycler, capable only of attaining a stage of enlightenment that reflects its masters' minds. If the goal of virtual reality engineers is the "eradication" of disabilities, then the fears of many in the field of disability studies are justified—it sounds like a cybernetic version of eugenics, the sort of march toward perfection through DNA manipulation that has already upset many. The utopia of a gravity-free environment, where sounds and sights are perfectly discerned, nobody stutters or speaks with an accent, where everybody looks like a fashion model and moves like an Olympic gymnast, takes facilitated communication to another, bizarre level at which it becomes facilitated living. Jack Nelson cites a 1992 survey by A. S. Atkins in which two dozen experts on virtual reality and direct mind interaction were asked about the outlook for the application of their work to the lives of people with disabilities. While thirteen of them felt that virtual reality could have a "very significant" impact by providing an environment in which the users would not be disabled, ten were concerned that it would be prohibitively expensive.[8] As James R. Fruchterman, another expert on the subject, predicts, "I want to make it clear that virtual reality will not make disabilities magically disappear. However, it will become a powerful tool for many people with disabilities. To a great extent, employment in a virtual office will remove many of the barriers that exist today.[9] One of my dearest friends in the disability community, a paraplegic whose life is a continuous hell of migraine headaches, is completely entranced by virtual reality. In 2005, this seems more like an escape than a solution to the economic and social problems with which he contends. Movies, television, magazines, and newspapers can all fit into the same category as diversions from real-life situations rather than tools for solving problems. Teachers I know also struggle at times with the awkward balance between being mere entertainers and effecting positive change in their students' lives. For those journalists, filmmakers, or software designers with higher aspirations than producing the next *Friends* or Play Station hit, the quality of the content in a virtual reality scenario, as in other forms, is of paramount importance. No guidelines or style sheets are sufficient to ensure that what fills the gaping maw of multimedia will adequately represent or serve people with disabilities, who, no matter what Ray Kurzweil says, will continue to exist. As splendid as it will be for them to carry around little pagers with LED screens for text messages translated simultaneously, the content of the messages that appear on screen will also be important. Some will want these messages to be inspirational or illusory. Others will settle for information and inclusion.

Appendix A

Guidelines for Portraying People with Disabilities in the Media

Fear of the unknown. Inadequate experience. Incorrect or distorted information. Lack of knowledge. These shape some of the attitudinal barriers that people with disabilities face as they become involved in their communities

People working in the media exert a powerful influence over the way people with disabilities are perceived. It's important to the 54 million Americans with disabilities that they be portrayed realistically and that their disabilities are explained accurately.

Awareness is the first step toward change.

Tips for Reporting on People with Disabilities

- When referring to individuals with disabilities use "disability," not "handicapped."

- Emphasize the person, not the disability or condition. Use "people with disabilities" rather than "disabled persons," and "people with epilepsy" rather than "epileptics."

- Omit mention of an individual's disability unless it is pertinent to the story.

- Depict the typical achiever with a disability, not just the super-achiever.

- Choose words that are accurate descriptions and have non-judgemental connotations.

These guidelines are used by permission. Copyright © 2002, National Center on Disability and Journalism.

- People with disabilities live everyday lives and should be portrayed as contributing members of the community. These portrayals should:

  Depict people with disabilities experiencing the same pain/pleasure that others derive from everyday life, e.g., work, parenting, education, sports and community involvement.

  Feature a variety of people with disabilities when possible, not just someone easily recognized by the general public.

  Depict employees/employers with disabilities working together.

- Ask people with disabilities to provide correct information and assistance to avoid stereotypes in the media.

- Portray people with disabilities as people, with both strengths and weaknesses.

Appropriate Words when Portraying People with Disabilities

Never Use
victim—use: person who has/experienced/with.
[the] cripple[d]—use: person with a disability.
afflicted by/with—use: person has.
invalid—use: a person with a disability.
normal—most people, including people with disabilities, think they are.
patient—connotes sickness. Use person with a disability.

Avoid Using
wheelchair bound/confined—use: uses a wheelchair or wheelchair user.
homebound employment—use: employed in the home.

Use with Care
courageous, brave, inspirational and similar words routinely used to describe persons with disabilities. Adapting to a disability does not necessarily mean someone acquires these traits.

Interviewing People with Disabilities

When interviewing a person with a disability, relax! Conduct your interview as you would with anyone. Be clear and candid in your questioning and ask for clarification of terms or issues when necessary. Be upfront about deadlines, the focus of your story, and when and where it will appear.

Interviewing Etiquette

- Shake hands when introduced to someone with a disability. People with limited hand use or artificial limbs do shake hands.

- Speak directly to people with disabilities, not through their companions.

- Don't be embarrassed using such phrases as "See you soon," "Walk this way" or "Got to run." These are common expressions, and are unlikely to offend.

- If you offer to help, wait until the offer is accepted.

- Consider the needs of people with d isabilities when planning events.

- Conduct interviews in a manner that emphasizes abilities, achieve ments and individual qualities.

- Don't emphasize differences by putting people with disabilities on a pedestal.

When Interviewing People with Hearing Disabilities

- Attract the person's attention by tapping on his or her shoulder or waving.

- If you are interviewing someone with a partial hearing loss, ask where it would be most comfortable for you to sit.

- If the person is lip-reading, look directly at him/her and speak slowly and clearly. Do not exaggerate lip movements or shout. Do speak expressively, as facial expressions, gestures and body movements will help him/her understand you.

- Position yourself facing the light source and keep hands and food away from your mouth when speaking.

When Interviewing People with Vision Disabilities

- Always identify yourself and anyone else who might be present.

- When offering a handshake, say, "Shall we shake hands?"

- When offering seating, place the person's hand on the back or arm of the seat.

- Let the person know if you move or need to end the conversation.

When Interviewing People with Speech Disabilities

- Ask short questions that require short answers when possible.

- Do not feign understanding. Try rephrasing your questions, if necessary.

When Interviewing People Using a Wheelchair or Crutches

- Do not lean on a person's wheelchair. The chair is a part of his/her body space.

- Sit or kneel to place yourself at eye level with the person you are interviewing.

- Make sure the interview site is accessible. Check for:

    Reserved parking for people with disabilities

    A ramp or step-free entrance

    Accessible restrooms

    An elevator if the interview is not on the first floor

    Water fountains and telephones low enough for wheelchair use

Be sure to notify the interviewee if there are problems with the location. Discuss what to do and make alternate plans.

Writing About Disability

One of the first and most significant steps to changing negative stereotypes and attitudes toward people with disabilities begins when we rethink the way written and spoken images are used to portray people with disabilities. The following is a brief, but important, list of suggestions for portraying people with disabilities in the media.

People with disabilities are not "handicapped," unless there are physical or attitudinal barriers that make it difficult for them to participate in everyday activities. An office building with steps and no entry ramp creates a "handicapping" barrier for people who use wheelchairs. In the same way, a hotel that does not have a TTY/telephone (teletypewriter) creates a barrier for someone who is hearing disabled. It is important to focus on the person, not necessarily the disability. In writing, name the person first and then, if necessary, explain his or her disability. The same rule applies when speaking. Don't focus on someone's disability unless it's crucial to the point being made.

In long, written materials, when many references have been made to persons with disabilities or someone who is disabled, it is acceptable for later references to refer to "disabled persons" or "disabled individuals."

Because a person is not a condition or a disease, avoid referring to someone with a disability by his or her disability alone. For example, don't say someone is a "post-polio" or a "C.P." or an "epileptic." Refer instead to someone who has post-polio syndrome, or has cerebral palsy, or has epilepsy.

Don't use "disabled" as a noun because it implies a state of separateness. "The disabled" are not a group apart from the rest of society. When writing or speaking about people with disabilities, choose descriptive words and portray people in a positive light.

Avoid words with negative connotations:

- Avoid calling someone a "victim."

- Avoid referring to people with disabilities as "cripples" or "crippled." This is negative and demeaning language.

- Don't write or say that someone is "afflicted."

- Avoid the word "invalid" as it means, quite literally, "not valid."

- Write or speak about people who use wheelchairs. Wheelchair users are not "wheelchair-bound."

- Refer to people who are not disabled as "nondisabled" or "able-bodied." When you call non-disabled people "normal," the implication is that people with disabilities are not normal.

- Someone who is disabled is only a patient to his or her physician or in a reference to medical treatment.

- Avoid cliches. Don't use "unfortunate," "pitiful," "poor," "dumb," "crip," "deformed," "retard," "blind as a bat" or other patronizing and demeaning words.

- In the same vein, don't glamorize or make heroes of people with disabilities simply because they have adapted to their disabilities.

Your concerted efforts to use positive, non-judgmental respectful language when referring to people with disabilities in writing and in everyday speaking can go a long way toward helping to change negative stereotypes.

Appendix B
Guidelines for Web Accessibility

This document provides a list of all checkpoints from the Web Content Accessibility Guidelines 1.0, organized by concept, as a checklist for Web content developers. Please refer to the Guidelines document for introductory information, information about related documents, a glossary of terms, and more.

This list may be used to review a page or site for accessibility. For each checkpoint, indicate whether the checkpoint has been satisfied, has not been satisfied, or is not applicable. A list of current W3C Recommendations and other technical documents can be found at http://www.w3.org/TR. This document has been produced as part of the Web Accessibility Initiative.

Priorities

Each checkpoint has a priority level assigned by the Working Group based on the checkpoint's impact on accessibility.

Priority 1. A Web content developer must satisfy this checkpoint. Otherwise, one or more groups will find it impossible to access information in the document. Satisfying this checkpoint is a basic requirement for some groups to be able to use Web documents.

Priority 2. A Web content developer should satisfy this checkpoint. Otherwise, one or more groups will find it difficult to access information in the document. Satisfying this checkpoint will remove significant barriers to accessing Web documents.

Priority 3. A Web content developer may address this checkpoint. Otherwise, one or more groups will find it somewhat difficult to access information in the document. Satisfying this checkpoint will improve access to Web documents.

Some checkpoints specify a priority level that may change under certain (indicated) conditions.

Priority 1 checkpoints

In general:

1.1 Provide a text equivalent for every non-text element (e.g., via "alt," "longdesc," or in element content). This includes: images, graphical representations of text (including symbols), image map regions, animations (e.g., animated GIFs), applets and programmatic objects, ASCII art, frames, scripts, images used as list bullets, spacers, graphical buttons, sounds (played with or without user interaction), stand-alone audio files, audio tracks of video, and video.

2.1 Ensure that all information conveyed with color is also available without color, for example from context or markup.

4.1 Clearly identify changes in the natural language of a document's text and any text equivalents (e.g., captions).

6.1 Organize documents so they may be read without style sheets. For example, when an HTML document is rendered without associated style sheets, it must still be possible to read the document.

6.2 Ensure that equivalents for dynamic content are updated when the dynamic content changes.

7.1 Until user agents allow users to control flickering, avoid causing the screen to flicker.

14.1 Use the clearest and simplest language appropriate for a site's content.

And if you use images and image maps:

1.2 Provide redundant text links for each active region of a server-side image map.

9.1 Provide client-side image maps instead of server-side image maps except where the regions cannot be defined with an available geometric shape.

And if you use tables:

5.1 For data tables, identify row and column headers.

5.2 For data tables that have two or more logical levels of row or column headers, use markup to associate data cells and header cells.

And if you use frames:

12.1 Title each frame to facilitate frame identification and navigation.

And if you use applets and scripts:

6.3 Ensure that pages are usable when scripts, applets, or other programmatic objects are turned off or not supported. If this is not possible, provide equivalent information on an alternative accessible page.

And if you use multimedia:

1.3 Until user agents can automatically read aloud the text equivalent of a visual track, provide an auditory description of the important information of the visual track of a multimedia presentation.

1.4 For any time-based multimedia presentation (e.g., a movie or animation), synchronize equivalent alternatives (e.g., captions or auditory descriptions of the visual track) with the presentation.

And if all else fails:

11.4 If, after best efforts, you cannot create an accessible page, provide a link to an alternative page that uses W3C technologies, is accessible, has equivalent information (or functionality), and is updated as often as the inaccessible (original) page.

Priority 2 checkpoints

In general:

2.2 Ensure that foreground and background color combinations provide sufficient contrast when viewed by someone having color deficits or when viewed on a black and white screen. [Priority 2 for images, Priority 3 for text.]

3.1 When an appropriate markup language exists, use markup rather than images to convey information.

3.2 Create documents that validate to published formal grammars.

3.3 Use style sheets to control layout and presentation.

3.4 Use relative rather than absolute units in markup language attribute values and style sheet property values.

3.5 Use header elements to convey document structure and use them according to specification.

3.6 Mark up lists and list items properly.

3.7 Mark up quotations. Do not use quotation markup for formatting effects such as indentation.

6.5 Ensure that dynamic content is accessible or provide an alternative presentation or page.

7.2 Until user agents allow users to control blinking, avoid causing content to blink (i.e., change presentation at a regular rate, such as turning on and off).

7.4 Until user agents provide the ability to stop the refresh, do not create periodically auto-refreshing pages.

7.5 Until user agents provide the ability to stop auto-redirect, do not use markup to redirect pages automatically. Instead, configure the server to perform redirects.

10.1 Until user agents allow users to turn off spawned windows, do not cause pop-ups or other windows to appear and do not change the current window without informing the user.

11.1 Use W3C technologies when they are available and appropriate for a task and use the latest versions when supported.

11.2 Avoid deprecated features of W3C technologies.

12.3 Divide large blocks of information into more manageable groups where natural and appropriate.

13.1 Clearly identify the target of each link.

13.2 Provide metadata to add semantic information to pages and sites.

13.3 Provide information about the general layout of a site (e.g., a site map or table of contents).

13.4 Use navigation mechanisms in a consistent manner.

And if you use tables:

5.3 Do not use tables for layout unless the table makes sense when linearized. Otherwise, if the table does not make sense, provide an alternative equivalent (which may be a linearized version).

5.4 If a table is used for layout, do not use any structural markup for the purpose of visual formatting.

And if you use frames:

12.2 Describe the purpose of frames and how frames relate to each other if it is not obvious by frame titles alone.

And if you use forms:

10.2 Until user agents support explicit associations between labels and form controls, for all form controls with implicitly associated labels, ensure that the label is properly positioned.

12.4 Associate labels explicitly with their controls.

And if you use applets and scripts:

6.4 For scripts and applets, ensure that event handlers are input device-independent.

7.3 Until user agents allow users to freeze moving content, avoid movement in pages.

8.1 Make programmatic elements such as scripts and applets directly accessible or compatible with assistive technologies [Priority 1 if functionality is important and not presented elsewhere, otherwise Priority 2.]

9.2 Ensure that any element that has its own interface can be operated in a device-independent manner.

9.3 For scripts, specify logical event handlers rather than device-dependent event handlers.

Priority 3 checkpoints

In general:

4.2 Specify the expansion of each abbreviation or acronym in a document where it first occurs.

4.3 Identify the primary natural language of a document.

9.4 Create a logical tab order through links, form controls, and objects.

9.5 Provide keyboard shortcuts to important links (including those in client-side image maps), form controls, and groups of form controls.

10.5 Until user agents (including assistive technologies) render adjacent links distinctly, include non-link, printable characters (surrounded by spaces) between adjacent links.

11.3 Provide information so that users may receive documents according to their preferences (e.g., language, content type, etc.).

13.5 Provide navigation bars to highlight and give access to the navigation mechanism.

13.6 Group related links, identify the group (for user agents), and, until user agents do so, provide a way to bypass the group.

13.7 If search functions are provided, enable different types of searches for different skill levels and preferences.

13.8 Place distinguishing information at the beginning of headings, paragraphs, lists, etc.

13.9 Provide information about document collections (i.e., documents comprising multiple pages.).

13.10 Provide a means to skip over multi-line ASCII art.

14.2 Supplement text with graphic or auditory presentations where they will facilitate comprehension of the page.

14.3 Create a style of presentation that is consistent across pages.

And if you use images and image maps:

1.5 Until user agents render text equivalents for client-side image map links, provide redundant text links for each active region of a client-side image map.

And if you use tables:

5.5 Provide summaries for tables.

5.6 Provide abbreviations for header labels.

10.3 Until user agents (including assistive technologies) render side-by-side text correctly, provide a linear text alternative (on the current page or some other) for all tables that lay out text in parallel, word-wrapped columns.

And if you use forms:

10.4 Until user agents handle empty controls correctly, include default, place-holding characters in edit boxes and text areas.

Notes

Preface *(page xviii)*

1. John Hockenberry, *Moving Violations: War Zones, Wheelchairs, and Declarations of Independence* (New York: Hyperion, 1995), p. 79.

1. *Heroes of Assimilation: Or How the Media Transform Disability* *(pages 1–23)*

1. "Negative Media Portrayals of the ADA," Beth Haller, *The Americans with Disabilities Act Policy Brief Series: Righting the ADA,* no. 5, February 20, 2003 (Washington: National Council on Disability), p. 2.

2. "Negative Media Portrayals of the ADA," p. 18.

3. James I. Charlton, *Nothing about Us without Us: Disability, Oppression and Empowerment* (Berkeley: University of California Press, 1998), p. 8.

4. Charlton, *Nothing about Us without Us,* p. 36.

5. Charlton, *Nothing about Us without Us,* p. 35.

6. "Negative Media Portrayals of the ADA," p. 1.

7. Joseph P. Shapiro, "Disability Rights as Civil Rights: The Struggle for Recognition," in *The Disabled, the Media, and the Information Age,* edited by Jack A. Nelson (Westport, Conn.: Greenwood Press, 1994), p. 59.

8. Tari Susan Hartman, interview with the author, July 2004.

9. Amy Harmon, "The Disability Movement Turns to Brains: Neurodiversity Forever," The Week in Review, *New York Times,* May 9, 2004, p. 1.

10. Erving Goffman, *Stigma: Notes on the Management of Spoiled Identity* (New York: Simon & Schuster/Touchstone, reissued 1986), pp. 123–124.

11. Henri-Jacques Stiker, *A History of Disability,* translated by William Sayers (Ann Arbor: University of Michigan, 2000), pp. 123–124.

12. Stiker, *A History of Disability,* p. 132.

13. David T. Mitchell and Sharon L. Snyder, *Narrative Prosthesis: Disability and the Dependencies of Discourse* (Ann Arbor: University of Michigan Press, 2003), pp. 35–36.

14. John W. Jacobson, James A. Mulick, and Allen A. Schwartz, "A History of Facilitated Communication: Science, Pseudoscience, and Antiscience: Science Working Group on Facilitated Communication," *American Psychologist,* vol. 50, no. 9, 1995, pp. 750–765.

2. *Whose Life Is It Anyway? The Use and Abuse of the Disibility Memoir (pages 24–49)*

1. Morrie Schwartz, *Morrie: In His Own Words* (New York: Delta Books, 1996), p. 89.

2. David T. Mitchell and Sharon L. Snyder, *Narrative Prosthesis: Disability and the Dependencies of Discourse* (Ann Arbor: University of Michigan Press, 2003), p. xii.

3. G. Thomas Couser, "Signifying Bodies," in *Disability Studies: Enabling the Humanities,* edited by Sharon L. Snyder with Brenda Jo Brueggemann and Rosemarie Garland-Thomson (New York: Modern Language Association, 2002), p. 117.

4. Helen Keller, *The Story of My Life,* edited by Roger Shattuck with Dorothy Herrmann (New York: Norton, 2003), p. 120.

5. Keller, *The Story of My Life,* p. 107.

6. Roger Shattuck, afterword to Keller, *The Story of My Life,* p. 439.

7. Shattuck, afterword to Keller, *The Story of My Life,* p. 431.

8. Mitch Albom, *Tuesdays With Morrie* (New York: Doubleday, 1997), p. 57.

9. Schwartz, *Morrie,* p. 92.

10. Michael J. Fox, *Lucky Man* (New York: Hyperion, 2002), p. 226.

11. Fox, *Lucky Man,* p. 5.

12. Richard M. Cohen, *Blindsided* (New York: HarperCollins, 2004), p. 147.

13. Cohen, *Blindsided,* p. 222.

14. Cohen, *Blindsided,* p. 225.

15. Cohen, *Blindsided,* p. 224.

16. John Hockenberry, *Moving Violations: War Zones, Wheelchairs, and Declarations of Independence* (New York: Hyperion, 1995), p. 27.

17. Hockenberry, *Moving Violations,* p. 24.

18. Hockenberry, *Moving Violations,* pp. 207–208.

19. Stephen Kuusisto, *Planet of the Blind* (New York: Dial Press, 1998), p. 180.

20. Kuusisto, *Planet of the Blind,* p. 183.

21. Jean-Dominique Bauby, *The Diving Bell and the Butterfly,* translated by Jeremy Leggatt (New York: Knopf, 1997), p. 5.

22. Bauby, *The Diving Bell and the Butterfly,* p. 103.

23. Bauby, *The Diving Bell and the Butterfly,* pp. 24–25.

24. Bauby, *The Diving Bell and the Butterfly,* p. 97.

25. George Steiner, *Errata: An Examined Life* (New Haven, Conn.: Yale University Press, 1997), p. 3.

26. Peter Brook, *Threads of Time* (New York: Counterpoint, 1998), p. 18.

27. Brook, *Threads of Time,* p. 195.

28. Brook, *Threads of Time,* p. 197.

29. Walter Abish, *Double Vision: A Self-Portrait* (New York: Knopf, 2004), p. 57.

30. Abish, *Double Vision,* p. 193.

31. Donald P. Spence, *Narrative Truth and Historical Truth: Meaning and Interpretation in Psychoanalysis* (New York: Norton, 1982), pp. 286–287.

32. Lauren Slater, *Lying: A Metaphorical Memoir* (New York: Random House, 2000), p. ix.

33. Slater, *Lying,* p. x.

34. Slater, *Lying,* p. 148.

35. Slater, *Lying,* pp. 65–66.

36. Slater, *Lying,* pp. 220–221.

3. Getting It on Paper: Revising the Disibility Story for the Print Media
(pages 50–68)

1. Cited by Mary Johnson in "Sticks and Stones: The Language of Disability," in *The Disabled, the Media, and the Information Age,* edited by Jack A. Nelson (Westport, Conn.: Greenwood Press, 1994), p. 33.

2 Frank Bruni, "Unraveling the Mortal Coil, in Plain View," *New York Times,* Week in Review, October 19, 2003, p. 1.

4. I'd Like to Thank the Academy: Losing Focus on Disibility
in Movies and Television (pages 69–108)

1. John Hockenberry, *Moving Violations: War Zones, Wheelchairs, and Declarations of Independence* (New York: Hyperion, 1995), p. 136.

2. John Callahan, interview with the author, May 2000.

3. "An Accurate Movie about Amnesia? Forget about It," *New York Times,* November 2, 2003, Arts and Leisure section, p. 28.

4. Jessica Yu, interview with the author, July 1999.

5. Jessica Yu, interview with the author, July 1999.

6. Aaron Sorkin, *The West Wing* (New York: Warner Books, 2002), p. 84.

7. Sorkin, *The West Wing,* p. 65.

8. Sorkin, *The West Wing,* p. 67.

9. Sorkin, *The West Wing,* p. 98.

10. Sorkin, *The West Wing,* p. 87.

11. Bryan Clark, *Whose Life Is It Anyway?* (New York: Dodd, Mead, 1978), p. 46.

12. Clark, *Whose Life Is It Anyway?* p. 113.

5. And Here's the Pitch: How Advertising Uses Disability
(pages 109–129)

1. Jack A. Nelson, "Broken Images: Portrayals of Those with Disabilities in American Media," in *The Disabled, the Media, and the Information Age,* edited by Jack A. Nelson (Westport, Conn.: Greenwood Press, 1994), p. 14.

2. Joseph P. Shapiro, *No Pity: People with Disabilities Forging a New Civil Rights Movement* (New York: Times Books/Random House, 1993), p. 12.

3. Richard Levy, *Give and Take: A Candid Account of Corporate Philanthropy* (Cambridge, Mass.: Harvard Business School Press, 1999).

4. S. Prakash Sethi, *Advocacy Advertising and Large Corporations* (Lexington, Mass.: D. C. Heath, 1977).

5. Brian Keller, interview with the author, April 2004.

6. Thomas Learner, interview with *WE* magazine, July–August 1999.

7. Beth Haller and Sue Ralph, "Profitability, Diversity, and Disability Images in Advertising in the United States and Great Britain," Economic and Social Research Council: 2001, pp. 6–13.

8. Michael Dietrich, interview with the author, May 1999.

9. Casey Martin, interview with the author, February 1999.

10. J. Lipman, "Disabled People Featured in More Ads," *Wall Street Journal,* September 7, 1989, p. 1.

11. Karen Goldman, "Dow Brands Criticized and Praised for Ad Featuring Disabled Child," *Wall Street Journal,* May 19, 1994, p. B8.

12. Phil Dourado, "Parity Not Charity," *Marketing,* 1990, p. 27.

6. Milestones, Mixed Messages, and Missed Opportunities: The Unfinished Business of the Disability Media (pages 130–156)

1. Tari Susan Hartman, interview with the author, July 2004.

2. John Seabrook, *Nobrow: The Culture of Marketing—the Marketing of Culture* (New York: Knopf, 2000), p. 28.

3. Catherine J. Kudlick, "The Outlook of *The Problem* and the Problem with the *Outlook,*" in *The New Disability History: American Perspectives,* edited by Paul Longmore and Lauri Umansky (New York: New York University Press, 2001), p. 209.

4. Robert Stone, "The Prince of Possibility," *New Yorker,* June 14 and 21, 2004, p. 89.

5. Erving Goffman, *Stigma: Notes on the Management of Spoiled Identity* (Englewood Cliffs, N.J.: Prentice-Hall, 1963), p. 25.

6. Tari Susan Hartman, interview with the author, July 2004.

7. WE: *The Short Happy Life of an Independent Magazine* (pages 157–195)

1. Cited in Charles A. Riley II, *High-Access Home: Design and Decoration for Barrier-Free Living* (New York: Rizzoli, 1999), pp. xviii–xix.

2. Rosemarie Garland Thomson, "Seeing the Disabled," in *The New Disability History: American Perspectives,* edited by Paul Longmore and Lauri Umansky (New York: New York University Press, 2001), p. 338.

3. Garland Thomson, "Seeing the Disabled," pp. 347–348.

4. Garland Thomson, "Seeing the Disabled," p. 341.

5. Garland Thomson, "Seeing the Disabled," pp. 363–364.

6. Garland Thomson, "Seeing the Disabled," p. 368.

7. Garland Thomson, "Seeing the Disabled," pp. 368–369.

8. Garland Thomson, "Seeing the Disabled," p. 372.

9. John Hockenberry, *Moving Violations,* p. 33.

10. F. D. Reeve, "Relatively Disabled," in *Points of Contact: Disability, Art, and Culture,* edited by Susan Crutchfield and Marcy Epstein (Ann Arbor: University of Michigan Press, 2000), p. 257.

11. John Stossel, *Give Me a Break* (New York: HarperCollins, 2004), p. 211.

8. *"On the Web We're All Equal": And Other Myths about Disability and Multimedia (pages 196–218)*

1 Jack Nelson, "Virtual Reality: The Promise of a Brave New World for Those with Disabilities," in *The Disabled, the Media, and the Information Age,* edited by Jack Nelson (Westport, Conn.: Greenwood Press, 1994), p. 202.

2. "Civil Rights and Information Technology: Where Do We Stand on Enforcement?" (Washington, D.C.: National Council on Disability, 2000), pp. 4–5.

3. The full text of the CAST guidelines can be found in appendix B to this book.

4. Dave Reynolds, "Ramping the Web," *Computer Companion,* Winter 2001–2002, p. 4.

5. Raymond Kurzweil, *The Age of Intelligent Machines* (Cambridge, Mass.: MIT Press, 1990), pp. 441–443.

6. Raymond Kurzweil, interview with the author, August 1999.

7. Cited by Nelson, "Virtual Reality," p. 201.

8. Nelson, "Virtual Reality," p. 204.

9. Cited by Nelson, "Virtual Reality," p. 205.

10. Harry Murphy, editor, *Proceedings: Virtual Reality and Persons with Disabilities* (Los Angeles: California State University at Northridge, 2004) p. 19.

Bibliography

Abish, Walter. *Double Vision: A Self-Portrait.* New York: Knopf, 2004.

Amsel, Rhonda, and Catherine S. Fichten. "Effects of Contact on Thoughts about Interaction with Students Who Have a Physical Disability." *Journal of Rehabilitation,* vol. 54, January–February–March 1988, pp. 61–65.

Augusto, Carl R., and Jane M. McGraw. "Humanizing Blindness through Public Education." *Journal of Visual Impairment and Blindness,* vol. 84, October 1990, pp. 397–400.

Baskin, Barbara H., and Karen H. Harris. *More Notes from a Different Drummer: A Guide to Juvenile Fiction Portraying the Disabled.* New York: R. R. Bowker, 1984.

Bauby, Jean-Dominique. *The Diving Bell and the Butterfly,* translated by Jeremy Leggatt. New York: Knopf, 1997.

Baynton, Douglas. *Forbidden Signs: American Culture and the Campaign against Sign Language.* Chicago: University of Chicago Press, 1996.

Bernatavicz, W. A. *Changing Attitudes toward the Disabled through the Media: What the Research Says.* Portland, Maine: Research and Advanced Study, University of Southern Maine, 1979.

Biklen, Douglas. "The Culture of Policy: Disability Images and Their Analogues in Public Policy." *Social Problems,* vol. 15, no. 3, 1987, pp. 515–535.

Biklen, Douglas, and Robert Bogdan. "Media Portrayals of Disabled People: A Study in Stereotypes." *Interracial Books for Children Bulletin,* vol. 4, no. 6, 1982, p. 7.

Bogdan, Robert. *Freak Show: Presenting Human Oddities for Amusement and Profit.* Chicago: University of Chicago Press, 1988.

Bogdan, Robert, with Douglas Biklen. "Handicapism." *Social Policy,* vol. 7, 1977, pp. 14–19.

Bogdan, Robert, with Douglas Biklen, A. Shapiro, and D. Spelkoman. "The Disabled: Media's Monster." *Social Policy,* vol. 13, 1982, pp. 32–35.

Bonnstetter, C. M. "Magazine Coverage of the Mentally Handicapped." *Journalism Quarterly,* vol. 63, 1986, pp. 623–626.

Boyer, Patrick, M.P. "No News Is Bad News." *First Report of the Standing Committee on the Status of Disabled Persons,* House of Commons, Ottawa, Canada, August 1988.

Bowe, Frank. *Handicapping America.* New York: Harper & Row, 1978.

Braithwaite, D. O. and T. Thompson, editors. *Communication and People with Disabilities.* Mahwah, N.J.: Lawrence Erlbaum, 2000.

Brolley, Dianne Y., and Stephen C. Anderson. "Advertising and Attitudes." *Rehabilitation Digest*, vol. 17, Fall 1986, pp. 15–17.

Brook, Peter. *Threads of Time*. New York: Counterpoint, 1998.

Byrd, E. Keith, and Timothy R. Elliot. "Feature Films and Disability: A Descriptive Study." *Rehabilitation Psychology*, vol. 30, no. 1, 1985, pp. 47–51.

Callahan, John. *Don't Worry, He Won't Get Far on Foot: The Autobiography of a Dangerous Man*. New York: Vintage, 1989.

———. *Will the Real John Callahan Please Stand Up?* New York: Morrow, 1998.

Campling, Jo. *Images of Ourselves: Women with Disabilities Talking*. London: Routledge and Kegan Paul, 1981.

Charlton, James I. *Nothing about Us without Us: Disability Oppression and Empowerment*. Berkeley: University of California Press, 1998.

Clark, Bryan. *Whose Life Is It Anyway?* New York: Dodd, Mead, 1978.

Clogston, John S. *Disability Coverage in Sixteen Newspapers*. Louisville, Ky.: Advocado Press, 1990.

———. "Fifty Years of Disability Coverage in the *New York Times*." *News Computing Journal*, vol. 8, no. 2, 1992, pp. 39–50.

Cohen, Richard M. *Blindsided*. New York: HarperCollins, 2004.

Conrad, Peter, and Joseph Schneider. *Deviance and Medicalization*. St. Louis: Mosby, 1980.

Cooke, Annemarie, and Neil Reisner. "The Last Minority." *Washington Journalism Review*, vol. 13, no. 10, December 1991, pp. 14–18.

Corker, Mairian, and Sally French. *Disability Discourse*. London: Open University Press, 1999.

Couser, G. Thomas. *Recovering Bodies: Illness, Disability and Life Writing*. Madison: University of Wisconsin Press, 1997.

Covington, George A. *Sensitivity Key to Interviewing: The News Media and Disability*. Washington, D.C.: The News Media Education Project/A National Workshop, p. 1.

Crow, L. "Helen Keller: Rethinking the Problematic Icon." *Disability and Society*, vol. 15, no. 6, 2000, pp. 845–860.

Crutchfield, Susan, and Marcy Epstein, editors. *Points of Contact: Disability, Art, and Culture*. Ann Arbor: University of Michigan Press, 2000.

Cumberbatch, Guy, and R. Negrine. *Images of Disability on Television*. New York: Routledge, 1992.

Cutlip, Scott. *Fund Raising in the United States*. New Brunswick, N.J.: Rutgers University Press, 1965.

Dattilo, John, and Ralph W. Smith. "Communicating Positive Attitudes toward People with Disabilities through Sensitive Terminology." *Therapeutic Recreation Journal*, vol. 24, first quarter 1990, pp. 8–17.

Davis, Lennard, editor. *The Disability Studies Reader*. New York: Routledge, 1997.

———. *Enforcing Normalcy: Disabilities, Deafness and the Body*. New York: Verso, 1995.

Deutsch, Helen, and Felicity Nussbaum, editors. *"Defects": Engendering the Modern Body*. Ann Arbor: University of Michigan Press, 2000.

Donaldson, Joy. "The Visibility and Image of Handicapped People on Television." *Exceptional Children*, vol. 47, no. 6, March 1981, pp. 413–416.

Driedger, Diane. *The Last Civil Rights Movement: Disabled People's International*. New York: St. Martin's, 1989.

Eiesland, Nancy. *The Disabled God: Toward a Liberating Theology of Disability*. Nashville, Tenn.: Abingdon, 1994.

Epstein, Julia. *Altered Conditions: Disease, Medicine and Storytelling*. New York: Routledge, 1995.

Ericson, R. V., P. M. Baranek, and J. B. L. Chan. *Visualizing Deviance: A Study of a News Organization*. Toronto: University of Toronto Press, 1987.

Feldman, David, and Brian Feldman. "The Effect of a Telethon on Attitudes toward Disabled People and Financial Contributions." *Journal of Rehabilitation*, vol. 51, July–August–September 1985, pp. 42–45.

Fichten, Catherine S., Joanne Hines, and Rhonda Amsel. "Public Awareness of Physically Disabled Persons." *International Journal of Rehabilitation Research*, vol. 8, 1985, pp. 407–413.

Fiedler, Leslie A. *Freaks. Myths and Images of the Secret Self*. New York: Simon and Schuster, 1978.

Fine, Michelle, and Adrienne Asch, editors. *Women with Disabilities: Essays in Psychology, Culture and Politics*. Philadelphia: Temple University Press, 1988.

Fleischer, Doris Zames and Frieda Zames. *The Disability Rights Movement: From Charity to Confrontation*. Philadelphia: Temple University Press, 2001.

Fox, Michael J. *Lucky Man*. New York: Hyperion, 2002.

Friedberg, Joan Brest, June B. Mullins, and Adelaide Weir Sukiennik. *Accept Me as I Am: Best Books of Juvenile Nonfiction on Impairments and Disabilities*. New York: R. R. Bowker, 1985.

Fries, Kenny, editor. *Staring Back*. New York: Plume, 1997.

Gadeken, Gary. "The Ray Charles Syndrome: Distorted Images of Disabled People in the Mass Media." *Dialogue*, vol. 28, Spring 1989, pp. 55–60.

Gakan, David. *Disease, Pain and Sacrifice: Toward a Psychology of Suffering*. Chicago: University of Chicago Press, 1968.

Gallagher, Hugh Gregory. *By Trust Betrayed: Patients, Physicians, and the License to Kill in the Third Reich*. New York: Henry Holt, 1990.

Gartner, Allen, and Joe Tom, editors. *Images of the Disabled, Disabling Images*. New York: Praeger, 1987.

Gaylin, Willard. *Doing Good: The Limits of Benevolence*. New York: Pantheon, 1981.

Gazsi, S. *A Parallel and Imperfect Universe: The Media and People with Disabilities*. New York: Freedom Forum Media Studies Center, 1993.

Gilman, Sander L. *Disease and Representation: Images of Illness from Madness to AIDS*. Ithaca, N.Y.: Cornell University Press, 1988.

———. *Seeing the Insane*. New York: Wiley, 1982.

Glucklich, Ariel. *Sacred Pain: Hurting the Body for the Sake of the Soul*. New York: Oxford University Press, 2002.

Goffman, Erving. *Stigma: Notes on the Management of Spoiled Identity.* Englewood Cliffs, N.J.: Prentice-Hall, 1963.

Goggin, G., and C. Newell. *Digital Disability: The Social Construction of Disability in New Media.* Lanham, Mass.: Roman and Littlefield, 2002.

Goldman, Charles. *Disability Rights Guide: Practical Solutions to Problems Affecting People with Disabilities.* Lincoln, Neb.: Media Publishing, 1987.

Grandin, Temple. *Thinking in Pictures and Other Reports from My Life with Autism.* New York: Random House, 1995.

Griffin, Clifford S. *Their Brother's Keepers.* New Brunswick, N.J.: Rutgers University Press, 1960.

Gusfield, Joseph R. *The Culture of Public Problems.* Chicago: University of Chicago Press, 1981.

Hahn, Harlan. "The Politics of Physical Differences: Disability and Discrimination." *Journal of Social Issues,* vol. 44, 1988, 39–47.

Halberstam, Judith. *Skin Shows: Gothic Horror and the Technology of Monsters.* Durham, N.C.: Duke University Press, 1995.

Haller, Beth. "How the News Frames Disability: Print Media Coverage of the Americans with Disabilities Act," in *Research in Social Science and Disability,* vol. 1. New York: JAI Press, 1999.

———. "Rethinking Models of Media Representation of Disability." *Disability Studies Quarterly,* vol. 15, no. 2, Spring 1995, 58–90.

Haller, Beth and S. Ralph. "Content Analysis Methodology for Studying News and Disability: Case Studies from the United States and England," in *Research in Social Science and Disability.* vol. 2. New York: JAI Press, 2001.

———. "Not Worth Keeping Alive? News Framing of Physician-Assisted Suicide in the United States and Great Britain." *Journalism Studies,* vol. 2, no. 3, 2001, 407–421.

Hartman, Tari Susan, and Mary Johnson. *Making News: How to Get News Coverage for Disability Rights Issues.* Louisville, Ky.: Advocado Press, 1994.

Hausman, Carl. *The Decision-Making Process in Journalism.* Chicago: Nelson-Hall, 1990.

Hevey, David. *The Creatures That Time Forgot: Photography and Disability Imagery.* New York: Routledge, 1992.

Higgins, P. C. *Making Disability: Exploring the Social Transformation of Human Variation.* Springfield, Ill.: Charles C. Thomas, 1992.

Hockenberry, John. *Moving Violations: War Zones, Wheelchairs, and Declarations of Independence.* New York: Hyperion, 1995.

Holmes, Gary E., and Ronald H. Karst. "The Institutionalization of Disability Myths: Impact on Vocational Rehabilitation Services." *Journal of Rehabilitation,* vol. 56, January–February–March 1990, 20–27.

Jacobson, John W., James A. Mulick, and Allen A. Schwartz. "A History of Facilitated Communication: Science, Pseudoscience, and Antiscience: Science Working Group on Facilitated Communication." *American Psychologist,* vol. 50, no. 9, 1995, pp. 750–765.

Johnson, Mary. *Make Them Go Away: Clint Eastwood, Christopher Reeve and the Case against Disability Rights.* Louisville, Ky.: Advocado Press, 2003.

Johnson, Mary, and Susan Elkins, editors. *Reporting on Disability: Approaches and Issues, a Sourcebook.* Louisville, Ky.: Advocado Press, 1989.

Johnson, Mary, and B. Shaw. *To Ride the Public's Buses: The Fight That Built a Movement.* Louisville, Ky.: Advocado Press, 2001.

Jones, Edward E., and others. *Social Stigma: The Psychology of Marked Relationships.* New York: W. H. Freeman, 1984.

Kailes, June Isaacson. "Watch Your Language, Please!" *Journal of Rehabilitation,* vol. 51, January–February–March 1985, pp. 68–69.

Katz, Michael B. *In the Shadow of the Poorhouse.* New York: Basic Books, 1986.

Keller, Helen. *The Story of My Life,* edited by Roger Shattuck with Dorothy Herrmann. New York: Norton, 2003.

Kerenyi, Carl. *Prometheus: Archetypal Image of Human Existence,* translated by Ralph Manheim. Princeton N.J.: Princeton University Press, 1963.

Kinsella, J. *Covering the Plague: AIDS and the American Media.* New Brunswick, N.J.: Rutgers University Press, 1989.

Kleege, Georgina. *Sight Unseen.* New Haven, Conn.: Yale University Press, 1999.

Kleinfeld, S. *The Hidden Minority.* Boston: Little, Brown, 1979.

Klobas, Lauri. *Disability Drama in Television and Film.* Jefferson, N.C.: Macfarland, 1988.

Koestler, Frances. *The Unseen Minority: A Social History of Blindness in America.* New York: David McKay, 1976.

Kolucki, Barbara. "Sharing the Street: Integrating Disability Awareness into Children's Television." *Rehabilitation Digest,* vol. 20, Winter 1990, pp. 3–7.

Krossel, Martin. "Handicapped Heroes and the Knee-Jerk Press." *Columbia Journalism Review,* vol. 27, no. 1, May–June 1988, pp. 46–47.

Kuppers, P. *Disability and Contemporary Performance: Bodies on Edge.* New York and London: Routledge, 2003.

Kurzweil, Raymond. *The Age of Intelligent Machines.* Cambridge, Mass.: MIT Press, 1990.

Kuusisto, Stephen. *Planet of the Blind.* New York: Dial Press, 1998.

Lane, Harlan. *The Mask of Benevolence: Disabling the Deaf Community.* New York: Knopf, 1992.

———. *When the Mind Hears: A History of the Deaf.* New York: Random House, 1984.

Levy, Richard. *Give and Take: A Candid Account of Corporate Philanthropy.* Cambridge, Mass.: Harvard Business School Press, 1999.

Lewis, C. S. *The Problem of Pain.* London: Geoffrey Biles, 1950.

Liachowitz, C. *Disability as Social Construct.* Philadelphia: University of Pennsylvania Press, 1988.

Linton, Simi. *Claiming Disability: Knowledge and Identity.* New York: New York University Press, 1998.

Longmore, Paul K. "Disability Rights Activists and Assisted Suicide." *Cornell Journal of Law and Public Policy,* vol. 7, no. 2, Winter 1998, pp. 280–285.

———. "Screening Stereotypes: Images of Disabled People." *Social Policy,* vol. 16, Summer 1985, pp. 31–37.

———. *Why I Burned My Book and Other Essays on Disability.* Philadelphia: Temple University Press, 2003.

Longmore, Paul, and Lauri Umansky, editors. *The New Disability History: American Perspectives.* New York: New York University Press, 2001.

Mairs, Nancy. *Waist-High in the World: A Life among the Non-Disabled.* Boston: Beacon Press, 1996.

Makas, Elaine, and Lynn Schlesinger, editors. *End Results and Starting Points: Expanding the Field of Disability Studies.* Portland, Maine: Society for Disability Studies and Edmund S. Muskie Institute of Public Affairs, 1996.

Marinelli, Robert P., and Arthur E. Dell Orto, eds. *The Psychological and Social Impact of Physical Disability,* second edition. New York: Springer, 1984.

Michalko, Rod. *The Difference That Disability Makes.* Philadelphia: Temple University Press, 2002.

Mitchell, David T., and Sharon L. Snyder. *The Body and Physical Difference: Discourses of Disability in the Humanities.* Ann Arbor: University of Michigan Press, 1997.

———. *Narrative Prosthesis: Disability and the Dependencies of Discourse.* Ann Arbor: University of Michigan Press, 2003.

Montgomery, K. C. *Targeting Prime Time.* New York: Oxford University Press, 1989.

Morris, David B. *The Culture of Pain.* Berkeley: University of California Press, 1991.

Murphy, Harry, editor. *Proceedings: Virtual Reality and Persons with Disabilities.* Los Angeles: California State University at Northridge, 2004.

Nelson, Jack A., editor, *The Disabled, the Media, and the Information Age.* Westport, Conn.: Greenwood Press, 1994.

Nielsen, Kim E. *The Radical Lives of Helen Keller.* New York: New York University Press, 2004.

Niesser, Arden. *The Other Side of Silence: Sign Language and the Deaf Community in America.* New York: Knopf, 1983.

Norden, Martin F. *The Cinema of Isolation: A History of Physical Disability in the Movies.* New Brunswick, N.J.: Rugers University Press, 1994.

Oliver, Michael. *The Politics of Disablement.* New York: St. Martin's, 1990.

———. *Understanding Disability: From Theory to Practice.* New York: St. Martin's, 1996.

Pernick, Martin. *A Calculus of Suffering.* New York: Columbia University Press, 1985.

Pointon, A., and C. Davies. *Framed: Interrogating Disability in the Media.* Bloomington: Indiana University Press, 1998.

Potok, A. *A Matter of Dignity: Changing the Lives of the Disabled.* New York: Bantam/Doubleday, 2002.

Price, Reynolds. *Feasting the Heart.* New York: Scribner, 2000.

Riley, Charles A., II. *High-Access Home: Design and Decoration for Barrier-Free Living.* New York: Rizzoli, 1999.

Rudofsky, B. *The Unfashionable Human Body.* Garden City, N.Y.: Doubleday, 1971.

Russell, Marta. *Beyond Ramps: Disability at the End of the Social Contract.* Monroe, Maine: Common Courage Press, 1998.

Ryan, M., and D. Owen. "A Content Analysis of Metropolitan Newspaper Coverage of Social Issues." *Journalism Quarterly,* vol. 53, 1976, pp. 634–640.

Sacks, Oliver. *An Anthropologist on Mars.* New York: Random House, 1995.

———. *Awakenings.* New York: Peter Smith, 1990.

———. *The Man Who Mistook His Wife for a Hat.* New York: Peter Smith, 1992.

———. *Seeing Voices.* Berkeley: University of California Press, 1989.

———. *Uncle Tungsten.* New York: Knopf, 2001.

Saxton, Marsha, and F. Howe. *With Wings: An Anthology of Literature by and about Women with Disabilities.* New York: Feminist Press, 1987.

Scarry, Elaine. *The Body in Pain: The Making and Unmaking of the World.* New York: Oxford University Press, 1985.

Schuchman, John S. *Hollywood Speaks: Deafness and the Film Entertainment Industry.* Urbana: University of Illinois Press, 1988.

Schwartz, Morrie. *Morrie: In His Own Words.* New York: Delta Books, 1996.

Scotch, R. K. *From Good Will to Civil Rights: Transforming Federal Disability Policy.* Philadelphia: Temple University Press, 1984.

Seabrook, John. *Nobrow: The Culture of Marketing—the Marketing of Culture.* New York: Knopf, 2000.

Sethi, S. Prakash. *Advocacy Advertising and Large Corporations.* Lexington, Mass.: D. C. Heath, 1977.

Shapiro, Joseph P. *No Pity: People with Disabilities Forging a New Civil Rights Movement.* New York: Times Books/Random House, 1993.

Sills, David. *The Volunteers,* New York: The Free Press, 1957.

Skocpol, Theda. *Protecting Soldiers and Mothers.* Cambridge, Mass.: Belknap Press of Harvard University Press, 1992.

Slater, Lauren. *Lying: A Metaphorical Memoir.* New York: Random House, 2000.

Snyder, Sharon L., with Brenda Jo Brueggemann, and Rosemarie Garland-Thomson, editors. *Disability Studies: Enabling the Humanities.* New York: Modern Language Association, 2002.

Spence, Donald P. *Narrative Truth and Historical Truth: Meaning and Interpretation in Psychoanalysis.* New York: Norton, 1982.

Sorkin, Aaron. *The West Wing.* New York: Warner Books, 2002.

Steiner, George. *Errata: An Examined Life.* New Haven, Conn.: Yale University Press, 1997.

Stiker, Henri-Jacques. *A History of Disability,* translated by William Sayers. Ann Arbor: University of Michigan Press, 2000.

Stone, Deborah. *The Disabled State.* Philadelphia: Temple University Press, 1986.

Stossel, John. *Give Me a Break.* New York: HarperCollins, 2004.

Strong, Marilee. *A Bright Red Scream: Self-Mutilation and the Language of Pain.* New York: Viking, 1998.

Sutherland, Alan T. *Disabled We Stand.* Bloomington, Indiana: Indiana University Press, 1981.

Thomson, Rosemarie Garland. *Extraordinary Bodies: Figuring Physical Disability in American Culture and Literature.* New York: Columbia University Press, 1997.

————, editor. *Freakery: Cultural Spectacle of the Extraordinary Body.* New York: New York University Press, 1996.

Titchkisky, Tanya. *Disability, Self and Society.* Toronto: University of Toronto Press, 2003.

Trent, James W. *Inventing the Feeble Mind: A History of Mental Retardation in the United States.* Berkeley: University of California Press, 1994.

Tysse, G., editor. *The Legislative History of the Americans with Disabilities Act.* Horsham, Pa.: LRP Publications, 1991.

Wagner, David. *What's Love Got to Do with It? A Critical Look at American Charity.* New York: The New Press, 2000.

Wendell, Susan. *The Rejected Body: Feminist Reflections on the Disabled Body.* New York: Routledge, 1996.

Wills, David. *Prosthesis.* Stanford: Stanford University Press, 1995.

Winfield, Betty Houchin. "FDR's Pictorial Image: Rules and Boundaries." *Journalism History,* vol. 5, no. 4, Winter 1978–79, pp. 110–114.

Wolfe, Kathi. "Heroes and Holy Innocents." *Utne Reader,* vol. 73, 1996, p. 24.

Yuker, Harold E., editor. *Attitudes toward Persons with Disabilities.* New York: Springer, 1988.

Zola, Irving Kenneth. *Ordinary Lives: Voices of Disability and Disease.* Cambridge, Mass.: Applewood Books, 1982.

Index